THE
BATTLE OF
LONG ISLAND

by Eric I. Manders

PHILIP FRENEAU PRESS

Monmouth Beach N.J.

1978

In print titles in the Philip Freneau Press
Bicentennial Series on the American Revolution

THE BATTLES OF SARATOGA
John R. Elting
LC No. 77-89325/ISBN 0-912480-13-0

THE BATTLE OF BRANDYWINE
Samuel S. Smith
LC No. 76-9405/ISBN 0-912480-12-2

THE BATTLE OF BUNKER'S HILL
John R. Elting
LC No. 75-3540/ISBN 0-912480-11-4

AT GENERAL HOWE'S SIDE 1776-1778
Friedrich von Muenchhausen/Ernst Kipping, trans.
LC No. 73-94002/ISBN 0-912480-09-2

BRITISH MAPS OF THE AMERICAN REVOLUTION
Peter J. Guthorn
LC No. 72-79889/ISBN 0-912480-07-6

THE HESSIAN VIEW OF AMERICA 1776-1783
Ernst Kipping
LC No. 72-161384/ISBN 0-912480-06-8

FIGHT FOR THE DELAWARE 1777
Samuel S. Smith
LC No. 74-130878/ISBN 0-912480-05-X

VALLEY FORGE CRUCIBLE OF VICTORY
John F. Reed
LC No. 70-76769/ISBN 0-912480-04-1

THE BATTLE OF PRINCETON
Samuel S. Smith
LC No. 67-31149/ISBN 0-912480-03-3

AMERICAN MAPS AND MAP MAKERS OF
THE REVOLUTION
Peter J. Guthorn
LC No. 66-30330/ISBN 0-912480-02-5

THE BATTLE OF TRENTON
Samuel S. Smith
LC No. 65-28860/ISBN 0-912480-01-7

THE BATTLE OF MONMOUTH
Samuel S. Smith
LC No. 64-56379/ISBN 0-912480-00-9

This Bicentennial Series
on the American Revolution
has been designed throughout by Paul R. Smith

Photography by Daniel I. Hennessey.

Copyright 1978 by Philip Freneau Press
Library of Congress No. 78-72581
International Standard Book No. 0-912480-14-9

CONTENTS

Chapter I NEW YORK   THE GRAND ARMY Chapter VI
Chapter II LEE   PREPARATIONS Chapter VII
Chapter III STIRLING   LONG ISLAND Chapter VIII
Chapter IV WASHINGTON   JUGGERNAUT Chapter IX
Chapter V THE HOWES   DELIVERANCE Chapter X
Bibliography, Notes, Appendix, Index

PREFACE

One problem of describing 18th Century society, whether in its own vernacular or by 20th Century usage, is a tendency to slide into ambiguity. So it might be helpful to begin with an understanding of some of the terms used in this narrative. In this way your concentration on the course of events need not be sidetracked by lengthy explanations within the text itself.

There is no ideal way to label the Americans of opposing views. Each side sincerely considered the other to be made up of unregenerate traitors. Both "Whig" and "Tory," when used descriptively, suggest membership in a political party, which was hardly the case. All in all, "patriot" and "loyalist" seem least objectionable, the first supporting the aims of the Continental Congress and the second adhering to the Crown. "Rebel" (and in some cases "Whig" and "Tory") will be used only as a pejorative, to reflect an attitude. The patriots did not consider themselves as rebels, but as defenders of their natural rights.

At one time it was de rigueur to maintain that the Anglo-Saxon political genius rested on a flair for local self government. In any event, it was nowhere better shown than in Revolutionary America. As the old colonial administration withered and died in New York, a structured system of committees emerged to fill the power gap and thereby circumvent anarchy. One of the new system's functions, of course, was to further the aims of the patriot cause. But in large measure it also met the workaday needs of any organized society, holding the fabric together until a legitimate constitutional arrangement could be worked out. The top layer of the system was occupied by the New York Provincial Congress, itself a kind of super-committee made up of delegates from all the province's fourteen counties (except, intermittently, the obstinately loyal Richmond and Queens). The Provincial Congress deputized and instructed New York's representatives to the Continental Congress and, in theory at least, it alone was empowered to process and discharge New York's Continental obligations.

Directives generally took the form of resolutions, and in a number of vital areas these were passed down to the several county committees for execution. The militia, for example, was organized on a county basis, and it was the county which raised, formed and equipped units for active military service as the need arose. The county, in its turn, relied for help on the township committee or district board. By its nature this bottom layer was the most visible of the entire civil structure, and the one held responsible for maintaining local order. Whenever disgruntled loyalists complained that their rights were being trammeled, it was usually the township committee doing the trammeling.

The militarily uninitiated might appreciate knowing that the soldiers did not fight as a mass, but were formed into companies. The companies were formed into battalions or regiments (most regiments contained only one battalion), the regiments into brigades and the brigades into divisions. Each level was a more or less permanent organization, operated by a commanding officer, his subordinates and his staff. A group of units *temporarily* thrown together under an officer is here called a detachment, except in such special cases as will become apparent.

It has almost become routine for Pennsylvania and New Jersey historians to designate their own twelve-months Continental units of 1775 and 1776 as "battalions." This serves, in part, to distinguish them from the "regiments" that were subsequently raised at the close of 1776 for the permanent Continental Line. While this nomenclature is parochially convenient, it defies incorporation into the larger picture without a degree of confusion. For our purpose, therefore, we will call any standard infantry unit a "regiment" if it has a normal complement of companies and is nominally commanded by a colonel—even if that post should be temporarily vacant in any given unit. "Battalion" is reserved for smaller units under a lieutenant colonel. Two such battalions may make up a regiment (eg, Miles's Pennsylvania Riflemen), or a battalion may operate as an independent entity (eg. Kachlein's Pennsylvania Associators).

The Royal Navy classified its warships by rate, 1 through 6. The first two rates, carrying 74 guns or more, were line-of-battle ships and were not assigned to the North American station. For the more lightly armed vessels we arbitrarily use a modern system wherein the 3rd and 4th rates (64 down to 50 guns) are called cruisers and the 5th and 6th rates (44 to 20 guns) are called frigates. These all presuppose three-masted, square rigged ships. Other types of vessels—bomb ships, brigs, schooners, sloops and tenders—are not in the rating system.[1]

Geography presents a special difficulty. With a few exceptions, the place name we use is the contemporary one, but with modern spelling: Kingsbridge instead of King's Bridge, for example, or Gowanus instead of Guiana and its variations. The major exception is Manhattan Island. It is so called today, and was so called in the Dutch period; but in the 18th Century it was invariably called New York Island. But "New York" appears repeatedly in the text as a province or state, and as a city. To tax you with an unfamiliar "New York Island" would be inexcusable pedantry. Another exception is the Tappan Sea; the modern Tappan Zee smacks of a self-conscious quest for ancient Dutch roots and seems out of place in the 18th Century. Nassau Island and Nutten Island had some contemporary usage, but they were more widely known as Long Island and Governor's Island, just as they are today. By the same token, the North River was also called Hudson's River, and we use the modern form of Hudson.

Those familiar with today's New York metropolitan area should remember that Brooklyn did not occupy the whole of Kings County in 1776, but was only one of six townships. Nassau and Bronx Counties did not exist at all, but were still part of Queens and Westchester. Richmond County, on the other hand, covered all of Staten Island, as it still does and was opposite Essex and Middlesex Counties in New Jersey. The entire west bank of the Hudson River south of the New York line was Bergen County, New Jersey.

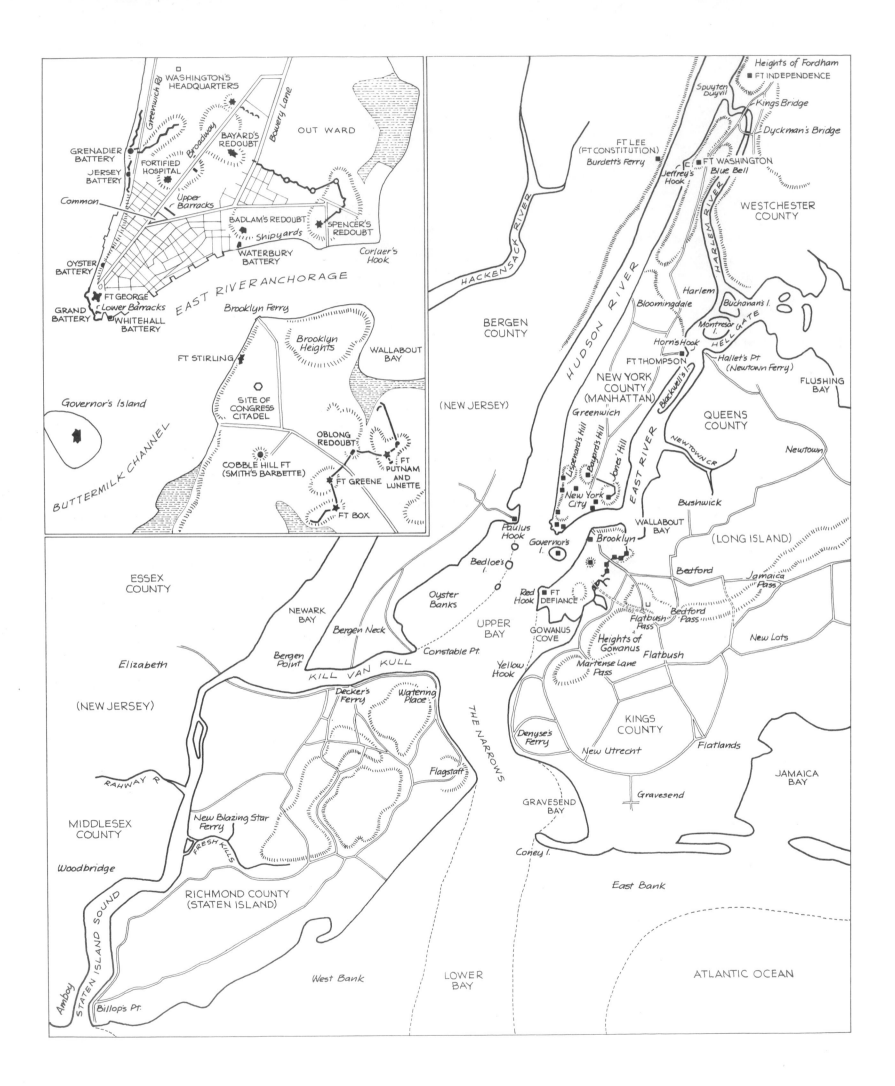

Chapter I

New York

Once the American War was perceived as somewhat larger than a local Yankee uprising, each side inevitably drew its attention to the strategic possibilities of New York City. New York, long before the outbreak of hostilities around Boston, had been the center of British colonial defense and headquarters for the North American garrison. Geography was the reason. The city was centrally located on the Atlantic seaboard, and so made an ideal base for coastal operations in any direction. Its (generally) ice-free harbor bay—some nine miles by three of navigable water—provided sea room for as many vessels as an 18th century power cared to sail into it.[1]

Moreover, New York's position at the mouth of the Hudson River made it "a kind of key to the whole continent, as it is a passage to Canada, to the Great Lakes, and to all the Indian nations." The observation is John Adams's, and he might also have pointed to the north-south orientation of the Hudson as well. Here was an unfordable barrier between New England and all the other colonies. Given control of the sea, anyone who also held this barrier could, if so minded, cut off any large scale communication across it and prevent either side from supporting the other. This leverage was the ultimate prize to be won.[2]

Despite its obvious potential, for much of 1775 neither side showed any great military interest in the place. The main theater of events, after all, was at Boston. It was from there that part of the British Army garrison had marched in April to seize patriot materiel cached at nearby Concord, and in the process opened the first round of general hostilities. Two months later, on 17 June, the garrison found itself locked in battle with a united provincial army representing the four New England colonies of Massachusetts, Connecticut, New Hampshire and Rhode Island.

As the Yankees fought and bled at Bunker's Hill, few if any were aware of their altered status as soldiers. The Continental Congress, barely reconvened at Philadelphia, had just adopted them as its own. George Washington of Virginia was appointed to the supreme command, and Congress assumed the right to name his subordinate generals, to commission his regimental and staff officers, to raise riflemen for his particular use, and to create articles of war for the general regulation of his newly converted "Continental" troops.

As affairs then stood—tactically, logistically and politically—any immediate effort by the British to re-establish their headquarters at New York was out of the question. The regular garrison there was actually withdrawn in June, when five thin companies of the Royal Irish Regiment boarded ship to augment the beleaguered forces at Boston. Within the month the Americans partially filled the vacuum by creating the New York Department as a separate military district under Major General Philip Schuyler, but his headquarters lay in Albany rather than New York City. Ultimately all the New York forces raised for Continental service were drawn northward for the invasion of Canada, leaving local military control in the hands of the New York Provincial Congress.

The Congress enjoyed a degree of military support from the city's "independent" militia, regimented under the command of Colonel John Lasher. These were spit-and-polish companies for the most part, quite distinct from the "common" militia wherein service was obligatory and which, in 1775, was barely getting organized. The independents were volunteers all, enthusiastic young gentlemen of means with snappy uniforms to match the company titles they chose: *Sportsmen, Bold Foresters, German Fusiliers,* and the like. But they turned out to be good, dependable soldiers for all their posturing, and cheerfully accepted whatever assignments fell their way.[3]

Under the circumstances their duties were somewhat limited. The Provincial Congress was not the only government on the spot, nor did it operate with an entirely free hand. The old colonial administration was still very much in evidence in the person of the royal governor, William Tryon, a bluff soldier-politician who had no intention of hauling down his flag. He continued to meet with his Council to keep the old government in a state of legal existence, though in the end he felt constrained to move his capitol out to a merchantman—*Dutchess of Gordon*—standing in the East River. It was a charade on the face of it, but Tryon was no fool. Behind all his paper shuffling he gave real aid and comfort to New York's sizable loyalist community. He actually set about raising soldiers for Crown service, within view of several patriot county committees.[4]

Any weaknesses afflicting the governor were political not martial, for he could hold over New York City the prospect of imminent bombardment. Constantly riding hard by the East River waterfront lay His Majesty's ship *Asia,* a man-of-war mounting 64 guns and commanded by Captain George Vandeput. The captain's standing orders were to assist in "supporting the legal Authority of Government, [and] protecting and securing the King's Stores and the Safety of his Majesty's faithful Subjects in the Province of New York." The King's stores meant the artillery pieces still ensconced at Fort George and its attendant Battery, curling around the toe of Manhattan Island. This was all Crown property, and Vandeput was determined that none of it fall into rebel hands.[5]

Some of it already had. On the night of 23 August a company of Colonel Lasher's independents helped the Continental artillerymen still in town to remove some guns from the Battery. This move provoked first an exchange of musketry with *Asia's* boat, and then a general cannonade from the ship itself. By the time it was all over three Americans were wounded, a British seaman had died, and wild-eyed citizens ran screaming through the streets in their nightrails. Property damage was kept to a minimum, partly because Vandeput had his guns trained on the Battery. But a few stray shots did manage to whistle through a roof or two, including the one on Black Sam Fraunces's tavern.[6]

The soldiers managed to get off with 21 pieces, all that were mounted, but the moral victory was clearly Captain Vandeput's. From that time forward the Provincial Congress lost all interest in any more of the King's stores. Even the captured guns were left untouched on the Common. A truce of sorts was solidified by degrees over the following months. As long as the Congress kept its hands to itself, or did not interfere "by threats or persuasion" with the agents contracted to provision *Asia,* then Vandeput would restrain himself from leveling New York City. Neither would he, unless provoked, cut off the market boat trade that kept the city supplied with food, forage and firewood. On the other hand, the Congress felt not in the least inhibited from organizing an armed militia as its own instrument, from raising and equipping troops for Continental service, or even from fitting out an armed vessel. But on balance the Royal Navy gained a certain psychological edge, and these were the prevailing conditions in December 1775 when the frigate *Phoenix,* 44 guns, arrived with some refinements.[7]

Captain Hyde Parker, Jr. was her skipper; he was Vandeput's

senior and carried orders to take the command of both vessels. But more than this, as he informed Governor Tryon, he had instructions to treat New York City "as in open Rebellion against the King" if any Crown officer "or other peaceable disposed Subjects" should be molested, if bodies of men should be raised and armed, if unauthorized military works should be erected, or if any Crown property should be seized or destroyed. Tryon lost no time getting this latest bullyragging into print and distributed so that the citizens—and the Congress—might better appreciate the consequences of civil disobedience.[8]

Meanwhile, the Americans were at last beginning to look at New York—and from two different vantage points. At Philadelphia the Continental Congress ordered a detachment from two Continental regiments, just raised in New Jersey, to garrison the Hudson Highlands upriver from the city. Fort Constitution had been under construction there since late summer. As it turned out, however, there were as yet no accommodations for billeting troops so the detachment was sidetracked instead to New York City, along with the rest of the two regiments, "till barracks can be fitted up for them in that fort." There was no sense of urgency in the move; New York would merely serve as a convenient depot until the Highlands were ready. That was on 8 December. A month and a half later both units were still in New Jersey, drumming up recruits and looking for enough firearms to make them effective for combat.[9]

By this time a much livelier interest in New York City was developing at Continental Army headquarters in Cambridge, Massachusetts. There two disparate individuals with briefly converging interests met at just the right moment, and between them set the course of the coming year's campaign. Major General Charles Lee, was the prime mover. If he was not the first to visualize New York as a Continental stronghold, then he would be the first to seize on the idea and transform it into a military imperative. All he needed for this alchemy was the proper catalyst, and he found it in the person of an old-school rebel named Captain Isaac Sears.

Captain Sears (whose title was nautical not martial; he was once a privateer skipper) had been part of a radical clique that kept New York City in turmoil for most of ten years before his activism grew tiresome. When hostilities finally opened his sometime colleagues found ways to channel their energies toward productive ends; but not Sears. In his view he was still raising liberty poles and picking fistfights with garrison redcoats. Responsible conduct was an indication of backsliding, and the *Asia* truce was a good case in point. He moved over to Connecticut, where a low opinion of Yorkers was widely cherished, and there proceeded to revive the good old Stamp Tax days. He knocked together a pickup troop of 75 or 80 freelance vigilantes, and with them swept into Westchester County to kidnap a judge, a preacher and a mayor who did not quite have their politics in order. Then he swung into the city and, joined by local Liberty Boys, took over Rivington's loyalist print shop and carried off his type. That done, he returned to Connecticut and waited for the applause. When instead he got criticism from New York authorities, it only convinced him they were a parcel of traitors after all. He decided to repair to Cambridge and turn them all in to the Army.[10]

Major General Lee, an old-country Englishman, fancied himself the Continental Army's military intellectual and the commander it ought to have had—a conceit kept alive by the knowledge that so many of his contemporaries agreed with him. Nor was he one to content himself with playing second fiddle. A remarkable insight into his unstable personality had been made by the Mohawk Indians some twenty years before. As a young English captain, Lee was given the name, "Boiling Water." But now (at the opening of 1776) he was just back from a tour of duty in Rhode Island, whose situation was very much like New York's. Newport also entertained a British man of war, *Rose,* 20 guns, carrying much the same orders as *Asia* and *Phoenix.* Lee

went about his business there as though the naval edict on open rebellion had never been issued, laying out defense works and forcing a test oath on leading Tories as well. The guns of *Rose* remained silent throughout. The lesson was not lost on Lee, and he returned to Cambridge hoping for a chance to repeat his performance elsewhere.

Enter Sears. We have no direct testimony on the information brought by Sears to Cambridge, but collateral evidence gives a good idea as to its content. Much of it was to the point. He could hardly have exaggerated, for example, the dangerous state of affairs in Queens County, where grim loyalists fondled their government muskets and awaited their day of deliverance. We know he mentioned some military stores in New York City—medicines, shirts, blankets—left behind by the Royal Irish and never seized by the Provincial Congress for Continental use. He probably reported the arrangement to provision the men of war, and may even have volunteered a current Yankee rumor that Yorker politicians were getting rich in an illicit trade with the enemy, and were prepared to turn their city over to the first corporal's guard of redcoats that showed up to claim it.[11]

Lee recognized his chance for a separate command. "Dear General," he opened an eye-rolling letter to George Washington, "The consequences of the enemy's possessing themselves of New York have appeared to me so terrible, that I have scarcely been able to sleep from apprehensions on the subject." He then lectured the commander-in-chief on the scope of his duties and responsibilities, and finally got down to business. He laid out a complete plan of action, and modestly offered his services to carry it out. The scheme had three main objectives: (1) to occupy and fortify the City of New York, (2) to defuse the loyalists in Queens County, and (3) to purge "the City and Long Island of the leading Tories"—without going into any details of identification. To accomplish these ends he would have to raise a corps of "volunteers" in Connecticut, and perhaps call in the New Jersey Continentals posted at Elizabeth. He closed the letter as dramatically as he had opened it, warning that "the delay of a single day may be fatal."[12]

As luck would have it, there did indeed prevail a sense of urgency in Lee's proposed mission. Intelligence had been coming out of Boston about "a Fleet now getting ready, under the convoy of the Scarborough and Fowey Men of War, consisting of 5 Transports and 2 Bomb Vessels, with about 300 marines and several flatt Bottom'd Boats." This suggested an amphibious operation in the works and, in the dead of winter, could only be for an objective somewhere to the south. It was not discovered till later that the reports were either wrong or misinterpreted, but for the moment they did put the spur to Washington's making up his mind.[13]

General Lee received his official orders from the commander-in-chief on 8 January. Mainly, they followed the scenario Lee had already worked out: "You will . . . with such volunteers as are willing to join you, and can be expeditiously raised, repair to the city of New York; and calling on the commanding officer of the forces of New Jersey for such assistance as he can afford, and you shall require, you are to put that city in the best posture of defence, which the season and the circumstances will admit, disarming all such persons upon Long Island and elsewhere, (and if necessary otherwise securing them,) whose conduct and declarations have rendered them justly suspected of designs unfriendly to the views of Congress." Further, Lee was to check out the fortification in the Hudson Highlands, and seize for Continental use the Crown stores still in the city, about which "Captain Sears can give you particular information."[14]

Lee had scarcely pocketed these orders when express riders were pounding out of Cambridge with dispatches for all the parties involved. Well, not quite all. There was one for the president of the Continental Congress, another for the governor of Connecticut, and even one for the colonel-commandant in New Jersey. But no official word whatever went out to the object of the exercise. Significantly, the letter for the New York Provincial Congress (addressed, actually, to its Committee of Safety) was placed in General Lee's own hand, to be presented with his orders when he got there.[15]

On 15 January a member of the New York Committee of Safety (sitting while the Provincial Congress was in recess for elections) brought in information "that a fleet of eighteen sail of transports, two men of war and two bomb ships, are sailed from Boston." This was the same fleet reported to Washington the week before, only grown larger with the telling and now well under sail. The Committee was alarmed enough to post a lookout to the Sandy Hook lighthouse, arrange for signals in case of a sighting, and charge all the pilots in town not to bring in "any transport with troops on board, or any ship of war, or ministerial armed vessel whatever." Then the Committee sat back and waited for an official warning from General Washington which, they had every confidence, was "on the way, and may be hourly expected."[16]

They were still waiting six days later when a second rumor crackled through the city wards, to the effect that General Lee was coming in with a Connecticut mob to provoke the British ships. Prudent citizens had no trouble working out the probable course of events. They could see the Boston war bearing down on them by land and sea. Wives and children were packed into dray carts along with household goods, and trundled out of harm's way. People of every class crowded the ferry slips to Long Island and New Jersey, some investing their last shillings in the fare. Within days Governor Tryon reported home that half the population had "withdrawn with their effects, hundreds without the means to support their families."[17]

The Committee dispatched a letter to Lee, demanding to know what he was up to and having him understand that New York would not be pushed into municipal suicide to no good purpose. The problem was not lack of pluck, they contended, but lack of powder, and Lee's presence with his troops could not alleviate that circumstance: "Our whole quantity of public powder is less than three tons. No works are erected to annoy the enemy in their present situation. Should it be practicable at this juncture to erect hasty works for that purpose, to what shift are we to betake ourselves after our trifling supply of ammunition should be expended?" General Lee, therefore, would kindly keep his troops "on the western confines of Connecticut" pending further discussion.[18]

The Committee's express found the general "on the Road" just east of Stamford. Handicapped by midwinter storms and a crippling attack of gout, Lee nonetheless had the command of a respectable body of troops. He had appointed Isaac Sears his adjutant (with the rank of lieutenant colonel) to do the necessary legwork, and the Connecticut government obliged by raising two regiments for him of 750 men each. One of these—Colonel David Waterbury's—was already in the field, having previously been raised for another mission since aborted. The only problem was that the recruiting orders promised Continental pay and Washington, seriously misreading his Yankees, had hoped the men would serve for out-of-pocket expenses only. Until the finances could be worked out, Colonel Andrew Ward was asked "not to move his Regiment from their Homes 'till further orders."[19]

Lee sent a mollifying if clumsy reply to the New York Committee, disclaiming any intent to open hostilities with the warships. His sole purpose, he said, was to "prevent the enemy from taking post in your Town, or lodging themselves in Long Island." However, if the Committee insisted, "I shall only carry with me into Town a force just strong enough to secure it against any designs of the enemy . . . the main body I shall leave on the Western Frontiers of Connecticut according to your directions." Lee was a professional soldier, however, and no stranger to guardroom lawyering. The force he considered just strong enough turned out to be everything he currently had: Waterbury's entire regiment, a few separate companies of genuine volunteers and a scratch troop of volunteer cavalry, all of which he started west along the Boston Post Road.[20]

The crisis came to a head on the first of February, when Colonel Waterbury presented Washington's long-pocketed letter to the Committee of Safety, outlining Lee's mission and begging their cooperation. They would have been well within their rights to refuse. Legally any military detachment, Continental or otherwise, fell under the direction of the appropriate host government. But George Washington's appeals always tended to have a certain softening effect. Besides, a three-man delegation from the Continental Congress had arrived in town only hours before the colonel, and it was fully prepared to assume responsibility for his troops. The Committee relented. By nightfall the vanguard of Waterbury's regiment was marched in and billeted at the old Crown barracks by the Common, while the odd-lot volunteers were left to make shift at Kingsbridge.[21]

A second and potentially greater crisis, only three days later, took on all the aspects of anticlimax. Major General Lee, so disabled by gout that he had to be carried on a litter, was escorted down Manhattan Island by the city light horse. At precisely the same time the long awaited Boston armada, whose menace Lee had been sent to counter, coolly dropped anchor in the East River. It consisted of a single frigate—*Mercury*, 20 guns—plus a storeship and two transports left riding off Staten Island. The military complement on board was less than a hundred men, hardly more than the general's bodyguard it in fact turned out to be. The expedition's commander was the second ranking British Army officer in America, Lieutenant General Henry Clinton.[22]

"He has brought no troops with him," Lee reported to Washington, "and pledges his honor that none are coming. He says it is merely a visit to his old friend Tryon. If it is really so, it is the most whimsical piece of civility I ever heard of. He informs us that his intention is for North Carolina, where he expects five regiments from England; that he only brought with him two companies of light infantry from Boston. This is certainly a droll way of proceeding; to communicate his full plan is too novel to be credited." The situation was peculiar all around, for if Tryon was an old acquaintance of Clinton so was General Lee. Thirteen years before they had been good enough friends for Clinton to give Lee a letter of introduction to Prince Charles of Brunswick, when Lee was looking for a career in continental Europe.[23]

The British general may have been indiscreet in revealing his long-range intentions, but he was also being entirely candid. While in port he indulged in no aggressive moves. There is no reason to believe he even went ashore, although there must have been that temptation, for the visit was a sort of homecoming. Clinton had lived here as a youth, when his father was New York's royal governor, and he had even commanded one of the King's garrison companies at Fort George. His talks with the current governor, however, were more than a revival of the good old days. Clinton and Tryon between them worked out a rough plan for an easy capture of New York, either by breaking Manhattan's link with the interior at Kingsbridge, or by occupying the heights of Brooklyn across the East River. Clinton even had some thoughts about advancing up the Hudson and seizing the Highlands while the American works there were still incomplete.[24]

General Clinton remained in port only eight days: on 12 February he weighed anchor and stood out to sea, taking his little convoy with him. Although neither man was aware of it, the paths of Clinton and Lee would cross once again, at Charleston, South Carolina. There, in five months time, Lee would find his old friend somewhat more belligerent than he was at New York.[25]

Chapter II

Lee

The problem with New York was its tactical vulnerability—"so encircled with deep navigable water," General Lee was to observe, "that whoever commands the sea must command the town." The Americans did not command the sea, nor were they ever likely to; but right now they did have at least a toehold on the land. It was Lee's business to understand the precise relationship between this particular land mass and this particular water system, and then determine how the one might be used to offset the advantages of the other.[1]

The salient feature was the harbor bay, so landlocked as to resemble a huge, ovoid lake. Its waters lapped the shores of eastern Staten Island, New Jersey's Bergen Neck, the southern tip of Manhattan (where New York City was perched), and the western extremity of Long Island. The relative positions of these three islands with each other, and with the stretch of Jersey mainland, create the very channels that separate them. The southernmost channel, "the Narrows," spreads between Long Island and Staten Island. It is the principal sea gate, opening into an arm of the Atlantic Ocean whose roadstead is marked by Sandy Hook lighthouse. Off the bay's western rim Kill van Kull (or "the Kills") separates Staten Island from New Jersey. It is the least of the channels, and was of no immediate concern to Lee. In the north yawned the mouth of the Hudson River passage to the continental interior, whose security was, of course, Lee's ultimate concern. But for the purpose of local defense he gave the Hudson a role of secondary importance.

His main interest was in the fourth channel, whose broad entrance is loosely plugged by Governor's Island and so divides into two smaller inlets. This is the East River—not a true river at all, but a strait connecting the harbor bay with Long Island Sound and so again with the open sea. New York's commerical anchorage lay just past Governor's Island, between the city and the Long Island shore. Here merchantmen were unladen and laden at a line of wharves stretching from the Battery to the shipyards at the Out Ward line (and here, incidentally, the three men-of-war currently rode at anchor).

The East River bends sharply at Corlaer's Hook and continues northeast to join the Sound at Hell Gate. This entrance is plugged in turn by Blackwell's Island, and the channel consequently split for almost two miles. Hell Gate is formed by a juxtaposition of Horn's Hook on Manhattan, part of Queens County's north shore and Montresor Island. The place was well named, for conflicting tides met here to create rips and whirlpools between the rocky shorelines. The pass was by no means impossible, and was in fact used regularly by smaller craft. But at times it could be a pilot's nightmare.[2]

Just north of Hell Gate opens a smaller strait which snakes through a cleft in the bedrock of northern Manhattan and the adjacent mainland. This is the Harlem River—again, not a true river, for it eventually squeezes into a narrow section called Spuyten Duyvil and then connects with the Hudson. It was not considered navigable, at least not its entire length, and neither was it fordable. But it was crossed by two spans: King's Bridge (which gave the entire area its name) and the newer Dykeman's Bridge. These were Manhattan's sole connections with the continent; New Jersey and Long Island could be reached only by ferry.

The day after General Lee's arrival he sent Captain William Smith, "an excellent, intelligent, active officer" and a competent engineer, to examine the ground at Hell Gate and on Long Island. Then he sat down with the delegation from Congress and another from the New York Committee of Safety, and by the next day they had a rough plan of action. "To fortify the town against shipping is impracticable," Lee reported to Washington, "but we

are to fortify lodgments, in some commanding part of the City, for two thousand men. We are to erect enclosed batteries, on both sides of the water, near Hellgate, which will answer the double purpose of securing the town against piracies through the Sound, and secure our communication with Long Island, now become a more capital point than ever, as it is determined to form a strong fortified camp of 3000 men in that island, immediately opposite to New York. The pass in the Highlands is to be made as respectable as possible. In short, I think the plan judicious and complete."[3]

This, basically, is the structure upon which the Americans would erect their defense of the Hudson River outlet. Lee realized there was no practical way he could prevent a landing of British troops on Manhattan Island. By securing the East River, however, he could confine the possible landing areas to the west side. Even so, New York City and its approaches could be so prudently fortified that "it must cost the enemy many thousands of men to get possession of it." In sum, such an attempt would mean Bunker's Hill all over again, but this time with a trump: "for should the enemy take possession of New York, when Long Island is in our hands, they will find it almost impossible to subsist."[4]

The main element of this plan was the Brooklyn peninsula, a rectangular knob which pushed out of Long Island's north shore and pointed one corner at New York City like a flattened arrow. By and large, the rectangle lay on a northeast-southwest line. The side that connected it to the island was defined at the eastern corner by Wallabout Bay and at the southern by Gowanus Cove. The rectangle's western corner was Red Hook (an island at high tide), which combined with Governor's Island to flank the southern inlet to the East River. But it was the northern corner, opposite New York, that attracted Lee's notice. Here a ferry linked the city to Kings County, and just beyond the ferry slip rose the scarped face of Long Island's northern plateau. Once properly fortified at the crest, Brooklyn's imposing heights could dominate the anchorage and render New York untenable.

If the plan were to be implemented at all, a dramatic expansion of the current garrison was needed to supply the necessary labor. General Lee invoked at once the authority of Washington's instructions to call upon "the commanding officer of the forces of New Jersey for such assistance as he can afford," and Waterbury's Connecticut volunteers had barely settled in when elements of the 1st New Jersey Regiment began crossing the Hudson. We last saw these Jersey Continentals in December, when some of them were diverted from taking post in the Highlands and ordered instead to New York City. Since that time the 2nd Regiment had departed the local scene for the Canadian front, but the 1st Regiment remained in New Jersey at Elizabeth, Brunswick and Amboy until they got Lee's summons.[5]

The general dismissed the ad hoc volunteers he had left at Kingsbridge, their terms of enlistment being rather sketchy. Instead he sent to Connecticut to call the men of Ward's regiment from their firesides, where they had been waiting ever since Waterbury's had marched off. New York, for its part, ordered down two regiments of minutemen (ie, service-ready militia) from Dutchess County and another from Westchester. The Continental Congress promised a detachment of Pennsylvania Associators (currently serving that province in lieu of militia) and another of Jersey minutemen. Lee was disappointed to learn that both these units were disbanded as quickly as they were raised—the one through a misunderstanding of its purpose and the other for lack of firearms. Congress tried to make up the loss by ordering out the 4th Pennsylvania Continentals, but this unit also had trouble finding arms. A three-company vanguard did not arrive at New York till the end of March.[6]

It is significant that the New York Committee of Safety did not activate Colonel Lasher's independent militia into Continental service, keeping them instead under its own direction. There were reasons. Once the first burst of patriotic enthusiasm was spent, relations between the Yorkers and General Lee deteriorated rapidly. Nor was there any improvement after the Provincial Congress resumed sitting, on 19 February. The principal sticking point was the continuing presence of the British warships. The Congress wanted them kept supplied; Lee wanted them cut off from all communication with the shore.[7]

Lee saw the problem as lack of backbone, but he was mistaken. In point of fact, Captain Parker's published orders about towns in open rebellion had been systematically defied. In the weeks since *Phoenix* dropped anchor the Provincial Congress (or its Committee of Safety) had risked a number of overt moves, any one of which might have triggered a bombardment of the city. It had, for example, continued forming its own militia and now detached three minuteman regiments for service against the King. It began raising a new quota of four Continental regiments, and completed the fitting out of its own armed vessel. It sponsored an expedition from out of province to quell the King's loyal subjects in Queens County. It formally, if reluctantly, allowed a Continental detachment to occupy the city, posted troops in the King's barracks, and then conspired with General Lee to erect fortifications. It even refused the provisioning of General Clinton's mini-squadron.[8]

Having taken so many risks without consequent retaliation, the Congress had clearly come to grips with its anxiety for the physical safety of the city. Its refusal to give up supplying the warships came to be based on other considerations. No doubt there was a certain distaste, born of a mercantile ethic, to break an agreement openly entered into. On the bread-and-butter level, there was no wish to see the Royal Navy out in the bay sweeping up the market boats plying out of New Jersey. Until a spring thaw would open the northern communications, the city depended on the harbor trade for almost everything it consumed.[9]

General Lee had no intention of waiting till spring, and the matter was brought to a head just a week after his arrival. In the broad daylight of a Sunday morning the men of his garrison began working the King's artillery out of the Battery. The big guns, none of them mounted on carriages, were hauled up Broadway to join the 21 pieces still parked on the Common since last August. There, in the heart of town, they would all be relatively safe from British seizure. In the course of the day a horde of civilians, men and boys alike, showed up and laid hold of the drag ropes "with an astonishing Uproar and the Work continued all Day long with an almost intire neglect of public Worship." At City Hall the Committee of Safety had some old fears quickened, and arranged to have the public records escorted out of town by a guard from Colonel Lasher's regiment.[10]

Perhaps drawing on his Rhode Island experience, Lee had early suspected the British ships were running a bluff. He countered it with one of his own. "The first house set in flames by their Guns," he promised, "shall be the funeral pile of some of their best friends." Now, with the brazen removal of the Crown artillery, was the time for the Navy to act if ever it intended to. *Phoenix's* tender pushed out to reconnoitre around the Battery, reported back to Captain Parker on the progress of the theft, and he—did nothing. There was some muttering about not wishing to indulge the Yankees (who openly pined to see New York laid waste), and a few days later all three ships were gone from the East River.[11]

Mercury, with General Clinton aboard, cleared that Sunday evening, picked up her transports and made for the open sea. But the other two did not go quite so far. *Asia,* with Governor Tryon's floating capitol under her stern, anchored in the harbor bay. *Phoenix* dropped through the Narrows and positioned herself off western Long Island. Captain Parker, after the removal of the guns, "thought it prudent to have the Ships in a Situation to Act." Nevertheless they continued to be provisioned as before, in spite of Lee's protests and petty harassments. The general's

paper war with the Provincial Congress on this subject lasted as long as his tenure in New York.[12]

In every other respect—provided the civil prerogative was not violated—the Congress stood ready to cooperate with Lee and "give him any necessary aid in the public service." A magazine was established for him, and a military hospital. A company of artificers (soldiers with useful trade skills) was raised on the Continental establishment. Tools and materials were provided without stint. A staff was appointed—barrackmaster, commissaries and wagonmaster—to take up the routine chores of garrison housekeeping. Buildings left unoccupied by the civilian exodus were condemned for use as troop quarters. And by no means least, the Congress instructed its commissariat to "issue one gill of rum per day for each man on fatigue."[13]

The first project was to modify the old Crown works. Fort George was the main structure, a square stone fort of 330 feet on the exterior line and bastioned at each corner. It had occupied the same spot in one form or another since 1615, "constructed on a small Nole just sufficient for the Work, which has two fronts to the Town and two to ye Water, one facing the East on one the North River." Two powder magazines were the only casemates, and they were damp. The water supply was insufficient, and part of the glacis had long ago been planted as a garden. The principal outwork—the Battery—was a chain of three bastions perched low on the water's edge, with a linking stone curtain that extended from the East River to the Hudson. The Lower Barracks completed the system, and were currently occupied by the Jersey Continentals (Waterbury's Yankees were quartered in the Upper Barracks, a mile up Broadway).[14]

General Lee could find no way to render the works "a fortification of offence against the enemy." Fort George was poorly situated to withstand the close fire of ships of the line. The Battery had no advantage of elevation, and could be raked by grapeshot its entire length. In fact, vessels might approach so near that a landing party could well overrun the low parapet, take possession of the fort, and have it "converted into a citadel, to keep the town in subjection." To thwart this potential embarrassment, Lee had the northeast and northwest bastions completely razed along with their connecting face "so that, being entirely open behind . . . it is impossible for the enemy to lodge themselves in and repair the fort." Just to make sure, a barricade was thrown across Broadway some 200 yards away and mounted with artillery to cover the interior.[15]

The actual labor on any new works had to wait for the reinforcements to come in. Meanwhile Lee, still crippled with gout, could hobble about well enough to keep engineer Smith busy with transit and chain. Plans were made to traverse and barricade all the cross streets leading in from the rivers on both sides of the town, supplemented by field works on a convenient protective ridge that partially screened the city from the Hudson. The East River anchorage was to be secured against the enemy "in such a manner that their ships will scarcely venture into it, or at least they cannot keep their station when in." This called for two batteries on a slope occupied by the Jewish cemetery, where the channel is the narrowest: one amid the shipyards at the foot of the slope; the other a larger, bastioned work on the crest. A third battery would be sunk in a wharf cellar closer to Manhattan's southern tip.

Three prominent heights spaced across the island on the city's north side caught Lee's eye. Bayard's Hill, in the center, and Jones's Hill, rising above Corlaer's Hook, would each accommodate a star-shaped redoubt and between them cover the Bowery Lane thoroughfare. Another work on Lispenard's Hill would do the same for the Greenwich Road on the west side. In fact, it was felt that all "the leading roads from the Hudson's River, whence the enemy can alone approach, must be obstructed to artillery." Not only that, but field works were to be thrown up "in certain regular steps . . . quite to King's Bridge." Kingsbridge itself was

9

to be "strongly fortified, to preserve the communication free and open with Connecticut."

By 15 February the upriver minutemen began filtering into the city a company at a time. The two Dutchess County regiments were quartered in town; the 2nd Regiment in a vacant hospital building and the 1st in some of the growing number of abandoned houses. The Westchester minutemen were posted to Horn's Hook, where they broke ground for a star fort large enough to hold 300 men. This would serve to control the pass at Hell Gate, and keep open the communication with Long Island. A complementary redoubt was planned to occupy one of the opposite shores, on either Montresor Island or Long Island.[16]

Ward's Connecticut volunteers did not arrive until the 24th, when they were immediately ferried over to Kings County and quartered in private homes. Their task was to prepare a retrenched encampment large enough for 5,000 men and "fortified by a chain of redoubts, mutually supporting each other, and which, also corresponding with the batteries on the New-York side, will prevent the enemy's entering or remaining in the East River." The intended number of redoubts in this chain was three; they would all be on the Brooklyn heights and oriented toward securing the anchorage. There was no immediate plan to prepare defenses against an attack from the Long Island interior.[17]

Finally, Lee executed his charge to "inquire into the state and condition" of the defenses in the Hudson Highlands, 50 miles upriver. Fort Constitution (present Constitution Island, across the Hudson from West Point) was still under construction; we have already seen that the works were not yet ready to accommodate the New Jersey Continentals in December. Little more had been accomplished by the time Captain Smith arrived on General Lee's behalf. He found the situation deplorable. The fort was poorly sited, poorly designed and, such as it was, poorly constructed. The current garrison consisted of three minuteman companies with a minuteman colonel for a commandant. Smith spent his tour laying out another work, to be located further downstream and "Nam'd after the brave Genl. Montgomery," New York's own martyred hero.[18]

By this time February was drawing to a close—and so was Lee's tenure as commanding officer at New York City. The Continental Congress had tapped him to head its newly created Southern Department, where the menace of Clinton's expedition was just starting to be felt. By 7 March the general was crossing the Hudson and on his way to the new assignment, his departure unmarked by ceremony of any kind. The Provincial Congress was plainly relieved to see the back of this abrasive Englishman who had instigated the Continental occupation of their city and then, for good or ill, stayed long enough to work out its plan of defense. Now it would be up to his successors to implement that plan. From this point on every spadeful of earth thrown over a man's shoulder, every plank laid into a gun platform would serve only to deepen the American commitment to its overall utility.[19]

Chapter III

Stirling

Lee's immediate successor was William Alexander, the self-styled Earl of Stirling and late commander of the 1st New Jersey Continentals. The new general was something of a local celebrity; his ties to New York were at once social, political and marital (his wife was a New York Livingston). He had, in fact, been raised in New York, and once counted Governor Clinton's son Henry in his circle of friends. Later, five of his early middle years were spent abroad in the quest of a lapsed Scottish earldom. His claim got recognition in Scotland, but failed to gain approval in the British Parliament. Alexander suspected political thimblerigging, so he came home and assumed the title anyway, and his country-

men thereafter addressed him as "My Lord." By the time the war opened he enjoyed a reputation as a high-rolling bon vivant, although his old regiment found him to be a bit of a martinet. When he took the New York City garrison in charge his commission as a Continental brigadier was only six days old.[1]

It was a hair-raising time for a new general in his first command—and an independent command at that. The elements of the big picture were beginning to shift and change. Washington had already notified Lee late in February that the British were preparing to evacuate Boston: "They have removed two Mortars from Bunker's Hill, and carried them, with a great Part of their heavy brass Cannon, on Board of their Ships. They have taken all the Topsail Vessels in the Harbour, into the Service. They are ready watered, and their Sails bent. All this Shew, may be but a Feint, but if real, and they should come your Way, I wish you may be prepared to receive them." The commander-in-chief had a measure of doubt that his adversary's next move would be an attempt on New York, but he could take no chances. "I shall keep a good Watch on their Motions," he promised Lee, "and give you the speediest Information possible."[2]

General Lee got this warning during his final days at New York, and somehow managed to lose it. But he did pass its content along to the Provincial Congress, except in the process much of the iffiness was deleted and the prospect of imminent invasion made a dead certainty. Understandably, the Congress was sparked to a flurry of preparation. A "magazine of provisions and military stores" was established in Westchester County, to be stocked with salt pork and peas. Powder mills were urged to step up production, and all the colony militia was put on alert as far north as Albany County. The Hampton townships were asked to post lookouts on Long Island's south shore "to give the earliest notice of a fleet upon the coast."[3]

The maritime front was coming alive in other respects as well, with the Royal Navy now enforcing a Parlimentary embargo "To Prohibit all Trade and intercourse with the several Colonies in North America." The frigate *Phoenix* was still moored off Long Island, just below the Narrows, where Captain Parker was trying a new ploy. Several loyalist harbor pilots had joined him, and he was using their boats to decoy inbound merchantmen so that he could snap them up as prizes. The Provincial Congress finally sent out its armed sloop *Schuyler*, with orders to patrol off the Jersey coast "between Egg Harbour and Sandy Hook, and protect all vessels coming into this port." Parker countered by arming his ship's tender and dispatching her to the same area. Meanwhile, a party of Ward's regiment was sent down from Brooklyn to surprise the pilot's beach camp on Gravesend Bay, but the place was deserted and the Yankees came back empty handed.[4]

Nor were *Phoenix's* decoys the only menace that incoming vessels had to endure. The Provincial Congress deliberately created a navigational hazard by having the Sandy Hook lighthouse blacked out, in the hopes of thereby hindering the invasion fleet. Major William Malcolm of the city Independents got this assignment, which he carried out with characteristic diligence and with the help of the Monmouth County (New Jersey) militia. The major "found it impossible to take out and save the glass . . . and therefore was obliged to break it." But he did make off with all the lamps, more than three casks of oil and some miscellaneous rigging.[5]

Apart from the beach camp raid, the new commanding general could do little except keep his small army scratching at the fortifications. There were too few hands to make very much headway, and prospects were not bright. Ward's and Waterbury's Connecticut regiments, whose ranks made up over half the labor force, were due to expire on 25 March. This already represented a two-week extension of their enlistments, and it was not likely they would stay longer than that. The three New York minuteman regiments furnished little more than 500 men between them, a number barely exceeded by the 1st New Jersey, plus a newly mustered company of New York Continentals. Not counting the New York artificers or new recruits not yet mustered into service, Stirling's total combat strength was 190 officers and 2232 men "present fit for duty." Another 378 were either sick or absent.[6]

Unsettling intelligence estimates began coming down from headquarters, where Washington now leaned to the opinion that New York would be the next British objective after all. "His Excellency . . . desires You will exert Yourself to the utmost in preparing for their reception," wrote an aide, who went on to express hopes that the Provincial Congress would cooperate "in using every endeavor to prevent their forming a lodgment, before his Excellency can come or send to Your Assistance—the fate of America depends upon this Campaign, & the Success of this Campaign will a good deal depend upon Your exerting Yourself with Vigour."[7]

Instructions from the Continental Congress added little comfort. The 3rd, 5th and 6th Pennsylvania Continentals were ordered to New York, as well as the 3rd New Jersey. But they were currently having as little luck in finding arms as the 4th Pennsylvania, which we have seen under marching orders since 20 February. Nonetheless, Stirling was expected to "exert the utmost diligence in erecting the works and perfecting the defences" according to Lee's master plan. He could, if he liked, call on New York, New Jersey and Connecticut for "some Militia," provided he did not overstep the bounds of his authority. "This large power," Congress hoped, "will be exercised with the greatest discretion as the exigence of affairs may require."[8]

Congress did not yet know that Stirling, on his own initiative, already had called on the neighboring provinces for militia reinforcements. The New Jersey Provincial Congress was currently in recess, however; no Committee of Safety sat daily to conduct public business, and the counties were reluctant to part with men they might very well need themselves. New Jersey counties of Essex, Morris and Sussex, after some wheedling, managed to send over a trickle of volunteers. At the same time Connecticut levied two regiments out of its militia "to repair by land or water to New York . . . to assist in securing and maintaining that place." They arrived just in time for the departure of Ward's and Waterbury's, so the net gain from New England was zero.[9]

But New York was the colony in immediate peril after all, and the bulk of any reinforcement might reasonably have been expected to come from within. The Provincial Congress worked out a program with Stirling, dealing mostly with raising and organizing a sufficient labor force. The three over-officered minuteman regiments in town, for instance, were to be filled with drafts out of the militia of Orange and Westchester Counties. In addition, the entire adult male population of New York City and Kings County would turn out, under penalty of a stiff fine, to work on the fortifications under Engineer Smith's direction. This meant everybody—merchant, mechanic, freeman and slave—and the work gangs would be organized through the existing militia organizations.[10]

New York patterned its militia on the dual system suggested by the Continental Congress in 1775, but with local variations. Under this system, virtually every male from 16 to 50 years was enrolled in a neighborhood training company. The enrollee was expected to provide himself with a prescribed array of arms and equipment, and to drill at regular intervals. In return, he had a voice in the selection of his company officers. His company joined with others to form regiments within each county, and the aggregate made up the "common" or "standing" militia. At the same time, each county was supposed to maintain a separate but complementary system of companies and regiments, composed of one fourth of the standing militia. While the officers of these units remained constant, the enlisted men were rotated every four months. These were the "minutemen," and their function was to go on active service as necessary without disturbing the integrity of the standing units.[11]

We have seen that the City and County of New York supported a third type, the "independent" militia companies of Colonel Lasher's regiment. These companies survived as a relic of the pre-war administration, when units just like them existed in metropolitan areas as a social convenience. Gentlemen of means could thus discharge their military obligations without having to hobnob with sweaty mechanics. The old snobbery still attached to Lasher's companies but to a much lesser degree; their very number tended to dilute their exclusiveness. In fact, so many new companies continued to form that a second regiment was created to accommodate them (Major Malcolm, the dismantler of Sandy Hook lighthouse, was of this unit; he would shortly succeed to its command). The city also kept up a troop of light horse, a type of cavalry "mounted on light, swift horses, whose men are but small, and lightly accoutred." We last saw the city troop escorting General Lee down Manhattan Island the day of his arrival.[12]

These two independent regiments served New York County in lieu of minutemen. In addition, there were three regiments of standing militia, distributed by company beats among the six wards of New York City proper (North, East, South, West, Dock and Montgomerie Wards), the Out Ward north of the city and Harlem township north of that. The patriotic spirit could run quite as high in these standing regiments as in the voluntary independents, but there was also a show of apathy and even mulish hostility. One beat embarrassed the county committee by electing an avowed loyalist for its company commander. Another polling was ordered, only to have the same man come out on top again. In the second election the vote was unanimous.[13]

Indifference, pure and simple, marked the general outlook in Kings County across the East River. There the freeholders still mostly considered themselves as Dutch, kept an inordinate number of black slaves, and were stubbornly disinclined to get involved in the political squabbles of their English neighbors. Seven companies made up the county's sole standing regiment; two from Brooklyn township and one each from Bushwick, Flatbush, Flatlands, Gravesend and New Utrecht. No provision was made for minutemen, but there was enough patriotic interest in the county to raise two troops of light horse. In the current emergency a patrol of these cavalrymen was to be "posted at some convenient height, near the west end of Nassau [ie, Long] Island, to reconnoitre the entrance of any enemy into Sandy Hook, or appearing on the coast."[14]

Patriotic sentiment ran much higher in Suffolk County, on the eastern two-thirds of Long Island. The Royal Navy had a strong bent for foraging livestock there to feed the Boston garrison, and this fostered a lively interest in local defense. The standing militia regiments were three. The 1st Regiment represented the western townships of Huntington, Smithtown, Islip and Brookhaven; the 2nd, Southampton and Easthampton on the south fork; the 3rd, Shelter Island and Southold on the north fork. More to the point, however, the county militia supported not only an active minuteman regiment, but a minuteman artillery company as well —the only one of its kind in New York.[15]

Between Kings and Suffolk lay Queens County, the most unabashedly loyalist county in America. Yet even Queens had areas where the Continental cause was embraced, and embraced quite fervently. One early militia unit in Jamaica, for example, volunteered itself "as a company of Minute Men, for the defence of American Liberty," and enough interest later developed in Newtown to raise a troop of light horse. Further, the citizens of northern Hempstead grew so incensed by their loyalist fellow townsmen that they erected a separate and independent district committee. It went by the engaging but unwieldy name of "Cow Neck, Great Neck, Etc." after the communities on Hempstead's north shore.[16]

The core of the problem in Queens County was a downright refusal to underwrite the General Association. This instrument,

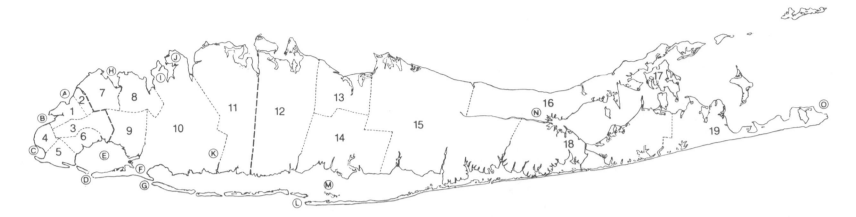

THE TOWNSHIPS OF LONG ISLAND IN 1776. Kings County: (1) Brooklyn, (2) Bushwick, (3) Flatbush, (4) New Utrecht, (5) Gravesend, (6) Flatlands. Queens County: (7) Newtown, (8) Flushing, (9) Jamaica, (10) Hempstead, (11) Oyster Bay. Suffolk County: (12) Huntington, (13) Smithtown, (14) Islip, (15) Brookhaven, (16) Southold, (17) Shelter Island, (18) Southampton, (19) Easthampton. Other points of reference: (A) Wallabout Bay, (B) Gowanus Cove, (C) Gravesend Bay, (D) Rockaway Inlet, (E) Jamaica Bay, (F) Rockaway, (G) Hog Island Inlet, (H) Flushing Bay, (I) Great Neck, (J) Cow Neck, (K) Jerusalem, (L) Fire Island Inlet, (M) Fire Island, (N) Riverhead, (O) Montauk Point.

basically, was the individual New Yorker's declaration of solidarity with his fellow citizens, in which he swore "to carry into execution whatever measures may be recommended by the Continental Congress, or resolved upon by the Provincial Congress for the purpose of preserving our Constitution." On the Association, and its general acceptance, rested the legitimacy of revolutionary government at every level. The first township committees in Queens realized early that they represented virtually nobody but themselves. This being the case, their delegates to the county committee could claim no constituency nor, in turn, could the county delegates to the Provincial Congress. As long as this situation prevailed the Congress could exercise little moral authority in the county except for those pockets that freely chose to accept it.[17]

Moreover, Queens had been unique in having a remnant of the old Crown militia still functioning, in direct competition with the sparse patriot units that were just beginning to form. The commander of the royalists was Captain Richard Hewlett of Hempstead, and his partisans armed themselves by openly robbing the patriot minority of any muskets handed out by the county clerk. Last September the New York Committee of Safety had sought to relieve the situation by sending a deputation to disarm the non-associators and impress their weapons for Continental use. A detachment from Colonel Lasher's Independents was first ordered along to provide muscle, but even this military support was held back in the end. As a result the disarmers collected little more than derision. "Had your battalion appeared," Hewlett told them, "we should have warmed their [back] sides."[18]

The counter-revolution culminated with the county elections of November, when the voters overwhelmingly declined any further representation in the Provincial Congress. They bore no grudge against their fellow New Yorkers, they further declared, but neither would they passively allow themselves to be disarmed. As if to emphasize the point, Captain Hewlett began distributing a quantity of powder, flints and musket balls which had been landed near his Rockaway home by one of *Asia's* boats. That was the final straw. The Congress resolved to settle the matter deci-

sively—but the trick was to do so without a miniature civil war which would surely involve the Navy.[19]

In the end it was decided that the delinquent voters should be "entirely put out of the protection of this Congress," and to let any appropriate action to be taken against them originate in Philadelphia. The Continental Congress obligingly took the cue, and by the middle of January it had a provisional regiment of New Jersey minutemen swinging through New York City for the Newtown ferry. The commander was Colonel Nathaniel Heard, and for some two weeks he marched the length of Queens with poll list in one hand and test oath in the other. By the end of the month he had collected over 800 signatures, enough muskets to arm a regiment, four royal militia standards and 19 ringleaders—seven more having slipped through the net. Neither of the warships stirred throughout, and Captain Hewlett could only retire with his partisans and hope for better times.[20]

Finally, General Lee felt constrained to make a contribution when, just before his departure from New York, he sent Isaac Sears into Queens County to apply another test oath. It was to be the old rebel's last Tory hunt. Taking with him a detachment of Ward's regiment, Sears tried to redo everything already done by Heard's minutemen, but on a smaller scale. Hapless delinquents were run to ground once more to have Lee's oath administered, "which they swallowed as hard as if it was a four pound shot." When he arrived in northern Hempstead, however, the hair-trigger patriots there indignantly had him recalled to New York. After that Sears continued on as Lord Stirling's adjutant, till at last the Cambridge Army arrived with its own staff system and put him out of a job.[21]

The resistance was crushed without loss of blood, and the patriot militia began to take shape. Two standing regiments were formed, however tardily—the 1st Regiment in Newtown, Flushing and Jamaica townships; the 2nd in Hempstead and Oyster Bay. There was no formal minuteman establishment other than the Jamaica volunteers, and the Newtown light horse was not commissioned till May. For the current emergency, the reliable district of northern Hempstead was asked to keep six horsemen posted as a lookout at Rockaway.[22]

Richmond County on Staten Island had also refused to select delegates to the Provincial Congress and, like Queens, was put under sanction. But Richmond tried to recant. Elections were rescheduled; the new Congress met and the county's delegates applied for admission, claiming that "⅞ths of the inhabitants" had signed the Association. The Congress was not impressed. When General Clinton was beating out to sea in February, Colonel Heard was asked to post his Jerseymen on Staten Island in case *Mercury* should call there to reprovision herself with livestock. It turned out to be a false alarm, but Heard took the opportunity to arrest some of the Richmond County delinquents and carry them off to Elizabeth.[23]

The county's new-found patriotic spirit was nipped in the bud. A standing militia eventually got organized, but only in a perfunctory manner. It consisted of a small regiment made up of one company from each of the four townships: Northfield, Southfield, Westfield and Castleton. There were no minutemen. No particular service was ever asked of Richmond County, and none was given.[24]

The character of any county's militia had to be somewhat influenced by continual recruiting for the Continental Army. The program tended to draw off the best motivated men of an active military age. This was so even in New York County, where a staunch patriot could find more agreeable service in one of the independent units. Colonel Lasher's regiment was given the option of entering Continental service as a complete body, but it declined. An officer of the 2nd Independents was given a recruiting warrant, but the county's Continental quota of eight companies had to be filled for the most part out of the standing militia. The quotas for the surrounding counties were in proportion to their population: three companies for Suffolk, one for Queens, and one company between Kings and Richmond.[25]

By the middle of March some of these militia companies were being mustered into service, adding to the respectable labor force now at General Stirling's disposal. The turnout of the New York citizenry had been gratifying. Men of every social rank assembled each morning to fife and drum; even those who could well afford to hire substitutes "worked so long, to set an example, that the blood rushed out of their fingers." With the militia officers acting as their foremen, the citizen gangs broke ground for breastworks and batteries almost as fast as Engineer Smith could trace them out.[26]

Stirling, under the spell of his predecessor's assumptions, clearly expected the first British move to be a direct assault on the city itself. Where Lee's priority had been to modify Fort George, Stirling's was to obstruct the side streets leading in from the rivers. "All the commissioned officers willing to take the direction of building a barricade," read general orders, "are desired to meet with Colonel Smith . . . and he will mark out their work for them." The job was completed in little more than a week, yielding strong breastworks "behind each of which a considerable Number of Men may be placed and kept covered from the Fire of the Enemy." Each was set well back from the water so as to afford a maximum field of fire. There was every confidence that any invaders would be cut down as they tried to clamber over the wharves.[27]

At the same time the other fortifications were by no means neglected, and the new general did not hesitate to modify Lee's plan. The Bayard's Hill Redoubt was started immediately to "command the Country from River to River and keep off any Enemy from that Quarter, and if any Enemy should get into the City this Fort will prevent there [sic] advancing into the Country." The new hospital, where the Dutchess County minutemen had lately been quartered, was converted into a magazine and extensively fortified. Extended lines were thrown up on the city's western ridge, overlooking the Hudson. These were the Oyster, Jersey and Grenadier Batteries. The works on the east side shaped up as Lee had planned, with a redoubt at one of the lower wharves, one in the shipyards and another on the covering hill by the Jewish cemetery. These were the Whitehall, Waterbury and Badlam Batteries. The Horn's Hook work was roughed out at Hell Gate and named Fort Thompson. At the southern end of Manhattan, Fort George and the Grand Battery were made a good deal more defensible by raising their parapets and providing embrasures for the artillery.[28]

The works on Long Island progressed just as rapidly, but with some changes from the original plan. Where Lee had wanted a chain of redoubts on the crest of Brooklyn's north scarp, an angular work named Fort Stirling was completed instead. Artillery was ferried over and mounted by the middle of March. With

that done, Colonel Ward's Yankees set to work with the Kings County farmers and their black field hands to erect a hexagonal citadel. It was to take up about five acres on the flat of the plateau, and named "the Congress." There were no plans in view to protect the entire Brooklyn peninsula against an attack from the land side. Stirling was concerned about a possible enemy landing at the Narrows, at the extreme western end of Long Island, but he could not stretch his available manpower so far as to cover that threat.[29]

Except for the citadel and the Fort George parapets, all these works were roughly complete by the time Stirling's brief tenure came to an end. On 20 March Brigadier General William Thompson arrived from Cambridge. He was Stirling's senior only by virtue of being three slots ahead in the promotion list of 1 March; even so, the command was handed over without rancor and perhaps with some degree of relief. Thompson was followed to New York by his old regiment of Pennsylvania riflemen—the 1st Continentals—plus two independent Maryland rifle companies and another from Virginia. The Pennsylvanians, now under Colonel Edward Hand, subsequently moved to Long Island and assumed the reconnaissance duties of the Kings County light horse. The three independent rifle companies were posted to Staten Island under Captain Hugh Stephenson.[30]

Stirling's first assignment in a subordinate role was to bring New Jersey into the general defense structure. He followed a plan of his own devising, whose aim was to protect the Jerseys against incursions and to secure the colony's communication with New York. The first aim was to be carried out by denying British access to Newark Bay and the river systems that fed into it. A redoubt at Bergen Neck would block the Kill van Kull inlet, supported by another on the Staten Island side. Works at Amboy and Elizabeth would secure the alternate channel, along Staten Island's west side. The New York communication would be secured by fortifying Paulus Hook and cutting roads across Bergen Neck to connect the principal ferry points. In addition, works were marked out on Staten Island with the hope that, upon completion, they could forestall a British lodgment there. With the interests of its own province now taken into account, the New Jersey Committee of Safety detached 2,000 militia for service, including the volunteers already sent to New York by Essex, Morris and Sussex Counties.[31]

General Thompson's term in a separate command was to be even shorter than General Stirling's. Only ten days after his arrival the Westchester minutemen at Horn's Hook stopped working long enough to watch a fleet of small craft work its way through Hell Gate pass. These were the topsail vessels of the coastal trade—sloops and schooners for the most part—inbound out of Norwich and New London. They had recently been hired as troop transports, and crowding their decks was Brigadier General William Heath's brigade from Cambridge. The Continental Army had begun to arrive.[32]

Chapter IV

Washington

The British Army, "in great haste and much disorder," evacuated Boston on St. Patrick's Day. The entire fleet of warships and transports, crowded with siege-weary troops and loyalist refugees, dropped down the harbor as far as Nantasket Road—and stayed there. General Washington did not know what to make of it: "The enemy," he admitted, "have the best knack of puzzling people I ever met with in my life." He fully expected an immediate descent on New York, yet he dared not strip Massachusetts of troops while the enemy remained in plain view. The entire procedure could, after all, be an elaborate feint to catch the Continental Army off guard.[1]

The general had already sent off as much of his army as he could spare. The riflemen, as we know, were quick-marched southward along with General Thompson, followed days later by five line regiments under General Heath. This vanguard had either reached New York, or was very close to it, when the British ships finally cleared the Massachusetts coast and stood out to sea. The fleet was barely under the horizon when Washington began feeding the rest of his army into the pipeline, "leaving only a convenient Space between each Division to prevent Confusion, and Want of Accommodation upon their March." Brigadier General John Sullivan's six regiments were ordered out first, then five more under Nathanael Greene, and then another five under Joseph Spencer. With Sullivan's brigade went Major General Israel Putnam, carrying orders to assume the command at New York City and to continue implementing Lee's defense plan. Washington did not move his headquarters out of Cambridge till 4 April. He left behind five Continental regiments as a permanent garrison for the Boston area.[2]

By the time he got to New York the first blood of the campaign had already been spilled. Two incidents had taken place, actually, the first of them a spoiling action directed against the prospect of British entrenchment. Governor Tryon, still living aboard *Dutchess of Gordon* in the harbor, now had so many fugitive loyalists in his care that he had to keep the overflow on one of Captain Parker's prizes. He thought they might be useful in countering the rebel fortifications, so he landed them on Bedloe's, now Liberty Island and started them throwing up works on the shore opposite New York City. General Heath could see what was going on, of course, and decided to dislodge the fugitives with a midnight raid. A detachment of the 1st Jersey Continentals got the assignment. The Americans landed at one in the morning, 3 April, to find the island deserted except for a handful of noncombatants. These they escorted into a cottage out of harm's way, fired the old quarantine hospital, demolished the new works, and carried off the entrenching tools. Four days later Tryon weighed anchor and dropped through the Narrows to join *Phoenix* off Sandy Hook.[3]

As Tryon sailed past Staten Island he was startled by the sound of small arms fire from the shore. Captain Parker's little squadron had lately been joined by the sloop *Savage,* and her skipper sent a boat ashore to take on fresh water. Another boat, from *Phoenix's* tender, went along on the same mission. It was Easter Sunday, and the sailors expected the usual lack of curiosity from the Richmond County militia. They had scarcely begun their work when a gun signalled them to come aboard, and moments later they found themselves sprinting for the beach with Captain Stephenson's Virginia riflemen in close pursuit. A complete surprise had been foiled by the signal gun, but the Americans did capture one of the boats and ten of its crew. The other boat carried off two of the British casualties under the covering fire of *Savage's* broadsides. The riflemen claimed a number of kills but they had in fact wounded only three seamen, suffering one wounded themselves from the British cannonade.[4]

General Putnam had taken command by this time, and the incident provoked him to put a final end to all communication with the warships, and to stop all further provisioning of them. Any citizens defying the order, he warned, "will be considered as enemies, and treated accordingly." The hapless British crewmen were promptly put on two-thirds rations, with no relief in sight. *Savage* had already brought word that the Army was not on the way to New York after all, but had gone instead to Halifax to pull itself together. With Continental troops now pouring into the area every day, *Asia* finally dropped through the Narrows under fire from the riflemen on shore. She spoke back with two 18-pounders, and then took up *Phoenix's* old station in Gravesend Bay. The upper harbor was left entirely clear of enemy ships.[5]

General Washington had come in the day before, on 13 April, and his arrival automatically made New York City the headquarters of the Continental Grand Army. In a physical sense the transformation had already occurred, for the place had long since become a garrison town: "deserted by its old inhabitants and filled with soldiers from New England, Philadelphia, Jersey, &c." An evening curfew was in effect, applying to citizen and soldier alike. The garrison itself had already been reduced to its professional core by General Putnam; purged of virtually every unit not originally raised on the Continental establishment. The militia, the minutemen, the levies, the gentlemen laborers with their blistered hands—all had been released from active duty and sent home. The remaining troops, all Continentals, were widely dispersed over Manhattan, Long and Staten Islands. They would have to be pulled together into some kind of cohesive military force.[6]

At this stage of the war there were two basic types of Continental units, each with its own peculiar subdivisions. The most numerous type by far comprised the 28 regiments of the late Cambridge Army: 26 of line infantry, one of riflemen and one of artillery—plus three independent rifle companies and another of artificers. All but the artillery and the independent companies carried regimental numbers, and all were tagged as "Continental" rather than by any provincial designation. But only the riflemen came from outside the four New England colonies, and any attempt to promote a sense of nationalism at the expense of local pride did not reckon with the enlistment patterns of colonial America. Of the 26 "Continental" infantry regiments, sixteen may be readily identified as from Massachusetts, five from Connecticut, three from New Hampshire and two from Rhode Island.[7]

All of these 26 regiments had started life together on New Years Day, and they were all to expire together on the last day of 1776. They had largely been raised out of the four distinct (albeit roughly Continentalized) New England armies of 1775, which in turn had largely been raised out of the several colony militias shortly after the war's beginning. In this way many of the existing Continental units could trace their lineage, however indirectly, to the provincial regulars who defended Bunker's Hill and, through them, to the minutemen who turned out for Lexington and Concord. A considerable number of the Yankee soldiers now walking the streets of New York had seen action at both of these engagements.

The riflemen had been raised by the Continental Congress last June to "march and join the army near Boston, to be there employed as light infantry." To a considerable extent, frontier counties of Pennsylvania, Maryland and Virginia provided the recruiting grounds, and the enlistment was for a year. The Pennsylvania companies were properly organized under field officers and were, in fact, the 1st Continental Regiment on the current establishment. The Marylanders and Virginians never got formally organized above the company level. As a body, the rifle corps was not quite complete. Last year one Virginia and two Pennsylvania companies had been detached to the Northern Army, and all three were lost in the assault on Quebec.[8]

The riflemen were military specialists, and they looked the part. Where the line infantryman aspired to a regimental coat and marching gaiters, the rifleman gloried in his fringed hunting shirt and Indian leggings. The infantryman was most effective when firing his musket in volleys; the rifleman could deliver a ball where he, as an individual, wished it to go. He was admired as an aggressive, self-reliant skirmisher—but he also had serious limitations. For one example, his weapon was his own personal property; it was designed for hunting game and could not be fitted with a bayonet. Once he got off his shot, the rifleman was vulnerable in a hand-to-hand situation until he could finish reloading. Then, too, under actual combat conditions he was not always quite the legendary deadeye. Stephenson's Virginians, firing point-blank into unarmed sailors clustered around their beached longboats, managed to wound only three, and none of them fatally.

The Continental Artillery Regiment had a leavening of Rhode Islanders, but in the main it was a Massachusetts outfit and its commander was Colonel Henry Knox. It was also three companies under strength, having left one at Boston and detached two more to the Northern Army. The loss was made up in part by attaching two New York artillery companies recently mustered into service—one on the Continental establishment and the other on the provincial. This last, Captain Alexander Hamilton's, was the only one to escape the recent purge of non-Continental units. Even so, there would never be quite enough artillerymen to go around, and the shortage eventually had to be made up by drafting men out of each infantry company in the army and training them to be artillerymen.[9]

By February Congress had begun dividing the colonies into military districts, and the second grouping of Continental regiments originated in the colonies of the Middle Department: New York, New Jersey, Pennsylvania, Delaware and Maryland. These also bore regimental numbers, but only on a colony-to-colony basis. There were fourteen raised in all: four in New York, three in New Jersey, six in Pennsylvania, and one in Delaware (Maryland had no Continental establishment as such). Four of these units—the 4th New York, 2nd New Jersey, 1st and 2nd Pennsylvania—had already been sent to the Northern Army and might be found anywhere between Albany and Quebec. Three more—the 3rd and 5th Pennsylvania (neither of them fully organized) and the Delawares—were for the time being kept at home. This left seven regiments under Washington's immediate command.

And of the seven, only the three New York regiments were to remain permanently. The 1st—Colonel Alexander McDougall's—was to have been composed exclusively of New York City people, but the recruiters could barely drum up enough men to get six companies mustered into service. The balance of the regiment had to be fleshed out with upriver men, plus the handful that could be lured out of Kings and Richmond Counties. The commander of the 3rd, Colonel Rudolphus Ritzema, was a City man; he had been McDougall's lieutenant colonel in 1775. Except for a few hardcore patriots from Queens, his current regiment was raised in the mid-Hudson region. The greater part of Colonel James Clinton's 2nd Regiment relieved the minutemen on duty in the Highlands. Three of its companies had been raised in Suffolk County, however, and they spent the entire campaign as a home guard for eastern Long Island.

The newly arrived Continentals of either type had barely settled into their town-house barracks when Washington was obliged to honor Congressional orders and detach ten regiments to shore up the hard-luck campaign in Canada. By the end of April all ten were aboard sloops and moving up the Hudson in two divisions, under Brigadiers Thompson and Sullivan. Among them was Stirling's old regiment, the 1st Jerseys, one of the first units into New York City and the one which had cleaned out the Bedloe's Island loyalists. They sailed with the 3rd Jerseys, six Cambridge Army regiments and as many of the 4th and 6th Pennsylvania as could be properly armed (the unarmed Pennsylvanians were posted on Long Island and had to catch up in July).[10]

Ten regiments and two general officers represented a sizable loss, and Washington felt his weakness keenly. His total paper strength hovered at 10,000 all ranks—only 2,000 more than the Continental Congress had considered adequate for New York when it was still a secondary post and the British Army was tucked away in Boston. To correct this situation, Washington took immediate steps to have the area militia—New York's, New Jersey's and Connecticut's—put on a stand-by footing. Meanwhile the little army could be put into a proper arrangement and set to work on the fortifications. Four brigades were organized under Heath, Spencer, Greene and Stirling. Israel Putnam, the only major general on hand, was second-in-command while Horatio Gates remained adjutant general. The troops were to be encamped on a line north of the city: "The first Brigade on the Right, the second upon the Left, and the fourth in the Centre." The Third Brigade, General Greene's, was sent over to Long Island.[11]

Each brigade, more or less, reflected the provincial origin of its commander. Thus General Heath's 1st Brigade contained five regiments of solid Massachusetts men. Spencer's 2nd Brigade had a Connecticut flavor, with four regiments from that colony and one from its northern neighbor. Greene's 3rd Brigade was slightly more cosmopolitan; it contained the Pennsylvania riflemen, two Rhode Island regiments and one Massachusetts. Lord Stirling's 4th Brigade held the only Middle Department regiments—the 1st and 3rd New York—plus one Connecticut and another Massachusetts. The Artillery Regiment was not included in the arrangement, but was quartered in the old Crown barracks till the fortifications could be fixed with guns and the regiment distributed to man them. The Maryland/Virginia rifle companies still patrolled the shores of Staten Island, while five companies of the 4th Pennsylvania waited patiently on Long Island for their muskets.

The lack of adequate firearms was endemic in the army as a whole, and the New York regiments were especially short. Few of the muskets laid out for last year's campaign had found their way back into colony stores. The 3rd Regiment could gather barely enough to arm a single company. "For God's sake," implored Colonel Ritzema, "exert yourselves in arming my regiment; I have a fine body of men." But the Provincial Congress could only lean on the county committees to come up with whatever household pieces still hung on fireplace walls. At one point the militia captains in Kings County were urged to make a house-to-house canvass, "and purchase at the cheapest rate they can be obtained for ready money, all such good muskets and firelocks, fit for the use of soldiers, as can be spared by the inhabitants." By such measures enough arms trickled in so that the Yorkers, if not completely armed, were at least brought up to the shortage level of their Yankee colleagues.[12]

An inventory of available artillery told much the same story. The total amount was impressive enough; it included all the guns taken from Fort George and the Battery, plus the ones brought down from Cambridge by the Artillery Regiment. Besides, a considerable number had been gathered by the Provincial Congress and sent up to Kingsbridge last year, while even now an "air furnace" in New York City was turning out excellent brass field pieces. But only a relative handful were large enough to be effective for coastal defense; an additional "Thirty pieces of Heavy Cannon" were needed to complete the fortifications. They might easily have been supplied out of ordnance lately captured by the Continental Navy at New Providence Island. As it turned out, however, Washington's counterpart in the naval branch, Commodore Esek Hopkins, had caved in to the pressure of narrow provincialism. The big guns were all mounted on the southern shore of his native New England, and the general in New York had to make do with what he had.[13]

The need of the moment, however, was for a diligent use of pick and shovel. The troops moved out of the city and into their encampments early in May, and work resumed on the fortifications. Most of the works on Manhattan Island had already been blocked out by Stirling's citizen army; they needed only finishing off and the mounting of artillery. The work on Jones' Hill, overlooking the back door to the East River anchorage, was the only original project found mostly incomplete. Spencer's Connecticut soldiers erected a star fort there, named for their commander, and supported by lines running around the crest of the hill and thence to the Bowery Lane. The front door to the anchorage was made more secure with newly opened works on Governor's Island, intended to complement the Grand Battery's command of the main channel. At the same time a smaller work named Fort Defiance was placed at Red Hook, on the Brooklyn peninsula. This would cover the shallower Buttermilk Channel and discourage any attack on Governor's Island from the rear.[14]

The guns on the Grand Battery's west side would be complemented by a strong outpost across the river at Paulus Hook, New Jersey. This, it was hoped, would effectively hinder any intrusion into the mouth of the Hudson. Should that actually happen, enemy vessels would still have to run the gauntlet of the Oyster, Jersey and Grenadier Batteries on New York City's west side. Beyond that, there was little immediate interest in anything north of the brigade encampments on either side of Manhattan Island. Even the roomy fort at Horn's Hook was left without a proper garrison. A subaltern's guard systematically patrolled the Kingsbridge area, but its stated purpose was to cut off deserters before they got over to the mainland.[15]

The scope of Washington's limited resources, in short, dictated that he focus his energies on the immediate problems of New York City. Red Hook, Governor's Island, Paulus Hook—all were designed primarily to modify General Lee's original defense plan and eliminate its most glaring weaknesses. But the most extensive embellishment was reserved for Long Island, where Greene's 3rd Brigade had pitched its camp. The Brooklyn peninsula—keystone of the entire defense structure—was virtually converted into a self-contained fortress and finally sealed off against attack from the land side. The architect of all this was Lieutenant Colonel Rufus Putnam, the general's cousin, who had lately superseded William Smith as the theater's chief engineer. Putnam opened a network of defenses across the base of the peninsula, about a mile and a half in length, and neatly straddling the Jamaica Road arterial that connected Brooklyn Ferry with the rest of Long Island. He tried to make the best use of whatever high ground he could find, anchoring one end of his line in the marshes of Wallabout Bay and the other in the Gowanus wetlands.

A chain of redoubts occupied the principal elevations. Fort Box, with a line of breastworks extending to the right of it, commanded the Gowanus area. Fort Greene overlooked the central plateau and was supported, across the Jamaica Road, by an unnamed work called simply "the oblong redoubt." Fort Putnam dominated the perimeter's high point, supported on the left by another unnamed work from which breastworks extended to the Wallabout marsh. A lunette or "half-moon" battery sat on a ridge that jutted out in front of the lines, and was joined to Fort Putnam by a passage called a "caponier." Off by itself on the extreme right a V-shaped battery, or "fleche," occupied a narrow spit and guarded the milldam across Gowanus Creek. Entrenched breastworks connected all the redoubts, their angles forming a broad cul-de-sac where the road passed through. The entire line was ditched in front, and further protected against direct assault by an abatis of sharpened timbers.[16]

Inside the Brooklyn lines, Fort Stirling still overlooked the East River anchorage while Fort Defiance commanded the Buttermilk Channel at Red Hook. No further labor was devoted to the huge Congress citadel, however, and that project was abandoned entirely. The only other interior work was Cobble Hill Fort (or Smith's Barbette), a circular redoubt built on a nipple of land to cover the approaches from Red Hook. Additional entrenchments were dug along the high ground facing the tidemill ponds on the peninsula's southwest side. The only outwork proposed was a battery at the Narrows, "provided Colo. Knox, after his arrangement of the Artillery should find there are any fit pieces of Cannon to be spared for it."[17]

In any event, the Brooklyn lines were meant to be the place where the army would make its stand on Long Island. "In case of an attack," warned General Greene's brigade orders of 17 June, "all these posts are to be defended to the last extremity." Yet directly in front of the lines, at an average distance of about two miles, the northern plateau ended in as formidable a natural barrier as a military engineer could wish for. This was Long Island's rugged central spine; a terminal moraine where the last glacial ice sheet had spewed its debris before retreating north. The Kings County section was called the Heights of Gowanus, so craggy and

thickly wooded it could be penetrated only through a limited number of passes. Properly deployed and supported, a modest number of defenders could seriously hamper an approaching enemy force. Beyond the woody heights a broad, flat plain stretched south and west some five miles until it slid into the Atlantic Ocean.[18]

The Pennsylvania riflemen were assigned to "scour" Long Island's south shore and cut off any communication between the loyalist community and the Royal Navy. Across the Narrows on Staten Island the Maryland and Virginia companies had much the same task. Their efforts were supported offshore by an independent naval squadron responsible directly to the commander-in-chief. Its ad hoc commodore was Lieutenant Colonel Benjamin Tupper of the 21st Continentals; his flagship was the armed sloop *Hester,* and the rest of his fleet consisted of the schooner *Mifflin* and a number of open whaleboats. The crews had all been drawn out of the ranks of the army. Further, New York's own mini-navy was now three ships strong, the sloop *Schuyler* having been joined by the sloop *Montgomerie* and the schooner *Putnam.* All three helped Commodore Tupper monitor the waters off New Jersey and Long Island, preventing the King's ships from being supplied locally and "being very usefull to protect the Vessels Bound here with Amonition and distress those Bound here with Stores from Great Britain and West India Ilands."[19]

The situation with Captain Parker's squadron had not changed appreciably. *Asia* still rode in Gravesend Bay and *Phoenix* off Sandy Hook, along with Tryon's *Dutchess of Gordon* and a collection of tenders and prizes. *Savage* had departed for Halifax early in May, convoying three prizes and carrying two companies of loyalists raised by Tryon for General Howe's service. A month later the frigates *Lively* and *Mercury* arrived with some welcome storeships. From time to time the frigate *Orpheus,* cruising between Long Island and Cape Henlopen, also looked in. Sandy Hook lighthouse, which was disabled last March by Major Malcolm, provided the well that kept the ships in fresh water. A sergeant and twelve men were posted there as a guard.[20]

With all systems operating as well as could be expected, General Washington was able to get away from the army and spend a few days in Philadelphia. It was more of a command appearance than a holiday; he went at the summons of the Continental Congress "in order to advise and consent with them on the present posture of affairs." A series of meetings began on 24 May, first with Congress as a whole and then with a committee appointed to confer with him and "concert a plan of military operations for the ensuing campaign." If there were any doubts concerning the tactical feasibility of defending New York, this would have been the time to raise them. But any weaknesses in the current plan, if pointed out at all, were evidently brushed aside. Washington came away with the understanding, stated or implied, that his objective was to hold New York as an American base.[21]

Nor did he come away empty handed. On 3 June Congress determined to augment his army to the tune of 23,800 men, all to be drawn for short-term service from the militias of seven colonies. The greater part, 13,800, were levied on Connecticut (5,500), New Jersey (3,300), New York (3,000), and Massachusetts (2,000). These forces would come in self-contained brigades under their own general officers. Yet while these troops were to be in Continental service and in Continental pay, they would by no means be on the same establishment as the regular Continental units currently making up the army. They were to serve as provincial auxiliaries only, distinguished from the regulars, as well as from the standing militia, by the name "New Levies."[22]

The remaining 10,000 were levied on Pennsylvania (6,000), Maryland (3,400), and Delaware (600). These were to make up a reserve pool called the "Flying Camp." On his way to Congress Washington had paused at Amboy, New Jersey "to view the Ground, and such places on Staten Island, contiguous to it, as

16

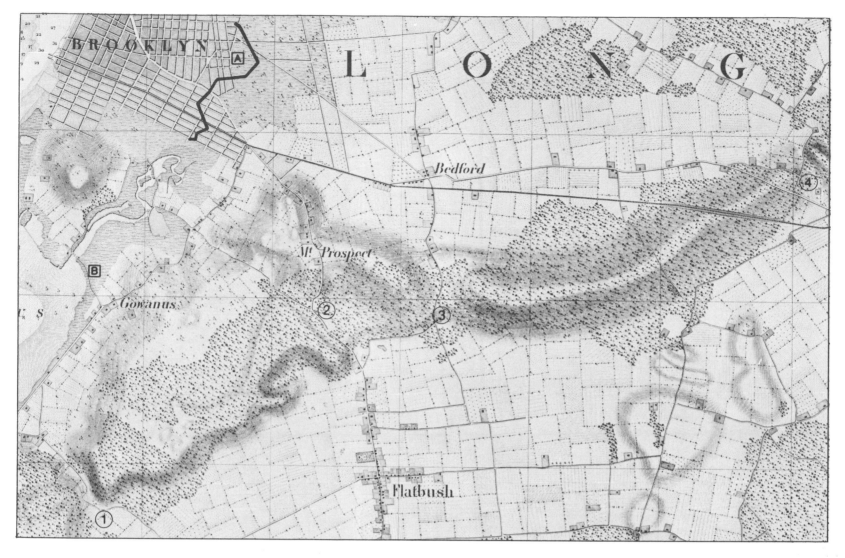

THE HEIGHTS OF GOWANUS. Detail of "Map of New-York Bay and Harbor and the Environs," Survey of the Coast of the United States, 1845. At this point in time the growing city of Brooklyn had already encroached on the site of the American lines (A). Even so, we are fortunate to have so accurate a portrait of the Kings County morain before its ultimate surrender to urban sprawl. Except for certain inevitable refinements, even the 18th Century road system remains largely intact (compare with Taylor's and Skinner's map Chapter VIII). The morass separating part of Grant's and Stirling's lines on 27 August (B) had evidently been drained and filled; it may, however be located on Bernard Ratzer's "Plan of the City of New York," 1776 (BrM 92/3).

In terms of modern orientation (1978), the gridded streets of the Borough of Brooklyn pay little heed to ancient roadbeds. The Martense Lane pass (1) generally follows the southwestern edge of Greenwood Cemetery. The site of Flatbush Pass (2) is intersected by Flatbush Avenue, where Prospect Park is separated from the Botanic Garden. Bedford Pass (3) follows the line of New York Avenue south of Eastern Parkway. Broadway cuts through the site of Jamaica Pass (4), north from Jamaica Avenue. A, B, 1, 2, 3, 4 and American Lines are additions to original map.

expanded Grand Army, a Continental brigadier would have to be appointed to the over-all command. General Hugh Mercer, sent up from Virginia, was the likeliest candidate.[23]

On the negative side, the army lost two of its key staff officers to promotion. The greater loss was that of Horatio Gates, now a major general, who had served the Continental Army since its inception in the capacity of Adjutant General. Washington had come to rely on him to keep the army a going concern, and at least reasonably responsive to orders. Now, just when his abilities would be most needed, he was appointed by Congress to head the floundering army in Canada. In addition, Quartermaster General Thomas Mifflin was appointed a Continental brigadier, also with the expectation of a line command. Both men were replaced in their respective posts by Colonels Joseph Reed and Stephen Moylan.[24]

Mifflin's brigade was created with the arrival, about 18 June, of the 3rd and 5th Pennsylvanians. Washington had reviewed these units at Philadelphia. They suffered from the universal complaint of the army, a shortage of arms. But for all that, they would be useful for a project he had in mind. "I have been up to view the grounds about King's Bridge," he wrote Congress, "and find them to admit of many places well calculated for defence, and esteeming it a Pass of the utmost importance have ordered Works to be laid out and shall direct part of the two Battalions from Pennsylvania to set about the erection immediately."[25]

Ultimately the plan involved fortifying a good deal of Manhattan's northern panhandle. The main citadel was built in a section called the Blue Bell, atop a granite elevation whose crest loomed a hundred feet above Harlem Heights and 230 feet above the Hudson River. At the base a triangular promontory poked into

may be proper for Works of Defence." By and large, this is where the Flying Camp was to be deployed, thereby putting a screen of armed men between any potential invader of New York and the capital city of Philadelphia. As with the New Levies, these troops would also be brigaded under their own provincial generals—two from Pennsylvania and one from Maryland. But inasmuch as the Flying Camp was to operate somewhat detached from the newly

17

the river, squeezing the channel into its narrowest breadth for miles in either direction. The work itself was a massive pentagonal fortress with extended outworks. Fort Washington ultimately became its name. But the soil covering here lay rather thin on the island's native bedrock, and the Pennsylvanians found themselves working all summer amid "perpetual clouds of dust."[26]

Further upriver, the Highlands had been inspected by Lord Stirling during Washington's absence. He gave Engineer Smith high marks for his layout of Fort Montgomery, suggesting only that the embrasures be faced with mortar and that outworks be planned for some nearby elevations. Fort Constitution, on the other hand, was deemed next to worthless. As Smith had discovered last February, it was located on an island off the east bank; it could only be salvaged, if at all, by covering it with a redoubt across the river at West Point. Moreover, while the 2nd New York was assembling its companies here, the old commandant—Colonel Isaac Nicoll—refused to give up his authority while there was a minuteman left in garrison. He was finally persuaded to go home, but only days before Colonel James Clinton arrived with Washington's instructions to assume Continental command.[27]

But no fortifications could be prepared against the enemy within. Washington had already been disturbed by a report that some riflemen had offered, for a bribe, "to set a Person on board one of the Men of War." He had only started getting to the bottom of it when the Provincial Congress came in with a potential time bomb. A conspiracy was afoot, they told him to corrupt the entire army—and his own hand-picked Company of Life Guards was not excepted. The evil genius behind the scheme was Governor Tryon, of course. And it did not take long, once the news was out, for his objectives to be blown out of all proportion by lurid rumor. One lieutenant of the 23rd Continentals, for example, was convinced the plotters "had conspired to Murther the General, blow up the Magaziens, & seize the Cannon of some of the Works, & hold possession of the Forts on Powles Hook. This was to be done on the First approach of the Enemy."[28]

But the bare facts were hairy enough, and were uncovered only incidentally during the civil investigation of a counterfeiting ring. A local gunsmith named Gilbert Forbes, it developed, had been engaged by Tryon as a recruiting agent. His mission was to sound out potential deserters and enlist them into the King's service. Since there was at present no practical way to get them out to the warships, the recruits would have to remain under cover for the time being. One of them, Thomas Hickey of the Life Guards, was currently in jail for passing bogus money. A fellow prisoner, testifying before a committee of the Provincial Congress, implicated him in the desertion scheme and so brought the whole affair to light. Hickey was turned over to the provost marshal, court-martialed for mutiny and sedition and, on 28 June, hanged in full view of the army.[29]

The general remained remarkably unflapped throughout the ordeal, and calmly restrained any impulse he may have felt to up-end the army in a search for would-be traitors. Perhaps he felt such a move would have been both demoralizing and untimely. Perhaps, too, he half-bought Hickey's plea that his part was only a shell game to swindle the Tories, "& afterwards consented to have his Name sent on Board the Man of War, in order that if the Enemy should arrive & defeat the Army here, & he should be taken Prisoner, he might be safe." At any rate, Private Hickey was the only soldier brought to trial, although four other Life Guards implicated with him quietly disappeared from the record. On execution day, Washington matter-of-factly made his report to Congress and then put the incident behind him.[30]

It was a poor time to have the army's self-confidence shaken, for the crisis was finally at hand. The general's intelligence regarding Halifax was slim, but he had grown expert in sorting out whatever data he had. By 10 June a rumor "that the Troops at that place were Imbarking for this, added to a thousand Incidental Circumstances . . . leaves not a doubt in my Mind but that Troops are hourly expected at the Hook." Much of the month was spent building gondolas and fire rafts to be used in the upper harbor, when the time came. Meanwhile three companies, complete with artillery, were sent down to destroy the Sandy Hook lighthouse lest it be jury-rigged into operation. The enterprise was directed by Commodore Tupper; *Hester* and the whaleboats provided naval support. But the tower walls were too thick, the artillery too light, and the crossfire too hot "from two men of war on one Side & the Light house on the other." The doughty Tupper tried to draw out a landing party so he could "meet them in the field or boats," but Captain Parker refused to bite. The whole affair had to be broken off.[31]

The rest of Tupper's vessels were on assigned stations: *Putnam* at Shrewsbury Inlet in New Jersey; *Mifflin* at Rockaway and *Schuyler* at Fire Island Inlet, both in Long Island. *Montgomerie* had been cruising at sea with no luck at all, and then came back to watch *Schuyler* snap up two prizes not a league from shore. The two American sloops thereafter threw in together, and had enough success to keep the Fire Island beach littered with contraband. On 27 June *Schuyler's* lieutenant proudly informed General Washington that they had retaken four prizes belonging to the British frigate *Greyhound*. Almost as an afterthought he mentioned intelligence "by one of the Prisoners that A fleet of 130 Sail, Sailed from Halifax the 9th Inst for Sandy Hook & that Genel How is on Board the Greyhound which We Suppos'd Pass'd us 3 Days Ago." After five months of anxiety the enemy was at the gate.[32]

Chapter V

The Howes

General William Howe had found it highly inadvisable to move his siege-weary army directly from Boston to New York. Not that there was no fight left in the redcoats. There was. But there were not enough of them to ensure a decisive outcome and end the war, and they lacked all the basic essentials for an extended campaign in a hostile country. That reality was brought home quite dramatically as they limped into the harbor at Halifax, Nova Scotia like a scene from Hogarth's "Gin Alley." Their pitifully few transport vessels were crowded to the gunwales with a jumbled mix of soldiers, camp followers, loyalist refugees, regimental baggage, artillery, ordnance stores, provisions, wagons, cavalry mounts—everything associated with the army that could possibly be taken aboard. Much, too much, had to be left behind for the rebels to salvage.[1]

Halifax held the only Royal Navy shipyard left in North America, but it was ill prepared to receive the horde. Provisions and accommodations were inadequate at best. Even after everybody had been sorted out, two thirds of the troops had to be quartered in the transports. They came ashore daily for fatigue and drill, reboarding at night to the bleak solace of a clay pipe (its tobacco provided by a *Society for the Relief of the Soldiers*, along with shoes, stockings and caps). Preparations for the forthcoming campaign went along in good order none the less, and the army tightened its slack ways in the routine of a stable garrison life. Muskets were systematically turned in for repair or replacement, while the production of paper cartridges was put on a full-time schedule. The "flank" companies—elite grenadiers and light infantry—were brought up to their mandated strength by skimming the best men from "line" companies.[2]

This bears some explaining, as it shows how the British Army organized itself on campaign. Each ten company standard infantry regiment (or "regiment of foot") contained one company of light infantry and one of grenadiers. These were the flank companies, so-called because they theoretically would occupy the flank positions when the regiment was drawn up in formal line of battle. The remaining eight companies thus made up the "line." But classic formations seldom recommend themselves outside the pages of drill manuals, at least not on the regimental level, and it had become the practice to detach the flank companies from their parent units and form them into provisional battalions of their own.

The light infantryman liked to think of himself as aggressive, intelligent and physically agile—a militarily refined counterpart, at this stage of the war, to the Continental Army's rifleman. His bob-tailed coat, modified jockey cap and functional equipment were reminiscent of the old colonial ranger, after whom he was originally patterned. The grenadier, on the other hand, was chosen not only for his strength, bravery and general military qualities but also for his extraordinary height, an asset which was further enhanced by adding a twelve-inch bearskin cap. The hand grenade itself had for some time been laid aside as a common battlefield weapon, but the grenadier still lingered on to assume the role of assault specialist. It is a quirk of combat psychology that defending troops, nervously standing their ground, tend to view their attackers as somewhat larger than life. The physical dimensions of the grenadier did nothing to diminish the effect.[3]

The Americans had no counterpart to the grenadier, nor did they really have any for the typical British soldier of any company. A recent British indulgence had allowed enlistments for three years (or for the duration "of the Rebellion now subsisting in North America"), but prior to that a recruit expected to sign up for life and spend his old age as a Chelsea pensioner. Howe's little army was made up exclusively of these old sweats. In one regiment of the period, over half the men were in their thirties and had seen better than fifteen years of active service. The recruit may have launched his career as a farm lad escaping drudgery, or a felon avoiding gaol, but in the end he became a thorough-going institutional man. Discipline was harsh and drill was constant. His pay, after running an imposing gauntlet of "stoppages," left him little or nothing in coin. It was a demanding lifestyle, but it made him one of the best professional soldiers in the world.[4]

The Halifax garrison (or at least that part of it earmarked for New York), contained eighteen regiments of foot. Washington's oldest unit—the 1st Continentals—dated its origin to 1775. Howe's oldest—the 4th King's Own—dated to 1680, and his youngest—the 64th Foot—to 1758. The difference is of more than antiquarian interest. The British recruit entered an established organization, and could learn much of his trade by emulating the men around him. In this way it was calculated to take three months to turn him into a proper soldier, where in a newly raised regiment it would take a full year. His inexperience, meanwhile, had little effect on the old-timers; they already knew how to function on a group basis. Eleven of the regiments had been mauled in varying degrees last year at Bunker's Hill, but they were still very much in business and all the wiser. Washington's ranks also held a respectable number of Bunker's Hill veterans, but the regiments they had served with that day were now all disbanded.[5]

The flank companies of all eighteen British regiments made up two battalions of light infantry and two of grenadiers. There also were five companies of Royal Artillery. They were not especially ancient as British units go, dating only to the formation of their parent 4th Battalion in 1771. Still, this gave them a five-year operating edge over Knox's Continental gunners, not to mention the advantages of professional training at Woolwich Academy. There was yet another unit Washington lacked: a regiment of cavalry, comparable to the 17th Light Dragoons, formed in 1759. Their general outlook on life is indicated by the regimental badge, a death's head with the motto *OR GLORY* underneath. The mobility of horsemen was their essential asset, to be employed mainly in the areas of reconnaissance and pursuit. But shock

tactics also formed part of their repertoire, involving a vigorous and skillful use of the saber. A well conditioned dragoon could lay a man open without batting an eye.[6]

Other than the regulars, there were three battalions of North American provincials in Nova Scotia. They were intended to remain there, along with two battalions of Marines, to act as a permanent garrison. There also were two independent companies of volunteers recently arrived at Halifax from New York with the *Savage* sloop. They had been raised under Governor Tryon's eye earlier in the year. Considering the names of their captains—Archibald Campbell and Alexander Grant—it is not surprising that they had a distinctively Scottish flavor. Recent immigrants to the mid-Hudson region had been button-holed with promises of land grants; those who enlisted were spirited aboard *Asia* for transshipment. Some had even gone off with General Henry Clinton in February to help raise their fellow Highlanders in North Carolina. Campbell's and Grant's companies were armed and accoutred from the Halifax stores, and ordered "to hold themselves in readiness to move with the army."[7]

They would not have to hold themselves in readiness for very long. The day before their arrival at Halifax, on 16 May, the frigate *Greyhound* had sailed in with nine provision ships under convoy. At that point General Howe had less than a week's supply of pickled meat on hand, and his depleted larder was inspiring painful memories of Boston with a sense of déja vu. One of *Greyhound's* ordnance vessels had been snapped up at sea by a Continental man of war, but he could get along without it. All that remained now was a shifting of cargo, and then he could be away before the weather closed him in. As he wrote to the colonial secretary, Lord Germain: "the fogs setting in upon the Coast may delay the Fleet upon its Passage, occasion a Seperation, & thereby prevent the Army from acting in full Force upon its Arrival."[8]

Everything else was ready to go. Howe had accumulated enough bottoms to ensure "a sufficient Quantity of Tonnage for the Removal of the Army from hence, without the Inconvenience of the Officer & Soldiers being crowded." The Halifax Army amounted to six thousand and more, but there would be over a hundred transports to accommodate them and their materiel—plus horse ships for the artillery and draught animals, and for the officers' mounts. The Death-or-Glory boys had some trouble finding enough forage for their horses; they would have to stay behind for now and catch up later.[9]

The general also had in hand Germain's promise of almost 13,000 reinforcements already at sea and on the way, and the prospect of getting most of General Clinton's troops from the southern expedition. Moreover, he could look forward to a close and comfortable working relationship with the Navy in the forthcoming joint operations. A new chief had just been appointed to the North American fleet: the Right Honourable Richard, Lord Howe, Vice Admiral of the White. This imposing title belonged to none other than General William Howe's older brother, Dick, known to his men as "Black Dick the sailor's friend."[10]

Curiously, the three principal figures of the coming campaign had a good deal in common. All three—George Washington and the Howe brothers—had that physical bearing which contributes no little to a commander's "presence." All were basically introverted, inclined to keep their own counsel. Yet they were popular with their men, respected by their officers and genuinely admired by their civilian colleagues. Each was a hero from the last war: George Washington as a dogged colonel of Virginia volunteers, William Howe as the dashing leader of Wolfe's vanguard at Quebec, and Richard Howe as a fighting ship's captain in a series of hair-raising exploits. Washington had been elected to the Continental Congress and the Howes to Parliament; the current situation of all three largely derived from these political stints. At this point they enjoyed the full confidence of their respective governments, yet none had commanded an army or a fleet before the

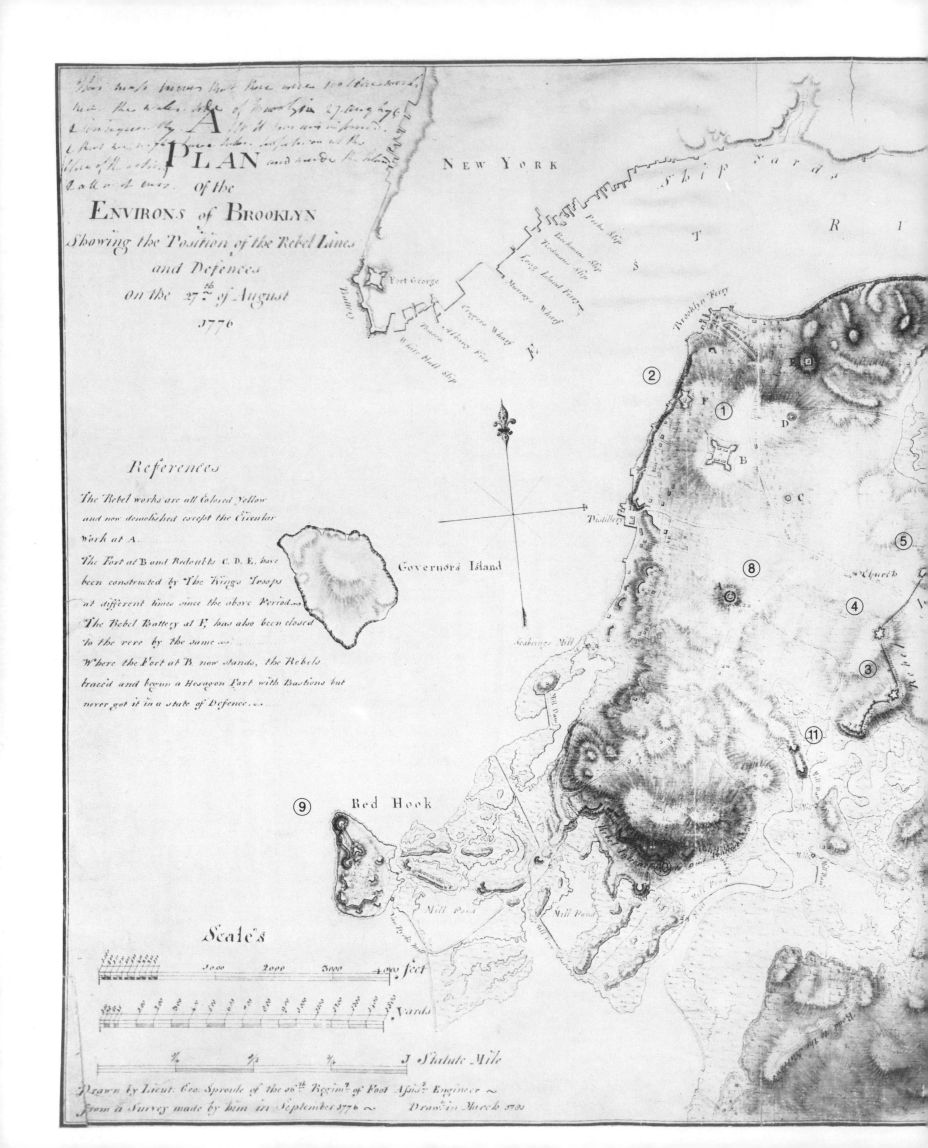

THE BROOKLYN FORTIFICATIONS. Lieut. George Sproule, a native Long Islander, drafted this map in 1780 based on surveys made before the American lines were demolished, in September 1776 (BrM 107/5). The works are laid out in exquisite detail: (1) site of General Lee's proposed Congress citadel, later occupied by the British fort shown here, (2) Fort Stirling, (3) Fort Box, (4) Fort Greene, (5) the oblong redoubt, (6) Fort Putnam, with its lunette extension, (7) the nameless ''redoubt on the left,'' (8) Cobble Hill redoubt (Smith's Barbette), (9) Fort Defiance, (10) entrenchments fronting Gowanus Creek, (11) fleches to cover the milldam crossing, (12) the breastwork at Flatbush Pass. Also included are (13) the British approaches thrown up shortly after the battle.

General Clinton, who succeeded Howe to the American command in 1778, still rankled at the outcome of the battle, and penned a notation on the upper left-hand corner: ''This map proves that there were no [close?] works near the water side of Brooklyn 27 Augt 76 & consequently SWH [Sir William Howe] was misinformed & that we might have taken possession at the (close of the action) and made the Island and all in it ours.'' His meaning is somewhat obscure. If by ''the water side'' he meant the Gowanus Creek system, it must be remembered that the only crossing—the milldam at (11)—had been destroyed during the battle by Col. Jonathan Ward of the 21st Continentals. If, on the other hand, he meant the line extending from the extreme left redoubt (7) to the Wallabout Bay marshes, then his opinion differs sharply with that of Capt. John Montresor of the Engineers. Montresor doubted the American left could have been easily breeched by assault (see Note 9 to Chapter X). Circled numerals are additions to the original map.

war. Washington had his own shortcomings in mind when he wrote of a subordinate: "His wants are common to us all; the want of experience to move upon a large scale." To some extent he could have been describing his adversaries as well.[11]

Ready or not, the large scale movements were irrevocably under way. At eleven in the morning on 10 June the Halifax Army weighed anchor and sailed off "in good health and great Spirets." There was a heady scent of victory in the wind. "The Marines are Very much mortified at being left behind," reported an officer of that corps, consoling himself that "no one doubt the least of our finishing this Bussiness before Christmas." The naval escort was under the command of Vice Admiral Molyneux Shuldham. His flagship was the cruiser *Chatham;* the rest of his squadron contained the frigates *Greyhound, Centurion* and *Rose,* the schooner *Tryal* and the sloops *Senegal* and *Swan.* General Howe was aboard *Greyhound,* and his fleet—"Transports, Victuallers &ca."—topped 120 sail as it was joined en route by early arrivals of his promised reinforcement. The weather cooperated beautifully. The entire armada was coasting Long Island completely intact, when *Schuyler's* people got wind of it and notified headquarters. By the evening of the 29th it was anchored behind Sandy Hook, absorbing Captain Parker's two ships and ending that skipper's independent command.[12]

Greyhound, with General Howe aboard, had separated from the fleet to reconnoiter, and so came in four days early. Howe used the waiting time to interview Governor Tryon and his growing loyalist entourage, gleaning all the intelligence he could about the American defenses and correlating it with information General Clinton had sent last February. Until now he had not known about any of the new American defenses, so he arrived with every intention of an immediate descent on Long Island. He had a sketchy knowledge of Fort Stirling and the defunct Congress citadel, but he was prepared to cope with them. Then he would occupy the Brooklyn peninsula with his Halifax Army and thus secure the East River anchorage. It would, in short, be Lee's plan in reverse. Even now, having learned about the new lines across the base of the peninsula, he did not judge them enough of an obstacle to warrant a change of mind. On Monday, 1 July, he ordered the fleet up to Gravesend Bay for a general debarkation.[13]

At this point, one of his subordinates pointed out the Heights of Gowanus in front of the American lines: "a ridge of craggy heights, covered with wood, that lay in the route the Army must have taken . . . which the Rebels would undoubtedly have occupied before the King's troops could get up to it." This was an obstacle Howe realized he must reckon with, and he grudgingly decided he lacked the resources to force his way through just yet. There would be time enough when all the reinforcements had come in. In the meanwhile, Staten Island looked to be a much better staging area than Long Island's coastal plain. It had plenty of fresh water for both the troops and the fleet, and at the same time was completely undefended. If the Americans wanted access to it they would have to cross from New Jersey over Kill van Kull.[14]

On Tuesday morning part of the fleet came to sail and began steering up through the Narrows and into the harbor bay. Captain Parker's *Phoenix* appropriately had the honor of taking the lead, followed by *Rose, Greyhound,* the *Senegal* sloop and ten sail of transports. The four flank battalions of grenadiers and light infantry were on board, and the warships were cleared for action. Just as the procession was well into the channel it was suddenly brought up short. The changing tide, combined with a drop in wind, put the transports "into great Confusion, all dropping upon one another without steerage way." They would have made sitting ducks for any shore artillery; some of them stood barely 700 yards off. But there were no heavy guns available to the Americans, and the Narrows had never been fortified. Colonel Hand's Pennsylvania riflemen dotted the western bulge of Long Island

and tried to pepper the nearest vessels, but the range was too great for them to be effective. Soon, the transports were signalled to drop down with the tide and put themselves out of danger.[15]

It was approaching nightfall, in pouring rain, when the flank companies were finally put ashore at the "Watering Place," now Tompkinsville, Staten Island. This is where Captain Stephenson's Virginians had tried to ambush the British seamen last April, but now the area was deserted. A rear guard had displayed signal flags at the Narrows earlier in the day, and then hauled them down to retire inland. General Washington had not been able to stretch his defenses to include Staten Island; the batteries and redoubts laid out there by Stirling had never taken physical shape. British chroniclers delighted in retailing the headlong flight of hundreds of Maryland/Virginia riflemen, but in fact recent enlistment expirations had left a skeleton force of barely 40 for all three companies. Along with a detachment of the 20th Continentals, they could do little more than round up local cattle and drive them over to New Jersey. Captain John Blanchard's light horse troop arrived from Elizabeth to lend a hand as impromptu cowboys. By Tuesday night the fattest beeves had been ferried across the Kills; after that "the Enemy . . . came on, & prevented our taking off the Lean."[16]

The movement of transports up the Narrows continued all Wednesday and into the following morning. The Pennsylvania riflemen resumed their popping from western Long Island. By afternoon General Greene got some 9-pounders into place at Denyse's Ferry, but yesterday's embarrassment with wind and tide did not repeat itself and the artillerymen had to cope with moving targets. The guns were either too light or too badly served to do any material damage to the ships. They had a certain nuisance value, however, and even managed to inflict a handful of casualties. Captain Vandeput had the satisfaction of returning their fire as *Asia* sailed past on Thursday noon, majestically bringing up the rear.[17]

Meanwhile, the debarkation continued at a steady pace, as one after another of the foot regiments poured onto Staten Island. The fleet's long boats provided most of the landing craft, but not all. Flat-bottomed boats had been trundled along from Halifax; huge structures, each propelled by sixteen oars and capable of hauling two companies of infantry in one trip. In addition, there were a number of roomy hay-boats which were supposed to have been destroyed last month by the Queens County militia, but the job was left half done. Their loyalist owners had managed to slip past *Mifflin* at Rockaway Inlet and then make their way to Sandy Hook. About twenty of these hay-boats were brought up the Narrows to help land the troops.[18]

Despite the last minute change in the choice of a landing site, General Howe's advance planning was quite thorough. The Halifax Army was already arranged into six brigades of three regiments each, not counting the flank battalions, the New York provincials and the artillery companies. Now, as each unit reached Staten Island it set off directly to a predetermined spot. The end result was a chain of posts along the island's north shore, stretching from the Narrows across to Billop's Point at the head of Raritan Bay. Special attention was given to the communication with New Jersey, and a number of ship's tenders were pushed into Kill van Kull to cover the ferries. A sharp little action took place at Decker's Ferry, now Port Richmond, on Wednesday, when the Americans brought a pair of field pieces up to Bergen Point and proceeded to rake the small craft from the shore. They killed a man and wounded four others aboard one tender, and put the vessel entirely out of commission.[19]

By the end of the week the brigades were deployed, and Staten Island was converted into a British armed camp. Almost at once the loyalists began to surface, including at least one delegate to the New York Provincial Congress. An entire company of men arrived from Shrewsbury under a half-pay officer and enlisted in the King's service. Even a few American riflemen turned up—

mainly old-country men—bringing in their weapons for a ten-dollar reward. The Richmond County militia, almost to a man, assembled and "took the Oath of Allegiance & fidelity to his Majesty." They were promptly reorganized as a loyalist militia, with their old rebel colonel as one of the new company commanders. They even revived their light horse troop to serve General Howe as a personal bodyguard.[20]

The British incursion, coming as it did on the heels of the depressing Hickey affair, caught General Washington emotionally off guard. "I could wish General Howe and his Armament not to arrive yet," he lamented, as Hickey was swung into eternity, "as not more than 1,000 Militia have yet come in, and our whole force, including the Troops at all the detached posts and on board the armed vessels . . . is but small and inconsiderable when compared to the extensive lines they are to defend." Even so mild a diffidence as this was wholly uncharacteristic, but it put the finger squarely on the crux of Washington's dilemma. How could the army, with its limited resources, cover all the possible invasion routes without being stretched to the point of dissolution?[21]

His immediate decision was to beef up the outposts, whereupon reinforcements were sent to Paulus Hook, Brooklyn and Governor's Island. General Mifflin was ordered to join his brigade at Fort Washington to push along the works there (he found them "well advanced, but not in a state of defence"). The city militia was brought into active service; New Jersey was called on as well for a suitable contribution. Within hours militia elements were marching in from the northern Jersey counties, and they were promptly posted to the Brooklyn lines.[22]

Meanwhile, the everlasting labor on the fortifications was to continue except, of course, in the event of an actual alarm. All points of entry to each work were to be blocked off with spiked frames and fascines. A perimeter was marked around each redoubt by placing small brush at a distance of twenty to thirty yards. In case of a direct assault by enemy infantry, this would be the killing ground—Bunker's Hill style. The first redcoats stepping into it would be treated to a volley of buck-and-ball: "one musket ball and four or eight buck Shot." A normal load excluded the buckshot but the stopping power of this combination was considered to be awesome at close range.[23]

During the crisis days of late June and early July attention was drawn to a full range of practical details, from supplying each man with 24 rounds of ammunition to making sure his canteen was kept filled with fresh water. From the day the British transports began plying up the Narrows, the troops were ordered to sleep with their muskets and to be at their alarm posts at four each morning, the city militia along with them. Not until the redcoats were landed and deployed on Staten Island could Washington drop his guard for a moment. But the strain had a certain tonic effect. By the time the first tense moments were over the American general was fairly licking his chops. By 10 July he confidently anticipated another Bunker's Hill: "they will have to wade thro' much Blood and Slaughter before they can carry any part of our Works, if they carry them at all; and at best be in possession of a Melancholly and Mournfull Victory." Two days later he was proposing an offensive operation against Staten Island.[24]

But manning the lines against enemy personnel was one thing; manning them against shipping was to be something else. Even as Washington was expressing his revived self-confidence, the irrepressible Captain Hyde Parker had the British admiral's orders to take his *Phoenix* up the Hudson River in company with *Rose*, the *Tryal* schooner and two tenders. The purpose of his mission was "to cut off and intercept any Supplies coming to New York, to give protection to His Majesty's well disposed Subjects," and generally sever the American communication with the Highlands and the Northern Army.[25]

The squadron weighed anchor at 3 o'clock Friday afternoon, 12 July. Fifteen minutes later Red Hook opened fire with its artillery, and then Governor's Island. Parker hewed close to the Oyster Banks on the bay's west side, putting as much distance as he could between his squadron and the forts. Once into the Hudson River channel, however, the full power of the American batteries was brought to bear in a thundering cannonade from Paulus Hook on the one side and all the western city redoubts on the other. The squadron ran the gauntlet handily, firing broadsides right and left as it sailed by. The action tapered off and then stopped completely as the last city battery was passed, only to start up again when the vessels approached the incomplete works at Fort Washington. By 5:30 Parker was past these as well, and completely out of danger. The ordeal had lasted two hours and fifteen minutes. At dusk the five vessels were anchored in a broad section of the Hudson called the Tappan Sea, over thirty miles upriver and virtually at the doorsteps of Forts Montgomery and Constitution.[26]

The affair, of course, made a laughing stock of American gunnery among the British. Observers counted 196 rounds fired out of the several forts: 27 from Red Hook, 16 from Governor's Island, 27 from Paulus Hook and 126 from New York City. This breaks down to an average of one round every 45 seconds, and each gun got off an average of four rounds for that portion of the time it had its target in sight. Parker entered the channel closer to the Jersey side, so it is not surprising that part of his damage was caused by Paulus Hook, and much of the rest by the elevated works at Fort Washington. Most of the rounds from the city batteries were seen to fall short. In all, *Phoenix* received "two Shot in our Hull & One in the Bowsprit & several through the Topsails, the Netting &ca in the Waste was Shot away." *Rose* had some of her rigging damaged, besides "one 18 Pound Shot in the Head of our fore Mast one through the Pinnace, several through the Sails and some in the Hull." Casualties were uncertain. A deserter subsequently reported that *Rose's* cook had a leg shot off, and "some others wounded." Stories quickly circulated that the civilian pilots of both vessels had been killed.[27]

For their part, the British could take very few honors in terms of gunnery. There were upwards of 70 carriage guns on board the men-of-war, and all of them seem to have been brought into play. Even so, no damage was inflicted on any of the American works, or any of the guns, nor were there any known casualties as a result of enemy action. As the squadron passed close by Paulus Hook the artillerymen there flinched momentarily from the visual and aural effects of the broadsides, but quickly returned to work their pieces. A number of buildings were hit in the city, indicating the squadron's shots went high and came in over the western ridge. Private houses were also damaged at Greenwich and Paulus Hook. Some rounds fell into the encampments, but the tents had been struck and there was no material damage other than the untimely end of an unfortunate milch cow. A ball or two was thrown into Fort Washington, also to no effect. The American casualties were all self-inflicted: six men were killed and three wounded when a cartridge exploded prematurely at the Grand Battery.[28]

One officer charged the killed and wounded men had been drunk "& neglected to Spunge, Worm & stop the Vent." In other words, there were still live sparks in the gun when the next cartridge was rammed down; its too-sudden ignition was the result of carelessness. Moreover, the same diarist noted, half the artillerymen in the city were off carousing instead of manning their guns. Even allowing for contemptuous embroidery the charge has some flavor of truth. Over 700 matrosses had recently been drafted out of the infantry; in complying with such a draft a company commander is not prone to send off his steadiest men. Even had there been time to train them all properly (and serving a gun called for exquisitely detailed choreography), lax discipline was not out of character for the army as a whole. Washington's greatest embarrassment was observing that "many of the officers and a number of men instead of attending to their duty at the Beat of the Drum; continued along the banks of the North River, gazing at the Ships.''[29]

While Parker's squadron was fighting its way up the Hudson, another vessel soared expectantly up the Narrows on a self-proclaimed mission of destiny. She was the cruiser *Eagle,* 64 guns, and her arrival sparked an impressive outburst of martial display. ''We were saluted by all the Ships of War in the Harbour, by the Cheers of the Sailors all along the Ships, and by those of the Soldiers on the Shore. A finer scene could not be exhibited.'' On board was Vice Admiral Lord Howe and he arrived with a cutlass in one hand and an olive branch in the other. Not only was he commissioned to take charge of all His Majesty's naval forces on the North American station, but he was also empowered, with his brother at his side, to open negotiations toward a peaceful settlement of the rebellion.[30]

His initial overtures collapsed in a calculated maneuvering of both sides to gain the moral edge. Two attempts to reach the American commander were made, the first letter addressed to *George Washington Esquire* and the second to *George Washington Esquire &c. &c. &c.* Both were refused on the grounds of insufficient identification of the addressee. The inference was clear: any communication for the general would have to bear his military rank. But to acknowledge the title would be to recognize the political authority which created it, and this the admiral was not prepared to do. So a routine interview was arranged between Washington and General Howe's adjutant, Lieutenant Colonel James Paterson, ostensibly to discuss the treatment of prisoners. Paterson inevitably brought the subject around to peace negotiations. The general replied abruptly that he had no authority that was not derived from the Continental Congress, that he knew the Howes' commission limited them to the granting of pardons, ''that those who had committed no fault wanted no pardon,'' and would the colonel care to partake of a small collation before returning to his duties?[31]

Washington was right; the Howes were in no position to promise anything until the political and military apparatus of the rebellion had been dismantled—Congress, the Army, everything. The Army, at least, was feeling rather good about itself just now, having recently celebrated the original Fourth of July. On the afternoon of the 9th all the brigades were drawn up on parade to hear the Declaration of Independence in its entirety. ''It was received with Joy, which they severally testified by three Cheers.'' When the troops were dismissed they were no longer in the service of the United Colonies, but of the independent United States. They gloried in the fact. That night a party of celebrants, soldiers and civilians, went down to the Bowling Green and joyfully pulled down the equestrian statue of their late monarch, George III.[32]

On top of that came an electrifying dose of good news from the south. General Henry Clinton, after sailing from New York last February, had rendezvoused off the Carolinas with an expeditionary force of seven regiments. They were fresh from Ireland, escorted over the Atlantic by Sir Peter Parker's squadron of the Royal Navy. Clinton's hopes of raising the North Carolina Highlanders were shattered when his recruits, en route to join him, were decisively trounced by the southern patriots. As if that were not enough, Clinton and Parker then tried a joint offensive against the city of Charleston and received much the same treatment. Best of all, the American commander who pulled off the victory was none other than that military prodigy who first laid out the defenses of New York City—''Boiling Water'' himself, Major General Charles Lee!

Chapter VI

The Grand Army

The huge augmentation of levies voted by the Continental Congress early in June had barely begun to trickle in during the invasion crisis. Actually raising the troops had been left, quite naturally, to the individual states (and that is what we shall call them, rather than colonies, now that the fact of independence has been noted). Too many of the state governments, in turn, sought to fill their quotas by a process of voluntary enlistment. It was an ill-timed gesture, one that managed to coincide with the early summer harvest. Prospective recruits had little interest in the army, at least for the time being. The war would have to wait till the crops were brought in.[1]

The New York Provincial Congress answered the call by dismantling its minuteman system. The idea of a dual establishment looked good on paper, but had just not worked out in practice. So the county minuteman regiments were all disbanded and the men sent back to their parent units in the standing militia. Only after that were four provisional regiments raised by levying quotas on every county north to Albany, and it was hoped the now unemployed minuteman officers would step forth to lead them. Two of the new regiments were formed immediately by drawing into active service, as complete organizations, the New York City independent militia battalions of Colonels Lasher and Malcolm. They were to be fleshed out with the drafted men of the three ward regiments, plus those of neighboring Kings, Queens and Richmond Counties.[2]

The Richmond contingent, as it turned out, was saved from marching by the timely arrival of the Halifax Army and the subsequent defection of the Staten Island militia. Kings County raised its allotted quota with no problem, but Queens found itself neatly perched on the horns of a dilemma. Last January's crushing of the loyalist uprising there had left the desired surface effect, but it had done nothing to change anyone's political views. The Queens militia held great numbers of unreconstructed loyalists, who stood in the ranks on muster day only to avoid payment of a stiff fine for delinquency. The county committee, understandably reluctant to send off its comparative handful of steady patriots, hit on the solution of drafting into service the most blatant of the British sympathizers. Once in the immediate presence of the Continental Army, and subject to the Articles of War, they would have no choice but to perform their military duties whether they wanted to or not.[3]

It was a short-sighted policy at best. The more determined of the draftees simply dropped from sight rather than bear arms in the rebel cause. The thickly wooded marshlands of Long Island's south shore offered them a perfect refuge, and the militia spent the better part of the month trying to flush them out. The old Jamaica minuteman company had an exchange of fire with defaulters in a Hempstead swamp, where they wounded one and took some prisoners. The whole situation alarmed the Provincial Congress, who could see not only a counter-revolution based on last year's model, but a tie-in with the current Hickey plot as well. General Washington was called on for troops, and by the end of June a detachment of Greene's brigade had joined the manhunt. The regulars had no better luck than did the militia; two separate parties combed the Hempstead woods for twenty miles and returned with only five prisoners. All the captured defaulters were collected and sent to General Greene's headquarters. They turned out to be a collection of individual tradesmen and farmers, some blatantly defiant, but none of them a part of any hostile military unit. Captain Hewlett, the old partisan, might have turned the fugitives into a guerrilla band to be reckoned with. But he had been on the Americans' most-wanted list since January and—wherever he was—did not choose to surface now.[4]

In one way or another the New York brigade met the wishes of

ARRIVAL OF VICE ADMIRAL RICHARD LORD VISCOUNT HOWE, 12 JULY. "Nothing could exceed the Joy," recorded Lord Howe's secretary, Ambrose Serle, "that appeared throughout the Fleet and Army upon our Arrival. We were saluted by all the Ships of War in the Harbour, by the Cheers of the Sailors all along the Ships, and by those of the Soldiers on the Shore. A finer Scene could not be exhibited, both of Country, Ships, and men, all heightened by one of the brightest Days that can be imagined." It was a grand day all around. In the morning PHOENIX and ROSE had passed up the Hudson River, thumbing their noses at American shore batteries along the way. British morale was at its zenith. Captain Lieutenant Archibald Robertson of the Engineers caught

little of the excitement in this rather placid sketch of the flagship EAGLE joining the fleet. Indeed, the occasion for celebration was more psychological than real. Howe came with no reinforcements. It would be another month to the day before Commodore William Hotham was to bring in the Hessians and Guards, and General William Howe had to postpone the season's campaign till his arrival. Robertson titled his work, "View of the Narrows between Long Island and Staten Island with our Fleet at Anchor and Lord Howe coming in. Taken from the heights above the Watering Place Staten Island, 12th July, 1776." It was from the base of this hill that the watering party from SAVAGE had run on Easter Sunday, with Captain Hugh Stephenson's Virginia riflemen in hot pursuit.

its commander, General John Morin Scott, to be the first to join the Army as a complete unit. The Kings County levies found themselves assigned to Lasher's regiment, the Queens levies to Malcolm's, and the Suffolk levies to an upriver regiment under Samuel Drake—the same colonel whose Westchester County minutemen had built the Horn's Hook fort last spring. Only half the fourth regiment was to serve with the brigade, however. Five companies were posted to the Highlands forts under their colonel, Cornelius Humphrey, and they stayed there for the rest of the campaign.[5]

The neighboring states of Connecticut and New Jersey relied entirely on volunteers to meet their quotas, and it was July before the two brigades could stand muster. The Connecticut General Assembly raised six new regiments to serve till Christmas Day, and added to them Colonel Philip Burr Bradley's battalion of state regulars which was already a month in service "for the special defence of this and the neighboring Colonies." General James Wadsworth, Jr. was appointed to command the brigade, with orders to march his first enlistees to New York while the rest were still raising. In the meanwhile, Connecticut's venerable Governor Jonathan Trumbull, a red hot patriot held over from the colonial regime, hit upon the idea of sending three regiments of militia light horse "under the command of Lieutenant Colonel [Thomas] Seymour, to march without loss of time" for the army at New York "and do duty with them until our battalions are completed, when, it is expected, they will be discharged."[6]

General Washington was grateful for the cavalrymen themselves—they numbered over 350—but he wanted no part of their mounts. Operating on interior lines as he was, his light horse requirements could well be taken care of by Captain Leary's New York City troop. Besides, a dry summer left barely enough forage on Manhattan Island for the artillery and commissary animals, which were already consuming prodigious amounts of oats and hay. A conference of his general officers took up the matter and agreed that the men should "be detained until the new Levies arrive, but the Horses sent home as soon as possible." When the troopers arrived they would have none of it. Their ancient militia law exempted them from duty as common foot soldiers. They refused to mount guard or perform any garrison chores that separated them from their mounts, nor had they brought even the simplest camp equipment for life in the field. What they really hoped for was to get in some rousing good Tory hunting and "purge the Colony of such vermin." Isaac Sears, had he still been around, would have been delighted. But Washington's patience was wearing thin. If his men refused to share the common lot, he abruptly told Seymour, "they can be no longer of Use here, where Horse cannot be brought to Action, and I do not care how soon they are dismissed." By 17 July, just a week after their arrival, the light horse was clopping back to Connecticut along the Boston Post Road.[7]

On the other side of New York, the New Jersey Provincial Congress organized its volunteers into a brigade of five regiments, and to command them, appointed General Nathaniel Heard—the old minuteman who once put the fear of God into Queens and Richmond. Recruiting hit a snag with the coming of the Halifax Army, when most of the state's militia was called out to reinforce New York. Once Staten Island was occupied, however, the Jerseymen howled that they were every bit as threatened as the Yorkers by the prospect of attack. Washington conceded the point, and returned all the militia to local control except the Morris County contingent. This he used to establish a post at Bergen Neck, "in order to prevent any communication, and to give the enemy obstruction in case they should attempt to land in that quarter." He hoped the remainder would be posted opposite Staten Island to guard the shoreline until the Flying Camp was established. He warned, however, that a clear distinction be made between Heard's brigade and the standing militia: "Every Man of the former, I expect with all Expedition."[8]

The Massachusetts General Court got around to raising its quota towards the latter part of June. In truth, the recruiting grounds were wearing thin. The state was currently manning not only eighteen Continental regiments, but three more of state regulars plus a system of coastal defense companies, and had also been asked to raise a six-regiment brigade for the Northern Army. Still, the militia of four counties was tapped to produce levies for New York, and in time three regiments were marching off under General John Fellows. They joined the Grand Army at the beginning of August.[9]

As the four brigades of new levies drifted into camp, all of them under strength, the Flying Camp was developing into an organizational nightmare. The Maryland and Delaware regiments were so slow in recruiting and arming that they did not join the Army till September. A show of good faith was made by the Maryland Convention, however, which ordered to the northward Colonel William Smallwood's regiment with a supplement of three garrison companies. These units were all state regulars; they had been in service since January to protect the rim of Chesapeake Bay from the inroads of the Royal Navy. Time and attention had been given to their training and discipline, and their first-rate officer corps had honed them to a keen fighting edge.[10]

The Pennsylvania Committee of Safety also sent forth its defense force of state regulars. There were three battalions, and they had been in service since March. Two of them were composed entirely of riflemen, joined in a single regiment under the command of Colonel Samuel Miles. The third, Colonel Samuel Atlee's Battalion of Musketry, was a standard infantry unit. Most of the riflemen had been raised in much the same territory as Hand's 1st Continentals, some of them even coming from the wild west area around Pittsburgh. Other companies, however, originated in such long-populated counties as Bucks and Philadelphia. Atlee's musketeers were also recruited to some extent in semi-frontier areas, at least as far west as Lancaster County.[11]

But it is the Pennsylvania levies who were born in the midst of confusion. The manpower pool from which they were to have been drawn was Pennsylvania's version of a standing militia—the voluntary Associators. However, before any recruiting could be done, a large body of Associators (those of three frontier counties and some guard details excepted) were thrown into New Jersey helter-skelter to meet the threat of Howe's invasion. There each individual unit was required to serve for six weeks, and then deliver up a set quota towards the Flying Camp before returning home. In this way the two types of units functioned side by side, except that the Associators came and went while the men drafted out of them stayed behind to be formed into regiments. The process took all summer, and was hampered by the Associators' general reluctance to serve any time at all. Desertions grew to such an alarming degree that guards had to be posted at the various river crossings to catch the shirkers in flight and send them back to duty. Even the celebrated Philadelphia city brigade, which General Lee had once been eager to have represented in his New York army, turned out in the end to be rather less dependable than the up-country militia.[12]

Still, it was through the Flying Camp that any effort at all was made to put the Halifax Army off balance. Washington had sounded out his generals on the idea of an assault on Staten Island by the whole Continental Army, but nobody except the commander-in-chief thought the move could be brought off successfully. It was decided instead to limit any such attempts to hit-and-run commando raids, "with a view to alarm the enemy and encourage our own Troops, who seem generally desirous that something should be done." Major Thomas Knowlton was posted in New Jersey with the 20th Continentals, a Connecticut unit. He had gained some experience at this sort of business back during the Boston siege, and now he was ordered to hand-pick a partisan corps from the ranks of his regiment and cooperate with General Mercer and whatever Flying Camp troops came to hand.

This would give the New Englanders, with their own long-standing ranger traditions, a representation in aggressive actions that so far had been somewhat limited to the "southern" riflemen.[13]

The effort was mounted the night of 18 July. Knowlton's Yankees, Miles's Pennsylvanians and a battalion of Philadelphia Associators were to cross the channel near Elizabeth, raise as much hell as they could with the British outposts, and then return to New Jersey at dawn the next day. But it never came off. The weather refused to cooperate, and the boats were too unseaworthy for the 300-yard crossing in a storm. By the following night, of course, the element of surprise would have been lost, so the troops were sent back to their billets till suitable assault craft could be assembled. By the time this was done all of Mercer's best Flying Camp units—the Maryland and Pennsylvania regulars—had been siphoned off to join the army at New York. Any further attempts against Staten Island never got past the planning stage. But there was some minor activity, including an artillery duel at Amboy on the 25th. It began with the appearance of some small craft in Raritan Bay, whose evident goal was to reach Staten Island. The American guns opened up on them, and the British guns in turn opened up on the Americans from across the channel. The cannonade continued "briskly during the Space of an hour." All but one shallop made it to port, but not before an Associator had been killed and two more wounded.[14]

Getting rid of Captain Parker's squadron in the Hudson River called for a combination of tactics. To all appearances the Tappan Sea was a British lake and Captain Parker was able to patrol it at will. Four days after his arrival he moved northward into Haverstraw Bay and even pushed one of his tenders within sight of Fort Montgomery (for which she almost took a 32-pound shot in her stern). But his capacity to carry out his assignment was somewhat diminished. The flow of materiel from New York City was stopped, and the Northern Army had to make do with local resources. On the other hand, the overland passes were still open for dispatch riders and such personnel—artificers, for the most part—that were moving north. Moreover, the loyal subjects Parker had come to protect did not materialize in any great numbers. Instead, the upriver New York militia turned out in force, and was even joined by militia from the adjoining counties of Connecticut and Massachusetts. Their continuing presence on either shore created an acute supply problem for the captain. His landing parties managed to hit some out-of-the-way farmsteads and so he was never entirely without fresh meat and cabbages. But the pickings were slim. His boats almost always ran into enough opposition to discourage an actual landing.[15]

The Americans assumed the British objective to be Poughkeepsie, some thirty miles farther up the river, where two Continental Navy frigates were currently under construction. The shipwrights there stopped work long enough to build a number of rafts and float them downriver. The idea was to lade them with combustibles, lash them together and string them out between Fort Montgomery and the opposite shore. Then, should Captain Parker try to run past the fort, the rafts would be ignited and in turn ignite his ships. It was a breath-holding situation for those who knew not nearly enough turpentine and saltpetre could be found to do a proper job. But piles of brush were placed along the river bank across from the fort, waiting to be set afire on the squadron's approach. These, at least, would present targets in stark silhouette to the Continental artillerymen, should a pass up the river be attempted under the cover of night.[16]

At the same time, hulks were being brought around from Connecticut to obstruct the lower part of the Hudson and prevent the squadron from rejoining the fleet. They were to be sunk in a line off Jeffrey's Hook, the promontory that squeezed the river below Fort Washington. Chevaux-de-frise were prepared as a supplementary measure—framed cribs weighted with stones and fitted with pointed timbers "to pierce and stop the way of vessels meet-

ing of them." The project offered technical difficulties which were not readily overcome, as "some [of] them sunk very well; others, rather irregular; and some of the hulks, which were strapped together with large timbers, separated in going down." The result was a gap, or a number of gaps, which left a wider passage for river traffic than was originally intended.[17]

While the British squadron was—it was hoped—being bottled up in the Tappan Sea, Commodore Tupper's five American ships still plied the coastal waters of New Jersey and Long Island, ready to pounce on whatever prizes might fall their way. So a second squadron was organized to operate in the inland waters around New York City, and it consisted entirely of row galleys. They were small craft, these, rigged somewhat along the lines of the coastal trade's topsail schooners, but with the added ability to maneuver by means of oars. Their armament generally consisted of heavy guns in the bow and stern, and lighter pieces along each gunwale. For this service the galleys *Shark*, *Crane* and *Whiting* were detached from the Connecticut Navy, plus *Washington* and *Spitfire* from Rhode Island, all working their way up through the East River channel. Two more, *Lady Washington* and *Independence*, were turned out locally and manned from the ranks of the Army. In addition, Pennsylvania sent a panel of experts to build fireships for use, when the time came, against Lord Howe's fleet in the harbor bay.[18]

By the beginning of August all the galleys except *Independence* had gone up the Hudson to intercept the British squadron. The peppery Tupper had been taken off *Hester* to assume command; his new flagship was Rhode Island's *Washington*. He found Captain Parker cleared for action and waiting off Tarrytown on Saturday afternoon, 3 August. The Americans had the numerical edge in terms of vessels, but the frigates enjoyed superiority in terms of concentrated firepower. In the end that proved decisive. After an hour and a half of sustained action the row galleys broke off and dropped down to Dobbs Ferry. There they counted two men killed and 14 wounded. There was considerable damage to rigging and spars; *Washington*, *Spitfire* and *Shark* had all taken shots in the hull. A good deal of reliance had been placed on *Lady Washington's* only gun, a huge 32-pounder, but it was split seven inches in the engagement. *Phoenix* recorded no casualties, while *Rose* had a Marine killed and four men wounded. Both vessels had been hulled; *Rose* also lost her starboard quarter galley and some rigging. Tupper and Parker both showed a willingness to begin again, but the fighting was over for the day.[19]

The matter was not taken up again for nearly two weeks, after *Independence* had escorted two fireships upriver from New York City. They fell on the squadron in a surprise attack off Fordham Heights, shortly before midnight on 16 August. One of the fireships tried to grapple *Rose* but fell athwart her tender in the effort to reach her. The tender burned to the water line, and *Rose* got off scot free. The second fireship actually grappled *Phoenix*; Parker skillfully maneuvered his vessel clear and suffered no damage. But the utility of the British squadron was clearly at an end. Two days later, running before a gale wind, the two frigates, the *Tryal* schooner and the remaining tender made a descent with the early morning tide, adroitly picking their way through the obstructions at Jeffrey's Hook. The rest of the way downriver they swapped artillery fire with the American batteries, repeating the actions of 12 July in reverse. By 8 o'clock they were anchored with the fleet off Staten Island. The row galleys, apparently caught by surprise, could only trail behind and take up their own stations in the East River.[20]

The entire Tappan Sea episode demonstrated to General Washington the weakness of his northern flank. His response embodied the last major embellishment of Lee's original defense plan. Completing the Hudson River obstruction was part of it, with the line of hulks covered on one end by a battery at Jeffrey's Hook and on the other by a redoubt at Burdett's Ferry. The Jersey work started out as a modest enough structure, but was quickly replaced by a more ambitious fortification first called Fort Constitution and then Fort Lee. Further north, the vital Harlem River crossing at Kingsbridge—the only link with the mainland—was protected by Fort Independence, thrown up on the southern tip of Fordham Heights in Westchester County. As a manpower reserve Governor Trumbull was asked to establish a New England version of the Flying Camp at the Byram River on the New York-Connecticut border.[21]

The New York Provincial Congress had moved out of New York City at the end of June and was now sitting at White Plains, in Westchester County, under a new name: the Convention of the Representatives of the State of New York. On 15 July the Convention passed a remarkably perceptive resolution to the effect "That, if his Excellency Genl. Washington think it expedient for the preservation of this State, and the general interest of America, to abandon the city of New York, and withdraw the troops to the north side of King's Bridge, that this Convention will cheerfully cooperate with him in every measure that may be necessary for that purpose." The suggestion was politely acknowledged, but evacuation was not in the general's immediate plans. Meanwhile the Convention could provide his northern flank with the augmentation he had been seeking. Four mid-Hudson counties were levied for a quarter more of their militia; they were organized into a brigade of five regiments and placed under the command of General George Clinton, Colonel James Clinton's younger brother. It was understood that the brigade's use would be limited to defending the lower Hudson, and Washington was more than satisfied to have them on that basis.[22]

All the reinforcements for the Grand Army were in camp by the third week of August. The five-regiment garrison left at Boston last April was broken up completely, two of the units transferring to the Northern Army and the other three to New York City. Another Continental regiment had been raised in Connecticut for service at Boston; it was commanded by the same Colonel Andrew Ward who had raised volunteers for General Lee. Washington countermanded Ward's marching orders and brought him instead to New York. Also ended were the long-standing home guard duties of the Delaware Continentals—an exceptionally well trained regiment—and Congress ordered them to camp as well. General Mercer sent from the Flying Camp all the Maryland and Pennsylvania regulars—Smallwood's, Miles's and Atlee's—and also included not only the 1st and 2nd Pennsylvania levies but one of the Associator battalions as well. This unit had marched in from Northampton County for its mandated six weeks of service, and was chosen for a more active role because it consisted entirely of riflemen.[23]

The Army was finally completed with the arrival of a brigade of Connecticut standing militia. In July Governor Trumbull had authorized Washington to call in all the regiments adjacent to the New York line, and the general took up the offer the following month. At this time the governor and his council obliged him by turning out not only these units, but virtually every regiment west of the Connecticut River. For the most part, however, the militia had been picked over extensively to make up not only the state's six Continental regiments but all the levies called for in the past months by Congress. The present thin brigade was under the command of General Oliver Wolcott. Many of the regiments had their colonels in Continental service of one kind or another, and so were lead on this occasion by lesser field officers.[24]

Each of the six additional brigades of levies, volunteers and standing militia came with its own general officer to command it: Scott, Wadsworth, Heard, Fellows, George Clinton and Wolcott. These, joined to the five existing Continental brigades of Heath, Spencer, Greene, Stirling and Mifflin, placed an unwieldy burden on the shoulders of both Washington and Israel Putnam—the only officers holding a rank higher than brigadier general. Congress relieved the situation by promoting Heath, Spencer and Greene to a major generalcy and appointing four colonels as new brigadiers. There was some necessary shuffling about of regiments, but by and large McDougall of the 1st New York took over Stirling's old brigade, while the Jersey laird received a new one made up of the Flying Camp men. Parsons of the 10th and Nixon of the 4th Continentals took over Spencer's and Greene's brigades, respectively. James Clinton of the 2nd New York stayed on as commandant in the Highlands, and his brigade—it had been Heath's—was actually commanded by Colonel Joseph Read. When the Grand Army was organized on 12 August James Clinton's, Scott's and Fellows's brigades were assigned to Putnam's division; Parson's and Wadsworth's to Spencer's; George Clinton's and Mifflin's to Heath's at Kingsbridge; Nixon's and Heard's to Greene's on Long Island. Stirling's Flying Camp detachment and Wolcott's Connecticut militia were maintained as separate entities.[25]

The Continental regulars, including the artillerymen and the regiments lately arrived, now numbered a little over 15,000. The new levies brought in about 9,700 more (some 4,100 short of the original quota), the Connecticut militia 5,200, the Flying Camp detachment 2,400 and George Clinton's New York brigade 2,000. To these must be added two regiments of Long Island levies, which will be discussed in their proper context and which have been reckoned to number 500, more or less, for both. So by the time everybody had reported in the grand total came to some 34,800 officers and men, returned as members of the regiments under General Washington's immediate command in New York City and its outposts at the Brooklyn lines, Red Hook, Governor's Island, Bergen, Paulus Hook, Fort Lee, Fort Washington, Fort Thompson at Hell Gate, Fort Independence, and the immediate environs of each.[26]

The Flying Camp, meanwhile, was in its usual state of turmoil. The levied regiments were filling ever so slowly as the Associators kept arriving under no particular system. They were joined during the summer by a four-regiment brigade of New Jersey levies whose term of service was to be exactly one month. After that each county was called on to field half its standing militia, which would serve for a month and then be relieved by the other half, the rotation to continue for an unspecified period of time. The Flying Camp was deployed at Amboy, Woodbridge and Elizabeth, and by the middle of August numbered over 4,000. These were all Associators and Jersey levies, indicating that the Pennsylvania levies raised thus far had been sent to New York City as part of the 2,400-man detachment. Nor does the figure include an improvised artillery battalion made up of Jersey regulars and Philadelphia militia, amounting to another 260. Over in Connecticut, the Byram River camp, which Washington had proposed, never materialized; the troops that would have composed it were now in Wolcott's brigade. The permanent garrison of the Highlands—five companies of the 2nd New York, with another five of Scott's brigade and some artillerymen—numbered about 750. The Continental detachment at the eastern end of Long Island accounted for another 235.[27]

CHAPTER VII

Preparations

Over on Staten Island, the Halifax Army was also losing its special identity as reinforcements began to pour in from every quarter. Some 400 kilted Scots had already been picked up at sea and so arrived in early July along with everybody else, and the rest of the month saw transports fetching their countrymen almost on a daily basis. They represented two different regiments. The 42nd Royal Highlanders—the Black Watch—was a veteran corps; it had seen a good deal of American service in the last war and in the Indian problems that followed. For its current assignment the regiment found itself on a bloated establishment of 1168 officers and men. Its sister regiment, the 71st Highlanders, was a newly raised unit with a complement of 2098 all ranks, divided into two battalions for easier management. Scotland had turned out to be the only part of the realm where there was no great scarcity of willing recruits, and both regiments were filled with men who had a far greater stake in this war than King George's meager army pay.[1]

The Scottish Highlands were still restive in the wake of Bonnie Prince Charlie Stuart's bid for sovereignty in the '45 uprising. His failure had touched off a systematic dismantling of the existing social order, a militant tribal system which depended in large measure on an almost mystical bond of fealty between the clansman and his chief. Even Dr. Johnson, himself no Celtophile, could reflect pensively on the changes wrought: "The clans retain little now of their original character; their ferocity of temper is softened, their military ardour is extinguished, their dignity of independence is depressed, their contempt of government subdued, and their reverence for their chiefs abated. Of what they had before the late conquest of their country there remains only their language and their poverty." Many who could scrape up the capital had already emigrated to the wilds of Nova Scotia, New York and North Carolina. The crofters who had to stay back for want of anything to sell could now gain their passage in return for a short-term enlistment in the army, and their regimental baggage subsequently turned out such unlikely equipment as churns and plow shares. They were realistic enough to see that any farmsteads coming their way would first have to be taken from defeated Yankee rebels. The prospect bothered them not at all.[2]

They were rather looking forward to it. Their transports had put out from Clyde with Boston as their destination, unaware of its evacuation. Admiral Shuldham had posted a screen of naval vessels to intercept and redirect them and some, as we have seen, joined the Halifax Army en route to New York. But others were not so lucky. Six transports missed the screen and got snapped up by Continental warships, resulting in the capture of more than 600 officers and men. The commanding officer of the 71st Regiment's second battalion was taken with them, and his major was killed in a show of resistance in Boston harbor. Massachusetts did not deal kindly with the prisoners; their agrarian objectives were too well known. Officers and privates alike were marched through village streets under a shower of ethnic slurs, stones and excrement, while their militia guard discreetly looked the other way. By the time the story reached Staten Island it had lost nothing in the telling, and the Highlanders there seethed. An American prisoner who escaped the island reported ominously "that the Scots troops are extremely incensed against us, and frequently say they will give no quarter."[3]

Nor were the Highlanders alone in their thirst to be in on the final kill. Major Robert Rogers, a walking legend from the old French war, was busy recruiting disgruntled refugees and shaping them into a new corps of Rangers. At the end of July the 17th Light Dragoons arrived from Halifax with their horses, and with their sabers whetted for a splendid fox hunt. Two days later General Henry Clinton arrived from the south, bringing with him the competent general, Lord Charles Cornwallis. His army contained seven regiments of the Irish establishment, two artillery companies, and a ragtag body of Virginia loyalists who were promptly turned over to Rogers. Clinton's people carried with them a hangdog stigma of defeat, all the more galling because the Charleston battle had been a ship-to-shore affair and they never even got into action. On their heels came a fresh brigade of Household Guards, a thousand volunteers picked from the cream of the British Army and smarting under all the indignities offered their sovereign by upstart rebels. When they found out the sovereign's equestrian statue had actually been pulled down and dismembered by the same upstarts "their impatience was beyond expression."[4]

Along with the troops came additional ships for Lord Howe's fleet, having served for the most part as convoy escorts. The

Highlanders misdirected to Halifax were brought down from there by the cruiser *Renown*, while others came direct from overseas with the *Flora* frigate. *Niger* accompanied the 17th Light Dragoons. General Clinton's regiments were escorted from South Carolina by much the same squadron that had brought them from Ireland, under the command of Commodore Sir Peter Parker and containing the cruisers *Bristol* (the flagship) and *Experiment*, the frigates *Solebay* and *Syren*, the bomb vessel *Thunder* and the schooner *St. Lawrence*. At the same time the frigate *Roebuck* arrived from the Potomac with Virginia's royal governor, Lord Dunmore, and his entourage.[5]

Except for the Guards, whose transports were only beginning to straggle in, the British expeditionary force was complete enough to put into a final arrangement. The original six brigades remained intact, except that each was given one of Clinton's Irish units to increase its strength from three regiments to four. The leftover unit, the 33rd, was brigaded with the 42nd Highlanders to form a reserve corps under Lord Cornwallis. The 71st Highlanders and the Guards (when they arrived) each formed its own brigade under a general officer. The flank companies which had come up with Clinton formed separate battalions, as did the Highlander grenadier companies, bringing the new totals to three battalions of light infantry and four of grenadiers. The provincial units—Rogers's Rangers and the two New York companies—were not brigaded with the regulars. The duties of the 17th Light Dragoons, of course, left them an independent unit as well. General Howe's forces, including the artillerymen, now topped 15,000 all ranks, and they would shortly be joined by another self-contained army of almost 9,000 more.[6]

This auxiliary force consisted of some of the best troops money could buy. Last year's recruiting drive had turned out to be a crushing disappointment for the British Army. Even the Irish regiments sent to General Clinton, supposedly on a wartime footing of 677 men, turned out to be every bit as under strength as the units in the old Boston/Halifax garrison. The British Army did not even enjoy the right of conscription from a standing militia, as did the Americans in their roundabout fashion, and further, there was some reluctance to strip the home islands of their fighting strength and leave them open to invasion by the traditional enemy across the English Channel. The only way to get around the manpower problem, it seemed, was to invoke the time honored practice of hiring professional mercenaries from any European state willing to strike a suitable bargain. Some of the initial overtures were turned down flat—notably by Russia, but six German territories embraced the opportunity.

Hesse-Cassel, a county of some 300,000 inhabitants, was the principal supplier. The Landgrave maintained a standing army there of seven cavalry regiments and 23 infantry, besides a few smaller corps of military specialists. Some of the older units dated back to the 17th Century. On 13 January he contracted to turn over to George III fifteen of his infantry regiments, plus four battalions of grenadiers (made up of detached companies, on the British model), two companies of riflemen called jaegers and a proportionate body of artillery. The whole amounted to 12,000, completely equipped and "put on the best footing possible." In return the Landgrave received, among other things, a stipulated fee for each man so furnished, with contingency payments to be made in case of extraordinary losses. The entire force was to be maintained as a distinct corps under its own officers. Lieutenant General Leopold Philip von Heister, a veteran of wars long past, was appointed to the overall command.[7]

The bulk of von Heister's soldiers were also veteran professionals, proud in the service of their Landgrave. But the regiments earmarked for service in North America had to be brought up to strength so as to meet the terms of the contract. German sovereigns had long made a game of enlisting each other's deserters, much in the spirit of neighborly competition. For the current exigency, hardnosed recruiting parties hauled in not only these military itinerants, but virtually any hapless prospect they chanced to meet, and the result was a mixed bag of local peasants, incidental travelers and barrack yard drifters. There was the inevitable number of genuine volunteers; men who signed on for reasons of liege loyalty, for adventure, or for other motives best known to themselves. At any rate, the initial sweep was so productive that the regiments of the first division were filled to overflowing.[8]

The division was mustered by the British minister plenipotentiary, Colonel William Faucitt, in March and April. He was impressed by the physical stature of the veterans, made all the more imposing by the presence of some scrubs: "but these are only 17 to 20 Years old, and all very stout and well put together." Some were a bit awkward in handling their muskets, "which could not be otherwise, as they are Recruits; . . . they have been drilled constantly twice a Day, ever since they have been in Cantonments." Faucitt was especially taken with the jaegers, whose ranks were filled entirely with experienced hunters, foresters and game keepers. The jaeger presented an ideal blend of the British light infantryman and the American rifleman. He was not only aggressive and self-reliant, but he was also thoroughly trained, disciplined and at home in the woods. His rifle was of a military design, somewhat shorter and less graceful than the American's, but the jaeger was no less skilled in its effective use.[9]

On 7 May General Howe's augmentation cleared St. Helen's on the English Channel: 92 sail of storeships and transports under the command of Commodore William Hotham. Serving as escorts were the cruiser *Preston* (the flagship), the frigates *Rainbow*, *Brune* and *Emerald,* the bomb vessel *Carcass*, the fireship *Strombolo* and the hospital ship *Jersey* (destined for infamy as a future prison hulk). The storeships held all the provisions and equipment needed by the general for the upcoming campaign. On board the transports were the provisional brigade of English Guards, eight regiments of Hessian infantry, three battalions of grenadiers, one jaeger company and a detachment of artillery. Two more Hessian regiments, late in arriving, sailed separately under escort of the frigate *Repulse*. It was to be a long voyage for all concerned.[10]

All parties knew very well the campaign would not begin in earnest till after the Hessians had arrived and gotten their land legs. General Howe's anticipation of the storeships in their convoy was especially keen; he was beginning to feel the same pinch on Staten Island that he had felt before in Boston and Halifax. The larder was getting low. It was comforting to watch his army grow, but until the men could be brought into action they only represented so many mouths to feed. Locally grown produce had been consumed in a matter of weeks, and the fat Jersey farms were effectively blocked off by the Americans' Flying Camp screen. Salt had risen to five times its normal price, and fresh meat had become so scarce, thanks in part to last June's roundup, that a cow was reported to sell for ten pounds sterling. The troops had to be put back on their standard fare of salt pork and moldy flour, all of it hauled 3,000 miles across the Atlantic. Moreover, there were not nearly enough camp kettles and canteens to go around, and life in the field would be virtually impossible without them.[11]

Howe did not contemplate Staten Island as a permanent station for his army, so he strove for no ambitious network of fortifications there. A redoubt was laid out for the protection of the watering place, so vital to the fleet, and works were thrown up to cover the ferry landings from New Jersey. That was about all. The general's mind was not on defensive measures; he was faced instead with the prospect of an amphibious operation against a hostile shore. Flat-bottomed boats had been put under construction, larger even than the monsters brought down from Halifax, till there were enough craft available to launch a first-wave landing capability of 6,000 men. He also saw to it that this first wave would not be without artillery support from the very outset. A number of platforms were pieced together, each supported by three pontoons, and each with a landing ramp fixed on its front. As soon as a platform had been towed to its destination and beached, the ramp would go down and the guns would roll ashore ready for action. Fifty pieces of artillery, mounted on field carriages, could be landed almost simultaneously.[12]

The immediate problem was to keep the army in fighting condition and out of trouble. Drill and fatigue took up most of each day, and off-duty men were confined to the immediate area of their billets. "'Tis a hard unpleasant Life this of a Soldier's, which is passed in a little paltry Tent which will neither keep out Wind, or Rain, or Vermin, and which seems to have little other Solace on this dusty Island than the Association of multitudes in the same Condition." Such Hessians as had arrived early found a modicum of solace in their Lutheran hymns. Their Anglo-Celtic allies took a somewhat more traditional tack. Admiral Howe's secretary almost had his carriage demolished one evening by "a Waggon full of tippling Highlanders." More gravely, there was the occasional rape of an unescorted farm girl. One officer inadvertently disclosed the prevalent attitude in a letter home: "they are so little accustomed to these vigorous methods that they don't bear them with the proper resignation, and of consequence we have the most entertaining courts-martial every day." The Staten Islanders, now that they had little left to sell, were growing tired of their liberators.[13]

In the American camps the relatively undisciplined Continentals managed to get into less trouble with the locals. An early assessment of them tended to hold up through the summer: "There are very few instances of so great a number of men together with so little mischief done by them. They have all the simplicity of plowmen in their manners, and seem quite strangers to the vices of older soldiers." Property owners, to be sure, were understandably outraged by the incidental destruction of their resources in the routine of garrison life, and there was some unwarranted bullying of vendors at the produce markets. But offenses against civilians were so few that even harried loyalists sought refuge in the Army's guard rooms. Not that the simple plowmen were above random pilferage. Farmers around the outposts noticed a sharp decline in their watermelon yield for instance, and on one memorable occasion General Putnam threatened to hang "every mother's son" caught red-handed in a locked wine cellar. But the recorded transgressions appear to be little more than pranks. On Long Island, General Greene was scandalized to find his troops skinny-dipping in one of the millponds and streaking "Naked to the Houses with a Design to Insult and Wound the Modesty of Female Decency."[14]

The men posted about New York City—which is to say the bulk of the Army—had immediately at hand the means of less innocent fun. The city spawned a district cynically styled "the Holy Ground," tenanted by hard-eyed "bitchfoxly jades, jills, haggs, strums, prostitutes" and the inevitable footpads who flocked with them. Even after all unlicensed dram shops had been closed down by the Committee of Safety, the place still posed a threat to internal order. Knock-down donnybrooks were a regular diversion, and the tempted soldier sometimes got more than he bargained for. Cases of venereal disease turned up rather soon among officers and men alike. Nor was it a man's health alone which was in jeopardy. One day "two Men were found unhumanly Murthered & concealed, beside one who was castrated in a barbarous manner." The dead men were considered avenged only when their comrades marched in and pulled down the buildings where the bodies had been found.[15]

However swimmingly the soldiers may have got on with the citizens (apart from their love-hate relationship with the Holy Ground), Continental officers had some difficulty tolerating each other. The problem grew out of sectional animosities. Yankees and Yorkers had been at loggerheads since the days of Puritans and Dutch patroons, the hostility kept alive over the years by a series of territorial disputes. The current bone of contention was a free and easy rapport between New England's enlisted privates and their officers, "who were in no single respect distinguished from their men, other than in the coloured cockades" that served as badges of rank. This leveling in a regular army appeared contemptible to aristocratic New Yorkers, and the Pennsylvanians agreed with them; not the riflemen—they carried their own brand of frontier yahooism—but the gallants of Mifflin's brigade who fancied themselves as wordly southern gentlemen. Interstate backbiting finally undermined Army morale to such an extent that General Washington offered to cashier any officer who indulged himself in the further practice of it.[16]

Another menace to the Grand Army's integrity came from a rather different quarter: infectious diseases which had the power to render the equivalent of whole brigades entirely unfit for service. Smallpox, for example, came very early on with the first arrivals from Cambridge, and by May had even caused some fatalities. But an epidemic was aborted by establishing a quarantine hospital at Montresor Island and isolating victims as quickly as their symptoms appeared. Inoculation was prohibited entirely; it was a tricky procedure which involved the contact of infected matter with the subject's own blood stream, and very likely to get out of control. In any case the subject would often be as useless to the Army as if the disease had been contracted naturally. Smallpox did not rage in New York to the extent it did, say, in the Northern Army, but new cases were turning up well into the summer.[17]

"Bloody flux" was a major problem. It probably represented a number of unpleasant intestinal disorders, marked by dysentery with bloody stools. One cause, at least, is easy to determine. The summer of 1776 was unusually warm, especially in July. Each soldier (acting in groups of messmates) was responsible for the storage and preparation of his rations, a policy of the times which often resulted in poor cooking of food that was already spoiled. Moreover, the city's resources of fresh water were taxed severely. By the end of July the public pumps were judged to be unhealthy and not fit for use. The difficulty was compounded by a disinclination to use the proper facilities. On Long Island (but it might have been anywhere) it was forbidden "in the most Positive Terms the Troops easing themselves in the Ditches of the Fortifications." New latrines were dug on a regular basis, and whole campsites were moved in a determined drive for a sanitary environment. Even so, a doctor of the General Hospital could still observe: "The Air of the Whole City seems infected. In almost every street there is a horrid smell."[18]

These ailments, and more, might have been tolerated as a normal fact of garrison life had it not been for the introduction of a new disorder loosely diagnosed as "putrid fever." This infection broke all medical norms, dangerously thinning the ranks and even rendering a key general hors de combat. It is often difficult to isolate it from the cases of dysentery already mentioned. Apart from diarrhea, the symptoms most commonly noted, high fever and extreme prostration, bear the earmarks of both typhoid fever and epidemic typhus. The groundwork for either disease—crowding, physical exhaustion, unchanged clothing—had been thoroughly laid throughout the late spring and summer. By the end of July so many men were down that the General Hospital could not handle them all. Each regiment had to establish its own hospital area, and nurses were sought by running a help-wanted notice in the press. The New York Convention helped by condemning country houses north of the city for hospital use. Still, the lot of the stricken men was deplorable. "In almost every barn, stable, shed, and even under the fences and bushes, were the sick to be seen, whose countenances were but an index of the dejection of spirit, and the distress they endured."[19]

In spite of the widespread infection, the case fatality rate was surprisingly insignificant. In time, the stricken could expect to return to duty, but the effects of both typhoid fever and typhus on the human system are debilitating and protracted. In each, the crisis occurs a week or two following contraction, after which the victim may expect a convalescent period of many weeks more. In this way the "fever" took huge portions of the Army completely out of action for extended periods of time. General returns of 5 May show 13% of the available rank and file on the sick list. This dipped to 12% in June, perhaps reflecting a stabilization of the early smallpox infection. But by 13 July the figure rose to 14%, and then to 17% only six days after that. On 3 August 26% of the men were down, with no let-up in sight (by 21 September the figure would top 33%). Nor was the disease any respecter of rank. "In some Regiments there are not any of the Field Officers capable of doing duty," the commander-in-chief reported on 16 August, less than a week before the opening of hostilities.[20]

For all its waning vitality, General Washington had little choice but to work his Army into the best fighting shape he could. The epidemic, ironically, netted him one gain: the sick men's arms were given to the unarmed well, thereby relieving that chronic shortage at last. As the summer wore along, picks and shovels were laid aside long enough to reacquaint the troops—Continentals, levies and militia—with the evolutions of dismounted drill. Each man got to fire twice at a target to give him the feel of his musket. On a larger scale, ground maneuvers were held on the east shore above the city, where units contested with each other in mock battle. At the same time the artificer corps labored to produce a fleet of flat-bottomed boats. They were neither as large nor as numerous as the corresponding British craft, but at least there were enough to divide between the city and Brooklyn so as to permit a respectable movement of troops across the East River in either direction.[21]

The Brooklyn garrison, as we have seen, had been enlarged to division strength and Nathanael Greene was promoted to Major General to accommodate his new responsibilities. His division held two brigades, one of Continental troops and the other of new levies. The Continentals, by and large, were the same units he had commanded as a brigadier. The 1st Regiment, Hand's riflemen, still patrolled Kings County south of Gowanus Heights to discourage any contact with the enemy on Staten Island. The 4th and 7th were posted on Governor's Island, the 9th at Red Hook, and the 11th and 12th occupied the lines. The 11th had recently been ordered to New Jersey to help block the threat of invasion there. Greene was anxious not to lose these veterans, and a bit of high-level foot dragging helped keep them in his command for the time being. All these Continental units came under their new Brigadier General, John Nixon. His colleague in the division was Nathaniel Heard, the old Jersey minuteman, whose brigade contained the five regiments of six-months volunteers from his own state. They were also on the lines. Serving with them was Colonel Fisher Gay's Connecticut volunteers, who somehow found themselves detached from their parent brigade in Manhattan. They were posted at Fort Stirling and the Cobble Hill redoubt.[22]

Also on duty were the remnants of the Kings County standing militia, serving as a show of good faith. Rumors had been circulating that the phlegmatic Dutch farmers intended to follow the lead of their Richmond County neighbors; not that they would welcome General Howe quite so enthusiastically, but should the British Army cross over to Long Island neither would they offer any active resistance. The New York Convention, in its current militant posture, rose up in sputtering indignation. A committee was appointed to look into the stories. If they should prove true, the committee was to disarm and arrest the backsliders, remove or destroy their stock of grain and, if necessary, "to lay the whole county waste." Further, this scorched earth policy was to be carried out by the Continental garrison, thereby eliminating any ideas of leniency. Under the circumstances, Colonel Van Brunt deemed it prudent to have his regiment on the lines at Brooklyn; at least what was left of it. By this time the Long Island militia was pretty well picked over.[23]

General Washington had long urged the Convention to run livestock off the island to prevent any replenishing of the enemy's larder. Considering there were nearly 100,000 head of cattle alone—not to mention horses, sheep and hogs—this was an assignment of Herculean proportions. Nevertheless, the Convention ordered out a fourth of the island militia from all three counties and put them under Colonel Josiah Smith of the defunct Suffolk minutemen. About all they could hope to do was to drive beeves and horses away from the coastal areas to a number of points in the interior where they could be conveniently guarded. The roundup was still in progress when Smith was ordered to pull his regiment together and march to the Brooklyn lines. He was joined there by yet another Long Island unit, levied from half the remaining militia of Kings and Queens Counties and commanded by Colonel Jeromus Remsen of Queens. Taking into account the June levy for Scott's brigade, the levies for these two regiments, and not forgetting the draft dodgers in the marshes, the standing militia of the two western Long Island counties was somewhat less than a quarter of its original strength.[24]

Brooklyn's security rested entirely in keeping the Royal Navy out of the East River anchorage. Given Captain Parker's recent nose-thumbing cruise up the Hudson, the prospects of doing so might have seemed grim. But the East River's entrance, plugged by Governor's Island, was a good deal more defensible than the Hudson's. The guns mounted there could be served to greater advantage, and there were plans under way to block the main channel with sunken hulks. The tricky Hell Gate pass, covered by Fort Thompson, tended to dispel any worries about an approach through the back door. And however contemptible the American row galleys might appear to the veteran British enemy, they at least represented a force-in-being to be reckoned with. Moreover, a number of fireships stood ready at the wharves, waiting to be brought into play. With the anchorage so safely in hand, Brooklyn seemed not so much an outpost as a contiguous extension of the main garrison on Manhattan.

The electric charge of impending battle was in the air, and morale soared. A summer of grueling labor had given the old Brooklyn garrison a territorial interest in their redoubts and their ditches. "I have the pleasure to inform you," wrote Greene to his commander-in-chief, "that the Troops appear to be in exceeding good Spirits and make no doubt that if they should make their Attack here we shall be able to render a good account of them." Fatigue details put the final touches on the lines, closing the last gaps between Fort Box and Fort Putnam. Civilians were evacuated from the potential combat zone. All the tidemills were dismantled; the Kings County farmers' stock was run off and their harvested grain either confiscated for Army use or stacked for quick burning. Dram shops were ordered closed: the only liquor dispensed was through the sutlers. Off-duty men were confined to their quarters, and to help keep them there, company rolls would be called "at least three Times a Day."[25]

General Greene was a competent officer with a sound grip on his tactical situation. A game leg had not prevented him from limping up and down his post till he was completely familiar with its topography, and he expected all his officers to do the same. Last year the Rhode Island Assembly had tapped him, a military neophyte, to command its provincial forces in the Boston siege, and his demeanor was such that he had enjoyed Washington's special confidence ever since. On 15 August he made out a routine intelligence report to headquarters, signed it, and then took to bed with "a raging fever." Three days later he tried to rally, but it was no use. The camp fever had struck, taking him completely out of the picture with his talents, his leadership, and his working knowledge of the Kings County terrain.[26]

CHAPTER VIII

Long Island

Commodore Hotham's convoy from England sailed through the Narrows and dropped anchor on 12 August, "with Sails crouded, Colors flying, Guns saluting, and the Soldiers both in the Ships and on the Shore continually shouting." Balky sailing conditions had kept him at sea for fourteen weeks. *Repulse,* escorting the tardy Hessian units, had caught up with him and both sections of the fleet arrived together after the (by now) customary search for General Howe at Halifax. Apart from a few cases of scurvy, originating in the vitamin deficiencies of shipboard fare, the entire division was in excellent shape. Even so, a period of recuperation was in order while the provision ships were unloaded and their cargo sorted out and distributed. To accommodate the newcomers two British brigades—the 1st and 5th—were placed aboard empty transports and their billets given over to the Guards and Hessians. For the next few days Flying Camp snipers could not resist squeezing off potshots across the Kill van Kull at mustachioed foreigners on the opposite shore.[1]

Sniping at hapless sentries was not considered the professional thing to do, and it only served to harden prevalent European attitudes toward those who would rebel against their lawful king. Moreover, embittered Scottish Highlanders started to work on their new German neighbors. Language barriers were overcome so far as to convince the Hessians, not yet adjusted to their alien environment, "that the Rebels had resolved to give no quarters to them in particular"—a notion that, unfortunately, had some currency in the American army as well. But the official American position took a different tack. The Continental Congress resolved to seduce the foreigners with propaganda leaflets, offering each potential deserter not only the rights and privileges of citizenship but a horse, a cow and 200 acres—plus payment for his arms and accoutrements. General Washington, who was to develop a flair for covert activities, implemented a scheme to slip the leaflets into the Staten Island camps disguised as tobacco wrappers.[2]

While the Hessians and Guards were finding their land legs on Staten Island, the naval phase of the British campaign was already under way. Captain Hyde Parker's squadron had not yet made its daredevil run down the Hudson to join the fleet. Parker was still stationed in the Tappan Sea with orders to cut off the American garrison from its upriver supply bases. No reports had come down since the day he left, and there was no way of knowing that his prime mission had failed and the plucky captain could do little more than hold his own. So to put an additional squeeze on the American larder Admiral Howe detached another squadron, of four vessels this time, and sent them around Montauk Point to create a naval presence in Long Island Sound. These were the frigates *Brune* and *Niger,* the sloop *Kingsfisher* and the armed brig *Halifax. Brune's* skipper, Captain James Ferguson, had the command. His aim was to disrupt the communication between Connecticut and New York, pose a threat to Long Island's north shore, and eventually work far enough west to block off the Hell Gate pass to the East River.[3]

Long Island's south shore also came in for a share of petty harassment, when five tenders made their way into Hog Island Inlet and landed a shore party to round up livestock. This was in southern Hempstead township, occupied by the hardcore Tories of Queens County, and the area had only recently been left wide open by the departure of Colonel Smith's levies to the Brooklyn lines. Word of the incursion somehow reached General Greene, who was trying to run his command from a sickbed. Greene sent 200 men of the 12th Continentals, stiffened by twenty riflemen and escorted by both troops of Kings County light horse, pounding down the Jamaica Road to investigate. They had some 25 miles to cover and did not reach Rockaway Beach till the next day, only to find the raiders had gone. Nevertheless they spent

WOODS

MARSH

OBLONG REDOUBT

FT PUTNAM

FT GREENE

BROOKLYN FERRY RD

FT BOX

DAM

BEDFORD

JAMAICA RD

PASS

ENTRENCHMENTS

BEDFORD RD

POND

FLATBUSH RD

CREEK

LI BREASTWORKS

ORCHARD

BYROAD

EAST WOOD

GOWANUS COVE

PASS

PASS

ORCHARD

BALD HILL

GOWANUS RD

FLATBUSH

PASS

MARTENSE LA

THE BATTLEFIELD AREA OF 27 AUGUST. Included are those topographic features which had a bearing on the course of events. Sections of this map are used to illustrate the progress of the battle in Chapter IX; they may be oriented to this larger view for greater clarity.

the rest of the week working their way east while they "Colected a good number of Cattle & Distroyed a grate number of Boats." At the village of Jerusalem the detachment was overtaken by an express rider who brought orders for them to return to camp, 42 miles back. The British had landed on Long Island in force and they were in danger of being cut off.[4]

Sending out the cattle drovers was among Greene's final acts on Long Island. The next day he was on his way over to New York City and his division was inherited by Major General John Sullivan. Last spring we saw Sullivan as a brigadier, taking six regiments upriver to Canada. Through a series of American catastrophes he eventually gained field command of the Northern Army, only to be bumped from that position by the arrival of a superior officer in the person of Horatio Gates. Smarting at the fancied slight, he humphed down to Philadelphia to turn in his resignation. There he was persuaded to stay on, and was reassigned to the Grand Army with a subsequent step up in grade. Washington was not happy with Sullivan's quitting his post in the north, but he did see the New Hampshire lawyer as an aggressive go-getter. On 20 August, after cooling his heels for a month, the new major general was assigned to command the Brooklyn lines till Greene was back on his feet. The move was not universally hailed, not even by members of the staff. Adjutant General Reed,

for one, recognized that Sullivan was "wholly unacquainted with the ground or country."[5]

Sullivan established himself immediately and, in the manner of all new commanders, proceeded to shake things up. He was dismayed to find the Brooklyn works were not yet entirely secure. It would take two or three days more of fatigue to finish them off to his satisfaction, and the process would tie up 500 men each day. Moreover, the woods immediately to the right of the lines represented a serious gap between those works and Red Hook. Two of the Jersey regiments would take their alarm posts there from now on, and occupy the entrenchments facing Gowanus Creek and its network of millponds. Meanwhile there were Gowanus Heights, rising two miles away and blocking direct access to the lines from the coastal plain beyond. If General Greene had ever considered occupying them as a first line of defense—and we must assume that he did—he later dismissed the idea in favor of letting the enemy batter himself against the enclosed perimeter of the prepared fortifications. But now his successor would see what he could make of them.[6]

The road coming up from Brooklyn Ferry ran right through the center of the American lines, where the four redoubts formed the pocket that was meant to be the principal scene of carnage. About halfway to Gowanus Heights it forked into three branches. The right branch ran due west between the Heights and the harbor bay, following the curve of Yellow Hook's shoreline from Gowanus Cove to the Narrows, and extended somewhat further than the western terminus of the Heights. This was the Gowanus Road, and it provided the overland connection between Denyse's and Brooklyn Ferries. At the southern edge of Gowanus Cove a narrow lane—the Martense Lane—broke off from the road, meandered through a hollow in the ridge and joined the Flatbush-New Utrecht road on the plain. Back at the fork, the left branch ran eastward on the plateau just north of the Heights, cut through Bedford village and eventually crossed the ridge about four miles from the lines. This was the Jamaica Road; it connected Brooklyn ferry with the mass of Long Island, and the place where it crossed the Heights was Jamaica Pass. This approach would bear watching if the British should land, say, at Rockaway Beach and work their way westward from Queens County.[7]

At Bedford the Jamaica Road was intersected by another thoroughfare, coming from Bushwick in northeastern Kings. This crossroad passed through Bedford, crossed the ridge, went on to Flatbush—about a mile south of the Heights—and then continued across the plain to Flatlands. The section running south out of Bedford Village was called the Bedford Road, and it crossed the Heights at Bedford Pass. Back at the fork again, the center branch could be seen as an extension of the Brooklyn Ferry Road. This was the Flatbush Road; it crossed the ridge through the wide notch of Flatbush Pass and then went on to join the Bedford Road just below the Heights. Should the British land in Kings County these approaches would be the likeliest routes of advance, with the Gowanus Road along the coast a strong alternate. In all, it seemed worthwhile to post troops on all three roads. Breastworks would be thrown up, protected in front by an abatis of felled trees. The function of these outworks would be to harass the invader and slow his progress, after which the advanced troops could fall back to the safety of the Brooklyn lines. This was to be the final embellishment of General Lee's original plan, and less than a week's time would prove it to be the most consequential of all.[8]

General Howe had already started embarking his troops on Sunday, 18 August. This was the day Captain Parker made his run home from upriver. The gale that brought him down also ushered in a spell of foul weather, so it was not till Wednesday that all the men were on board the transports. These made up the 2nd, 3rd, 4th, and 6th British brigades (the 1st and 5th were already afloat), the Guards, the 71st Highlanders and the two New York provincial companies: "about Eleven thousand eight hundred and fifty English foot, Near five hundred Artillery and about 120 Light Horse, with fifteen hundred Foreigners under Col. Donop." The cavalry, of course, was the 17th Light Dragoons, and Donop's foreigners were the three Hessian grenadier battalions and the jaegers. Left on Staten Island for the time being were the rest of the Hessians—now organized into three brigades of their own—and Lord Cornwallis's British reserve. The Richmond County militia was called out; a number of suspected backsliders were disarmed and the remainder was sent to man the outposts with the Hessians and with Rogers's new provincial corps. The Rangers were still in the recruiting stage and not yet ready to take the field.[9]

General Washington was kept posted on the embarkation, for the most part by Colonel Hand's observations from Long Island. By five Wednesday evening the 21st the rifle commander reported "at least fourteen sail of transports, some of them crowded with men, now under sail; and more, from the noise, are hoisting anchor." These all dropped through the Narrows and into the lower bay. Later in the evening an American agent crossed over from New Jersey, bringing hard intelligence that 20,000 soldiers were now on board. A night attack was in the offing and it was to be "on Long Island and up the North River." Further, 15,000 men left on Staten Island were to cross the Kills and descend on Bergen Point, Elizabeth and Amboy. This spy was vouched for by General Livingston, commander of the New Jersey militia and soon to be that state's first constitutional governor. His man claimed to have been well inside the British camp and "heard the orders read, and heard the Generals talk of it . . . that they appear very determined and will put all to the sword."[10]

The threat of a night assault was taken seriously, and a continuation of the week's nasty weather promised early nightfall and a moonless sky. But at seven o'clock a fierce thunder storm rolled across the area like a cliché out of some Greek tragedy. "Several claps struck in and about the city; many houses damaged; several lives lost." A captain and two lieutenants of the 1st New York were electrocuted by a single lightning bolt, "the points of their swords for several inches melted." Additional fatalities and some injuries were later reported in both New York and on Long Island, while one of the row galleys in the East River had its mast completely shattered. The moral effect of all this on a basically religious army was not especially significant, at least not outwardly, but the event had to give some pause to the long-faced Puritans. "When God speaks," one of them wondered, "who can but fear?"[11]

The storm blew over in three hours, leaving in its wake a moderating trend with localized rain squalls. All night the transports rode at anchor off Long Island, shepherded by part of the fleet. Promptly at daybreak Thursday morning the 22nd, they warped into Gravesend Bay with the frigates *Phoenix, Rose,* (both once more in the thick of the action) and *Greyhound,* and the bomb vessels *Carcass* and *Thunder.* All the men-of-war hove in close, their broadsides turned to rake the shore. In addition, the bomb ships had the capacity to lob exploding shells among any defending troops, being so constructed as to withstand the massive recoil of their mortars. Farther up the shoreline *Rainbow* trained her guns on Denyse's Ferry, where last July American 9-pounders had pelted the invasion fleet. There were no guns mounted there now, but *Rainbow* kept her station in order to enfilade the Gowanus Road and play hell with any reinforcements coming down that way.[12]

As the ships positioned themselves in the grey dawn, Lord Cornwallis's reserve—the 33rd Foot, the 42nd Highlanders, all the British grenadiers and the 3rd Light Infantry Battalion—clambered aboard their flat boats at Staten Island and were towed across the channel to Gravesend Bay. They made up the advance corps, and they hit the beach about nine in the morning with General Clinton at their head. At precisely the same time Admiral Howe fired a signal gun from *Phoenix* (she was his flagship for the occasion) and hoisted a blue and white flag. Immediately the first division of landing craft, laden with redcoats, pulled for the shore. The entire landing fleet consisted of "seventy five flat Boats with eleven Batteaux and two Gallies"—the last two items being the craft built during the summer. The boats serving the transports had been organized into ten divisions, and these into two waves, all under the immediate direction of Commodore Hotham. As the first wave pulled out, its emptied transports dropped away to make room for the second team of transports and boats. "Every thing, relative to the Disembarkation," gloated Admiral Howe's secretary to his diary, "was conducted in admirable Order, and succeeded beyond our most sanguine Wishes."[13]

The 71st Highlanders and the embarked light infantry got ashore first (after Cornwallis's vanguard, of course), followed by Donop's Hessians and then the remaining British forces. As quickly as knots of arrivals waded through the surf, Clinton marched them up the beach and formed them on the flat plain of New Utrecht township. By noon the debarkation was completed; in less than three hours some 15,500 men and forty pieces of artillery were landed and reasonably prepared for offensive operations. All that remained was for the Navy to dry its canvas and begin ferrying over the baggage, supplies, wagons, draft animals and mounts. When General Howe arrived with his staff from aboard *Preston* he found himself in command of an army in boyish high humor. "The Soldiers & Sailors seemed as merry as in a Holiday, and regaled themselves with the fine apples, which hung every where upon the Trees in great abundance."[14]

By Thursday afternoon Howe was deploying his forces to occupy the southern part of Kings County, posting them in extended order along a road running across New Utrecht, Gravesend and Flatlands townships. This made a line about eight miles long, anchored on the left at Denyse's Ferry and on the right by the marshes lying between Jamaica Bay and Flatlands village. At the same time Cornwallis was detached with his reserve corps, two battalions of light infantry, all of Donop's Hessians and six field pieces, and sent upcountry to probe Flatbush Pass. He was ordered not to force the pass should he find it occupied by American troops, but instead fall back on Flatbush village and take his post there. The makeup of Cornwallis's detachment suggests that enough draft animals had been landed to pull his artillery, but there were as yet no mounts for the 17th Light Dragoons. This, ideally, would have been the unit to use, either for reconnaissance or to cut off the retreating American riflemen.[15]

Hand's riflemen, about 300 strong, had been alerted by their picket guard at dawn. They quickly assembled near the beach but, as the British reserve waded ashore, retired in good order through New Utrecht village and continued up the road leading to Flatbush. Behind them they left a scorched earth of flaming grain shocks and hay ricks till the smoke could be seen in New York City, all the while keeping an eye on Cornwallis's vanguard trailing them. When they reached the Martense Lane juncture they left the main road and, assuming themselves to be the objective, laid an ambush in the woods where the Lane crosses Gowanus Heights. This was the rifleman's natural element of cover and concealment, but as Cornwallis approached somebody's rifle went off and gave the game away. Cornwallis paused only long enough to assess his danger and then marched past the road juncture and kept on to Flatbush. Hand could only dog his left flank, staying to the edge of the wood and sending a detachment ahead to burn grain. Captain James Hamilton had the charge of this task, "which he did very cleverly, and killed a great many cattle."[16]

General Washington, we may assume, received his first news of the landing in the prescribed manner: two guns fired from the Cobble Hill fort at Brooklyn. Verbal reports started coming in soon after, brought by panting runners from the rifle regiment and hurried across the East River to headquarters. But they gave the American commander a false account of Howe's field army, and the misinformation was to stay with him and influence his tactical decisions in the crucial days ahead. The figure given was "about eight thousand." Inasmuch as yesterday's intelligence put 20,000 British troops on board the transports, it seemed apparent that some 12,000 were still afloat and poised for a descent elsewhere. The move against Long Island was therefore suspected as a feint "to draw our Force to that Quarter, when their real design may perhaps be upon this." It was the St. Patrick's Day riddle all over again, and again Washington was uncertain which way to jump.[17]

He could not, however, ignore the occupation of Flatbush; his garbled intelligence left him with the impression that Cornwallis's vanguard actually represented the entire enemy strength. Reinforcements were therefore ferried over to Sullivan late Thursday afternoon. But rather than disrupt the brigade deployments in New York City, with a consequent shifting of men to unfamiliar alarm posts, six individual regiments were detached piecemeal. It is difficult to identify all of them with certainty, but they included Miles's Pennsylvania riflemen, Silliman's Connecticut levies, and the 10th and 17th Continentals from Parson's brigade. No provisions had been readied for them to take along, yet their morale was excellent and they climbed into their flat boats "in high Spirits." Once on the other side the Continentals were posted to the advance lines at Gowanus Heights along with Miles's two battalions, while Silliman's Yankees occupied a wood near the shore at Red Hook. They all spent a sleepless night with muskets in hand, listening while opposing sentries occasionally popped rounds at one another.[18]

If Cornwallis's advance position appeared unstable, he actually felt himself in little danger of being cut off and captured. Should the attempt be made he was strong enough to hang on while General Howe brought up the main body, and it was not likely the Americans would risk a decisive engagement on the plain. But Cornwallis presented a tempting target for harassment, and the temptation was not resisted. Activities began first thing Friday morning, when the 17th Continentals were pushed to the edge of the wood facing Flatbush and supported by artillery. At dawn Hand's riflemen filtered through them and opened "a Scattering fire on the Enemys Advanc'd Sentrys." These were the Hessian jaegers, and for the first time American and German riflemen faced each other in open combat. "The Idea which we at first conceived of the Hessian Riflemen was truly ridiculous," recalled one American officer a few days later, "but sad experience convinces our people that they are an Enemy not to be despised."[19]

It is impossible to reconcile the conflicting accounts of either side, but it appears that an initial assault by the Continental riflemen was driven off when field pieces were brought up to support the jaegers. A second attack in the afternoon had somewhat greater success. Hand's people, supported by their own artillery, actually drove Cornwallis's picket back to Flatbush village. They came within an ace of capturing the Hessian guns when they were prematurely ordered to retire, but they did pick up a number of small arms and even brought back enemy corpses to prove their close contact. At the same time they fired some country houses where the jaegers had taken shelter and so eliminated their future use as outposts. Afterward the 42nd Highlanders threw a breastwork across the Flatbush Road a half mile to the rear of the original picket line and mounted it with two guns. For the rest of the day there was "a Considerable Number of shots Exchang'd between the Artilery of the two Armys."[20]

With his vanguard thus occupied, General Howe proceeded to raise the Royal Standard. By proclamation he offered the King's protection to all the Islanders who "have been compelled by the leaders in this rebellion to take up arms against His Majesty's Government." All they had to do was repair to army headquarters at New Utrecht and "be received as faithful subjects." They could then return home with certificates documenting their fidelity, and if they chose to take up arms in the King's service they would meet with every encouragement. There is no evidence of any great clamor to take the offer, at least none so dramatic as Staten Island's capitulation last month. But the militia of Kings County's four lower townships was effectively neutralized nonetheless, and some of the individuals who did come in were to prove invaluable as guides.[21]

By Friday General Washington started making daily visits to Long Island. He left sometime before the afternoon skirmishing, still convinced that the bulk of the British troops were aboard the transports awaiting only a favorable mix of wind and tide for a general descent on Manhattan. But the Connecticut militia was now showing up in respectable numbers, and he could afford to detach four more regiments to Sullivan with orders for them to return immediately should Lord Howe's fleet "push up to the City." Meanwhile, General Heath had already been ordered to detach a combat team from the Harlem-Kingsbridge sector "of about Eight hundred or a thousand light active men, and good Marksmen" and send them with some light artillery to cover Manhattan's west side. Heath built this force around the 3rd and 5th Pennsylvania, pulling them out of Fort Washington and beefing them up with picked men from his other Continental units and from George Clinton's New York levies. General Mifflin had the command, and he marched the detachment down to Bloomingdale, about half way to New York City. This Out Ward hamlet offered the likeliest point of attack from the Hudson River. Mifflin was prepared, as events dictated, to repulse a landing there, to continue south and reinforce Washington, or to return to his former station.[22]

With his new reinforcements General Sullivan could permanently cover each of the main approaches with two regiments. For the Friday night picket Johnston's and Martin's Jersey levies were assigned to the Gowanus Road, and the 11th and 12th Continentals to Flatbush Pass. Remsen's Long Island levies joined Miles's Pennsylvanians at Bedford Pass. During the night something happened to spook Remsen's people, who immediately pulled foot and retired in disorder to the safety of the Brooklyn lines. The alarm may have been triggered by the midnight arrival of the cattle drovers sent to Queens County last Monday, now returning to camp after a forced march of 40-odd miles in less than twelve hours. They had stopped only once to rest and eat, apparently just this side of the county line. Shortly after their break they learned that a patrol of British dragoons was on their trail, but the Kings County light horse stayed by and escorted them through Jamaica Pass, screening the last leg of their march. For their timidity Remsen's sprinters were reduced to the shame of serving exclusively as a labor battalion, "to which they are to attend from day to day." Totally lost in the night's events were the facts that a body of men had gained easy access to the Brooklyn plateau through Jamaica Pass, that the British dragoons probably knew about that pass, and that the steadiest troops alive will panic with a real or fancied threat to their rear.[23]

The skirmishing across no-man's land continued all through the weekend, by day and night, involving not only small arms but artillery as well. In terms of numbers, and forgetting the private agonies of those afflicted, the resulting casualties were insignificant to either side. Colonel Ephraim Martin of the Jersey levies was shot through the chest in one engagement; he survived, but never rejoined the service. The American riflemen did what they were best at: "They climb trees, they crawl forward on their bellies for one hundred and fifty paces, shoot, and go as quickly back again." General Washington witnessed these freelance tactics on his Saturday inspection of the outposts, and he was not at all impressed by their effectiveness. He ordered a stop to them, citing among his reasons a courting of the enemy's contempt, a waste of ammunition and a breakdown of unit integrity. Aggressiveness was certainly to be encouraged, but only in organized parties under proper leadership and with specific objectives.[24]

Washington had to change his mind, at least to some extent, about the immediate danger to New York City. Reports were starting to come in that the Staten Island encampments were being struck and that the fleet was dropping through the Narrows. The obvious suggestion in this was that "they mean to land the Main Body of their Army on Long Island, and to make their grand push there." Six more regiments were fed across the East River, and by Sunday they had to be formed into two provisional brigades with the ten already sent on Thursday and Friday. The original Brooklyn garrison—Nixon's and Heard's brigades—remained intact, with Smith's and Remsen's Long Island levies attached to Nixon's. But then Lord Stirling was sent over to command Miles's and Atlee's Pennsylvania regulars, Haller's and Cunningham's Pennsylvania Flying Camp levies (they were barely getting organized), and Lasher's and Drake's New York levies. At the same time Brigadier General Samuel Holden Parsons arrived to take charge of Silliman's, Chester's and Gay's Connecticut levies and the 10th, 17th, 21st and 22nd Continentals. Any more units coming over were to go to Stirling.[25]

So many units were now on Long Island that Major General Israel Putnam—the Grand Army's ranking officer—pressed his right to command them. Putnam, at least in his outward appearance, was the precise opposite of Washington's ideal model of a Continental officer of any grade. He was rough in manner, blustering in speech and barely literate. Still, he was a noted ranger veteran of the last war, the hero of almost as many stories as the legendary Rogers, and more recently remembered as the minuteman general of Bunker's Hill. Washington seemed fond of

him and actually considered him "a most valuable man and a fine executive officer." So he got the Long Island command, thereby bumping Sullivan to the status of an executive whose function was to carry out orders rather than originate them. It was the second time this summer Sullivan had been demoted under identical circumstances; despite every effort his nose remained understandably out of joint.[26]

But at least he had the satisfaction of seeing his recent innovations solidified as official policy. A vital shift in emphasis moved the primary defense perimeter from the prepared works of the Brooklyn lines—which General Greene had once vowed to defend "to the last extremity"—to the natural barrier of Gowanus Heights. The idea now was not to stall the invader at the passes but to stop him cold. On Sunday General Putnam received orders to deploy his unruly riflemen in the woods next to Red Hook, where their frontier individualism would not be an embarrassment to the Army. "The Militia [ie, the levies] are most indifferent Troops (those I mean which are least tutored and seen least service) will do for the interior Works, whilst your best Men should at all hazards prevent the Enemy's passing the Wood [ie, the wooded Heights] and approaching your Works." There either was no apparent need for proper fortifications at the passes or it was felt there was no time to prepare them, but "The Woods should be secured by Abattis &c. where Necessary to make the Enemy's approach as difficult as possible."[27]

At the same time, Washington tried to introduce an auxiliary force onto Long Island. On Saturday, still under the impression that Cornwallis's Flatbush garrison was the whole British field army, he wrote Connecticut's Governor Trumbull asking could his state "throw a Body of about one thousand or more Men across the Sound, to harass the Enemy in their rear or upon their Flanks?" This proposed force would also prevent foragers from gaining supplies in the interior; "The Cattle," he suggested, "to be removed or killed." It is remarkable that he did not ask the New York Convention for the patriotically oriented Suffolk County militia to carry out this assignment. Or, if he sensed the east Islanders feared for their own livestock, he could have called in his three Continental companies of the 2nd New York. They were still posted in Suffolk County as a cattle guard under their energetic regimental commander, Lieutenant Colonel Henry Beekman Livingston.[28]

With the major part of the Connecticut militia already at New York City or on the way there, Trumbull apparently could not see his way clear to send any part of his state's Eastern Division to Long Island. By this time Captain Ferguson's squadron was poking its way into the Sound. The troops, plying across in whaleboats, could easily have been intercepted and the risk may have seemed too great. But the New York Convention coincidentally came up with much the same idea, and on its own initiative. All the "horses, horned cattle and sheep" south of the morain ridge in Queens County were to be driven to the Hempstead Plains and put under guard, while the area's grain was to be stacked in the fields for burning. Detailed to pull this off—and in the Tory stronghold!—was half the 1st Suffolk Regiment, as many of the remaining Queens militia as could be persuaded to turn out, and the three light horse troops of Kings and Queens. Further, General Washington was to be asked for Smith's and Remsen's levies to help out. The whole project was to be organized and executed by the Convention's own absent President, Brigadier General Nathaniel Woodhull, who had resumed active command of his 3rd Brigade of New York Militia (Suffolk and Queens Counties).[29]

By Sunday the 25th General Howe had his British forces settled in and resupplied for the campaign, and it was time to bring over his Hessian auxiliaries under General von Heister. Two brigades of three regiments each—Mirbach's and Stirn's—crossed the Narrows in flat boats "with their Field Artillery and Baggage," and landed on the beach of Gravesend Bay. The third brigade, Lossberg's, remained behind to secure Staten Island with the Richmond County militia, Rogers's corps, and sundry British recruits, convalescents and odd-lot detachments brought up from the south. Mirbach's and Stirn's joined Donop's brigade at Flatbush the next day. They added about 4,300 to Howe's field army, bringing his total strength on Long Island to almost 20,000. The number left on Staten Island could not have amounted to much more than 3,000. [30]

Monday, 26 August, found Washington as much in the dark as ever concerning his enemy's actual strength. He tended to overestimate the total numbers and underestimate the part on Long Island, by as much as 10,000 or more in either case. He seems to have been only vaguely aware of Howe's deployments. No patriotic civilians of record came in to report their observations. The 17th Light Dragoons had set up a screen against infantry patrols and the only local cavalry, the Kings County militia troops, were off cowboying with General Woodhull. Deserter interrogations revealed that "there was about 8 or 9 thousand Men Landed," and Lieutenant Colonel Nicholas Covenhoven, on leave from Remsen's regiment, returned to camp with much the same tale. On his way home he had been picked up and taken to General Howe. He was not detained, as a field officer of rebel militia might have expected to be, but was asked only to send in provisions from his farm. While at British headquarters he "understood from the officers that 8,000 men had landed the first day." The coincidence is extraordinary. Could Covenhoven—wittingly or no—have been a double agent with a planted story? Washington's early acceptance of the 8,000 figure was common knowledge. Its continual popping up might almost suggest that Howe was deliberately reinforcing the American commander's low estimate so as to keep him worried about a nonexistent force ready to strike New York. [31]

General Woodhull had penetrated Kings County and was driving cattle eastward into Queens. Fresh orders from the Convention had altered the nature of his assignment. He was now to position himself on Gowanus Heights somewhere near the county line—or anywhere else he thought appropriate—"for preventing the incursions and depredations of the enemy." To accomplish this he had about forty stalwarts gathered in Queens, a hundred more from Suffolk and another fifty of the Kings County light horse. Washington had promised "that he would immediately give orders that Col. Smith's and Remsen's regiments should march into Queens county to join Genl. Woodhull," but they never arrived. About all the Yorker could do was to post his handful individually as "guards and sentries from the north side to the south side of the Island." If nothing else this screen could try to isolate Kings County from the rest of Long Island and so intercept any loyalists making their way to the British lines. On a worldlier level, they would keep the more obstinate animals from drifting back home. [32]

Suffolk County blamed its poor turnout on Captain Ferguson, whose squadron was working its way through Long Island Sound and snapping up coastal shipping en route to New York. On the 25th Ferguson landed a party at Brookhaven township to pick up provisions, and the seamen went about the business of shooting cattle to take aboard. The news spread quickly. Most of the detachment intended for Woodhull immediately backtracked to take care of the local threat, and the next day they prevented the British from taking a sloop that had run aground to avoid capture. Woodhull could therefore not only expect no further help from his own home county, but he himself was asked to send reinforcements! "Our women," explained the commander of the 1st Suffolk Regiment, "are in great tumult." [33]

General Washington spent all Monday the 26th on Long Island. In the course of the day he was followed across by Smallwood's Maryland regulars with two attached independent companies, Haslet's Delaware Continentals, Kachlein's Associator battalion of Pennsylvania riflemen, and a detachment of a hundred volunteers from the 20th Continentals under the partisan Knowlton (this group fancied themselves as Yankee rangers with a specialty in night patrols). It is difficult to determine how far the Army had been savaged by camp fever this late in the month, or even to what extent the newly arrived Pennsylvania, Delaware and Maryland units were infected. But a 30% disability rate seems likely, and a rough estimate might thus put the total number of officers and men now in the Brooklyn lines and their outworks at about 9,000. The three regiments at Red Hook and Governor's Island would add less than a thousand more. [34]

The fever was taking out an alarming number of field officers. Colonel Fisher Gay of Connecticut was already dead; others were too sick to accompany their units to Long Island. There were barely enough healthy ranking officers in the whole Army to hold a court martial for Lieutenant Colonel Herman Zedwitz. Smallwood and Haslet, with their lieutenant colonels, had to sit on that trial from the 25th through the 26th, while their regiments were in the field. Zedwitz, commander of the 1st New York Continentals, had recently offered his services as an agent in place to Governor Tryon, and the offer had found its way instead to General Washington. It was a nasty business to take care of at this critical period. It had as much potential for disrupting Army morale as the late Hickey affair. Zedwitz was found guilty of "holding a treacherous correspondence with, and giving intelligence to, the enemies of the United States." Taking his pitiful defense into consideration, the court apparently thought him more of a fool than a traitor and sentenced him only to be cashiered. The whole incident passed over with little stir. [35]

Before Washington returned to his New York headquarters on Monday evening, the day before the battle, he and Putnam studied the enemy position at Flatbush. They may even have watched von Heister's two Hessian brigades relieve Cornwallis, who then left the immediate area with all the British forces. The arrival of fresh troops led the American commanders to "apprehend they would in a little time make a general attack." We do not know, however, whether or not Washington personally supervised Putnam's deployments before leaving the Island. Curiously, yesterday's orders to remove the riflemen from the outworks and to post only the steadiest troops there went ignored. Tonight it was Parsons's turn to command the Heights as Brigadier General of the Day, and his units were very much a mixed bag of Continentals, state regulars and levies, drawn piecemeal from all four of the Long Island brigades. [36]

It had become General Putnam's policy to cover each of the three likeliest approaches with 800 men, and to put another 300 in the woods between Red Hook and the interior lines. Monday night's deployment was not quite so evenly distributed as this might suggest, beside which the Army's riflemen were posted on each flank of the outer perimeter. Hand's 1st Continentals occupied the Red Lion Inn at the end of the Martense Lane, and a half mile up the Gowanus Road they were supported by detachments representing most of Atlee's Pennsylvania regulars, most of the Flying Camp levies and most of Lasher's New Yorkers. Flatbush Pass, where the main thrust was expected, was held by Johnston's New Jersey levies and the 11th and 12th Continentals, supported by a battery of field pieces. Bedford Pass, less than a mile to the left, was held by Chester's Connecticut levies and the 22nd Continentals. Miles's two battalions of riflemen occupied the ridge on the left flank "to watch the motion of the enemy on that part, with orders to keep a party reconnoitering to and across the Jamaica Road." Sentries were placed at intervals from one flank to the other so as to "keep a constant communication between the three guards on the three roads." From Hand on the right to Miles on the left, about 3,000 Americans were deployed at Gowanus Heights and its western passes, all wearing a sprig of green in their hats in lieu of a common uniform. [37]

Some time before, Miles's patrols had penetrated the British screen on the plain so far as to discover there were more troops

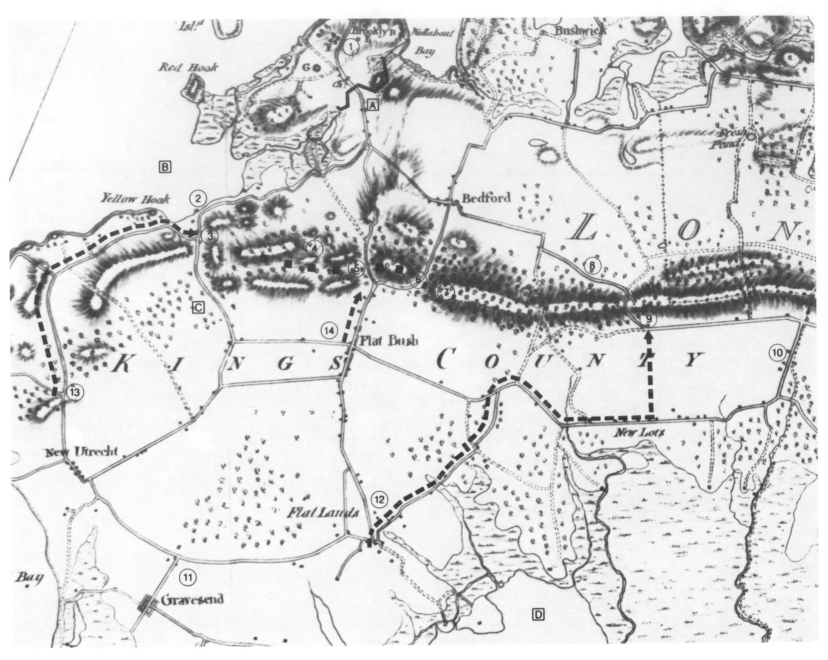

NIGHT OF 26/27 AUGUST, 8:00 PM—2:00 AM. Detail of George Taylor's and Andrew Skinner's "A Map of New York & Staten Islds And Part of Long Island," 1781 (BrM 112/3). (A) American lines, (B) Gowanus Cove, (C) Martense Lane, (D) Jamaica Bay. American deployments: (1) Gen. Putnam's division at the Brooklyn peninsula, (2) New York and Pennsylvania detachments on the Gowanus Road, (3) Maj. Burd's Flying Camp levies at the Red Lion (Martense Lane pass), (4) line of pickets on the "communication," (5) Col. Johnston's three regiments on the Flatbush Road (Flatbush Pass), (6) Col. Wyllys's two regiments on the Bedford Road (Bedford Pass), (7) Col. Miles's riflemen in the eastern wood, (8) Miles's picket guard on the Jamaica Road, (9) mounted patrol at Howard's (Jamaica Pass), (10) Gen. Woodhull's Long Island militia on the county line road. British deployments: (11) Gen. Percy's division on the New Utrecht-Flatlands road, (12) Gen. Clinton's line of march, (13) Gen. Grant's line of march, (14) Gen. von Heister's line of march. A—D, 1—14, American Lines, routes of march and positions of troops are additions to the original map.

on the Island than those occupying Flatbush. Colonel Covenhoven, in his espionage activities for Washington, saw "many regulars" posted at Flatlands to the southeast. They were the two battalions of 71st Highlanders and a detachment of light infantry, and they were in an excellent position to make a diversion through Jamaica Pass once the general engagement was started. To forestall any unpleasant surprise, five officers on horses—the only cavalry now available—mounted a guard at this opening. All of them were locals; three were the adjutant and two subalterns from Lasher's regiment. The other two were volunteers who had served in last year's campaign and whose commissions were now inactive. Should the Flatlands garrison turn up at the pass their natural course would be to gallop back to Parsons's line and give the alarm to Miles. Then the Pennsylvania riflemen could change their front and cover the Jamaica Road till reinforcements came up from the reserves at Brooklyn.[38]

There was one major change during the night. The 1st Continentals had been on constant duty since Thursday's landing and they had now reached the end of their physical endurance. Shortly after midnight they were pulled off the right flank and sent to the interior lines to get some sleep. Haller's Flying Camp regiment—and possibly Cunningham's as well—took their place at the Red Lion.[39]

About the same time Knowlton's Yankee rangers filtered through Flatbush Pass with an eye to snapping up some Hessian sentries for interrogation. They were just about to spring the trap on an enemy guard post when they "were fired upon by a party of American Militiamen, who did not understand their duty, and who immediately took to their heels." The incident has no particular significance in itself; Hessian privates were not necessarily privy to the details of staff planning. But it does serve to illustrate the everlasting lack of discipline and coordination that plagued the American Army, even those entrusted with its first line of defense. It was the essence of Washington's complaint against freelance skirmishing.[40]

CHAPTER IX

Juggernaut

Howe's second-in-command, Lieutenant General Henry Clinton, was also dismayed by the *petite guerre* situation at Flatbush. He felt the hit and run firefights served only to give the Americans "courage, confidence, and service," while his own troops were taking losses "without any one good end likely to be answered by it." There was, in fact, very little about the campaign's management that suited Clinton, and he was so tactless about saying so that he and his chief were currently not on speaking terms. Even before the Hessians and Guards arrived Clinton had proposed to take and hold Kingsbridge, and thereby cut off Washington's only terrestrial connection with the mainland. Howe listened and seemed at first to agree, but then said no; offensive operations would have to wait for reinforcements and for the camp equipment coming with them. Even then he did not follow Clinton's advice, but committed his entire field army to Long Island, pushing Cornwallis so close to the American lines he was "exposed to affront in a very awkward situation."[1]

On Friday the 23rd Clinton personally reconnoitered the American positions. By Saturday he had a handle on all the defended areas and had discovered Jamaica Pass, either by his own observations or by reports of the dragoon patrols. For the topographical situation behind Gowanus Heights he would have had to rely on his maps, on descriptions furnished by locals, and on his own memory of long-ago days as the Governor's son. But it was Jamaica Pass that most caught his eye, and by Sunday he had developed a plan to secure that opening and use it to hit the left flank of Washington's outer line and roll it up like a soldier's blanket.

Clinton's plan was essentially a classic double envelopment with frontal demonstrations. At a given signal, a thrust was to be made up the Gowanus Road to gain the western end of Gowanus Heights and proceed eastward along the ridge. The defenders of Flatbush and Bedford Passes would simultaneously find their attention thoroughly occupied by the Flatbush garrison. Once activities had begun, the bulk of the British Army would burst out of Jamaica Pass, seize the plateau between the outer and inner American perimeters, and at the same time fall on the outer left flank and rear. While this was going on, the fleet was to demonstrate against the East River shore batteries as if to force its way into the anchorage. All the attacks were intended to be "vigorous but not too obstinately persisted in, except that which is designed to turn the left flank of the rebels, which should be pushed as far as it will go."[2]

The whole operation depended, from first to last, on an awesome combination of audacity, skill, secrecy, timing, clement weather and plain good luck. Clinton showed his plan to Sir William Erskine of the 71st Highlanders and asked him to present it to the commander-in-chief. This Erskine undertook to do, only to meet with cool hostility. But Howe had developed no workable alternative. He toyed with Clinton's plan overnight before calling its author to headquarters. Erskine's arguments had won out. Clinton was told to organize a strike force and use it to secure Jamaica Pass that night. Then he was to wait there till Howe brought up the rest of the Army on Tuesday morning. At that time Major General James Grant would move up the Gowanus Road with two detached brigades to turn the American right, and General von Heister would go to work on the Flatbush/Bedford complex with his Hessians. Howe would also consult with his brother about the Navy's part in the affair.[3]

When Lord Cornwallis was relieved by von Heister's Hessians on Monday evening the 26th, he marched down the Flatbush-Flatlands road with his reserve corps and with his attached battalions of British light infantry. At Flatlands he was assigned to Clinton's strike force, but with some organizational changes in the reserve. Cornwallis kept his 33rd Foot (under the British system of multiple appointments he was its Colonel), while the 42nd Highlanders were detached and sent across the county to the British left. Their places were taken by their countrymen of the 71st Highlanders, possibly as a courtesy to General Erskine for his role in selling the plan. At the same time the rest of Clinton's force was being assembled until he had, in all, the 33rd Foot, the 71st Highlanders, General James Robertson's 1st Brigade (4th, 15th, 27th and 45th Regiments of Foot), all three battalions of light infantry, all four battalions of grenadiers, the 17th Light Dragoons, and a detachment of the Royal Artillery Regiment with fourteen guns. This division of Howe's field army—which was just its vanguard—already held more troops than were posted along the entire length of the American outer line.[4]

Clinton's column marched out of Flatlands at 8 p.m. the 26th "by half-battalions, ranks and files close." The light infantry took the lead, followed by the grenadiers, the 33rd Foot, and then the 1st Brigade. The Highlanders fanned out through the open country on the left flank to provide a screen against enemy patrols. The most direct route to Jamaica Pass came uncomfortably close to the American left; any activity on it might have been detected by Miles's riflemen. Instead Clinton's loyalist guides detoured over a road which skirted the woods and wetlands surrounding Jamaica Bay, by way of New Lots village. The column covered barely more than a mile an hour in the darkness, "halting every minute just long enough to drop asleep." Shortly before midnight a rattle of small arms fire from the rear startled Clinton and gave a few minutes of concern (it was probably Knowlton's sentry trap being foiled at Flatbush). He was relieved to get past New Lots, leave the road altogether and cut northward through the same fields where Woodhull's militia had been driving cattle only hours before. Woodhull was then less than two miles east along the county line road, all unaware of his chance to become a national hero by closing in and peppering Clinton's exposed right flank from out of the dark. Any sound of musketry at this point would have eliminated the element of surprise from Clinton's plan.[5]

A cold front moving through the area had caused an unseasonable drop in temperature, and Tuesday morning saw Clinton's soldiers shivering in the dark fields. Shortly after 2 they had quietly halted less than a quarter of a mile from Howard's, a popular roadhouse that catered to travellers on the Jamaica Road. It stood only a few hundred yards south of the pass through Gowanus Heights, and Clinton suspected it would make a likely outpost for a picket guard. He was right. Captain W. G. Evelyn's light company was sent through the grass to investigate; they did their job so competently that the five mounted Yorkers huddled there were all captured in one instant, and with barely a sound. The prisoners were hustled back to Clinton, who browbeat them into admitting that Jamaica Pass was unoccupied. Still not entirely convinced, Clinton sent a patrol across the ridge by way of a footpath to confirm the story. Only then did he secure the gorge with a battalion of light infantry and deploy the rest of his division eastward along the Jamaica Road. (Just a few miles away General Woodhull still knew nothing of Clinton's presence. During the night a party of 49 Oyster Bay loyalists easily slipped through his screen and fairly stumbled over the British column.)[6]

At the first light of dawn the entire vanguard was moved into the gorge and deployed against a possible attack. They were still in position two hours later, when the second division arrived under the command of Lord Hugh Percy. This was the main body of the Army and it held General Robert Pigot's 2nd Brigade (5th, 28th, 35th, 49th Regiments of Foot), Valentine Jones's 3rd Brigade (10th, 37th, 38th, 52nd Regiments), Francis Smith's 5th Brigade (22nd, 43rd, 54th, 63rd Regiments), Edward Mathew's Brigade of Guards and another detachment of Royal Artillery with fourteen more guns. The baggage train brought up the rear to indicate all the camps had been struck and there was no intention of returning to them. And at Percy's side, rode the commander-in-chief himself, General Howe.[7]

Over on the opposite end of the American lines, General Grant had already begun his part of the operations. His troops were his own 4th Brigade (17th, 40th, 46th, 55th Regiments), General James Agnew's 6th Brigade (23rd, 44th, 57th, 64th Regiments), the 42nd Royal Highlanders, the two New York provincial companies and a detachment of Royal Artillery with ten guns. Grant had spent much of the last war fighting Indians out west, and his experiences with frontier shirtmen had not left him with a high regard for American military expertise. Early last year he rose in the House of Commons to announce that Americans knew nothing about fighting, and offered to march unhindered from Maine to Florida with 5,000 men. All he was expected to do this morning, however was to march along Gowanus Heights from the Red Lion east to Flatbush Pass.[8]

He got off to a rousing start. At about 2 o'clock (just the time Clinton's division was approaching Howard's), Grant fell on the Red Lion after a stealthy night march of his own up the coast road from Denyse's Ferry. His timing was excellent. He had had the American outpost under observation for at least three hours, and must have been delighted to see Hand's tough riflemen relieved at midnight. Only one British regiment—"about 2 or 300 men"—was detached to make the assault, catching the new replacements psychologically off guard by a sudden strike from out of the dark. There was some scattering fire later dignified as a skirmish, but the confusion had its predictable effect on the green Flying Camp levies. They broke and ran for their lives, spreading their panic to the supporting troops up the Gowanus Road, and leaving Major Edward Burd to be captured with a lieutenant and a handful of men.[9]

General Grant did not follow through on his cheap little victory, nor did he intend to. The Martense Lane was now completely clear of American troops, but in the darkness there was no way of knowing what activity was taking place on the road leading to their lines. Grant's assigned mission, in any case, obliged him to sit tight till morning. If there were any rebels on his front at that time he was to keep them occupied on the one hand and, on the other, work his way along the Heights for a link-up with von Heister's Hessians. Meanwhile he could only deploy his brigades across the Gowanus Road as advantageously as the hour allowed, and then wait to see what would happen next.

It was daylight before the first American reinforcements arrived. Major Burd had sent runners to alert Putnam that his Red Lion outpost was under attack. General Parsons, the Brigadier of the Day, immediately made his way down the Gowanus Road to inspect the situation. He found the whole picket guard retiring in disorder; not only the Flying Camp men from the outpost, but Lasher's Yorkers and Atlee's Pennsylvania regulars as well. He was able to stem the tide long enough to shame some twenty fugitives into returning with him, and he posted these "on a height" about half a mile in front of Grant, who appeared to be advancing. There he was joined by Colonel Samuel Atlee. Part of

Atlee's regiment was fresh from the Brooklyn lines, but he also appears to have intercepted most of the fugitives and turned them around. Some of the others may also have returned with Lord Stirling, who shortly arrived with a fresh detachment of the Flying Camp, Smallwood's Maryland regulars and Haslet's Delaware Continentals, followed in due course by Huntington's 17th Continentals and by Kachlein's Pennsylvania Associators. At any rate, Stirling now took command of the American right wing.[10]

Concerned that Grant might attack while he was shuffling his odd-lot units into position, Stirling pushed Atlee forward to hold a section of the Gowanus Road that crossed a morass in his front. As a countermove, Grant advanced part of his 4th Brigade to the opposite side of the morass and had his artillery play on the Pennsylvanians with round shot and grape. Atlee nonetheless stood his ground "without any kind of cover," trading musket volleys across the swamp with Grant's forward men, while behind him Stirling posted the American brigade. The Marylanders and Delawares occupied a lateral ridge running up the slope of Gowanus Heights. Parsons went up to the wooded crest at the far end of this ridge with the 17th Continentals. When everyone was reasonably settled, Atlee broke off fighting—he had taken only one casualty—and retired to his assigned position in the woods between Parsons and the Delawares. Kachlein's riflemen were placed in extended order in front of the entire line to act as skirmishers. When Captain-Lieutenant Benajah Carpenter's artillery company rolled up, his two guns were unlimbered far enough up the slope to command the road in front of Grant. The Flying Camp units, with as many of Lasher's Yorkers as were still in the field, were probably held in reserve. It was now about 7 o'clock.[11]

By this time, or shortly after, General Sullivan had gone down to Flatbush Pass, where the main attack was still expected. But when he looked out across the plain from the high ground there all he could see were blue-coated Hessians, their regiments drawn up in column. General von Heister had them waiting under arms a half mile in front of Flatbush. Mirbach's brigade (Knyphausen, Rall and Lossberg regiments) stood on the left, Stirn's brigade (Donop, Mirbach and Erbprinz regiments) stood on the right. Before them were Donop's grenadiers (Linsingen, Minnegerode and Block battalions) and before them, Wreden's jaeger company. Each unit had two light field pieces, as support guns, on its own front. The artillery was presently duelling with the guns at the American breastworks in the pass, neither side doing the other any great harm.[12]

On the extreme American left, Colonel Samuel Miles could hear the cannonade; some of the stray Hessian rounds were even passing over his camp. He decided, without waiting for orders, to take the 1st Battalion of his Pennsylvania rifle regiment to the scene of the action. But to get there he would have had to cross Bedford Pass, where he ran into Chester's Connecticut levies and Colonel Samuel Wyllys's 22nd Continentals. Wyllys, his senior by virtue of holding a Continental commission, ordered Miles back to his assigned position. Miles obeyed, but on his way there he learned from his own pickets that British troops were coming down the Jamaica Road. He immediately set off to meet them, but approached the road so obliquely that he came out at the rear of Lord Percy's second division, "the baggage guard just coming onto the road." At this point he sent Major Ennion Williams, who was mounted, to order up the 2nd Battalion, and it was probably also Williams who then pressed on to warn General Putnam, picking his way through the cover of the woods.[13]

So far the riflemen had not yet been discovered. Miles called a hasty council of his officers and offered them three choices. They could (1) cut their way through the enemy baggage guard, make their way to Queens County and cross to Manhattan at the Newtown ferry. Or, (2) they could wait till the column had passed and do the same. Or, (3) they could try to gain the front of the column and fight their way to the Brooklyn lines. The first choice

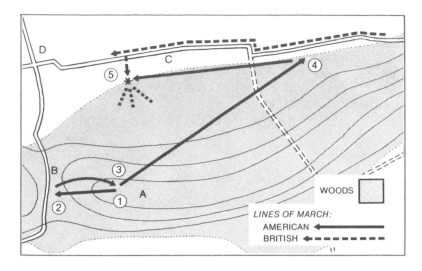

ACTION IN THE EASTERN WOOD, 7:00 — 8:30 AM. (A) Eastern wood, (B) Bedford Pass, (C) Jamaica Road, (D) Bedford. (1) Col. Miles marches 1st Battalion Pennsylvania riflemen to Bedford Pass. (2) Miles is ordered back to his original position by Col. Wyllys. (3) Miles learns of British presence on Jamaica Road and marches to intercept. (4) Miles sights rear section of British column. (5) Miles overtakes head of British column; clashes with light infantry and is dispersed.

smacked of futility (Miles had information from a captured British flanker that a whole brigade guarded the baggage), and the second of cowardice; so the third course was taken. When they came out of the woods again, after a half mile's force march, they ran into the British light infantry. The riflemen fired a ragged volley from the tree line and were immediately pursued back into the woods, their empty pieces now useless against bayonets. There Miles's command fell apart, as individuals and small knots of men either hid in the brush or tried to make their way to the lines. Lieutenant Luke Brodhead managed to capture a British major and hold him "for some hours" before he himself was found and captured. Colonel Miles avoided capture till 3 in the afternoon, but was taken prisoner with Lieutenant Colonel James Piper, a captain, eight lieutenants, the surgeon and his mate, and 120 men. The rest of the 1st Battalion, about half its strength, somehow made it to safety.[14]

As soon as Percy's division had arrived earlier in the day, General Howe's juggernaut marched through Jamaica Pass and stopped for some cold breakfast before starting operations. Once in motion again, however, there was nothing to stop it. By half past 8 it had had its brush with Miles's Pennsylvanians and was in full occupation of Bedford village. From that point Cornwallis's reserve corps swung into action, fanning out across the plateau. The light infantry, with the 71st Highlanders, worked south along the Bedford Road toward the Heights; the grenadiers continued west with the 33rd Foot to secure the Flatbush Road. These two moves were intended to block the Americans from any retreat to their lines. At 9 o'clock two guns were fired as a signal to Grant and von Heister that the trap had been closed.[15]

While all this was going on, Miles's 2nd Battalion was marching through the woods in search of their colonel and the 1st Battalion. The men were strung out awkwardly in Indian file when, through a garbling of orders, the battalion broke into two sections, each losing contact with the other. When they became separately aware of the overwhelming enemy force on the Jamaica Road, the two parts further divided by taking different directions. One kept moving east, and may have run afoul of British mopping-up parties who were ferreting out the dispersed members of the 1st Battalion. A good many, however, appear to have got around the rear of the enemy column and up to the Newtown ferry. The

other section, under Lieutenant Colonel Daniel Brodhead, came out of the woods onto the Bedford Road. There Brodhead caught sight of a Continental artillery company manhandling a field piece and a howitzer into position so as to oppose the advancing light infantry. How it came to be there remains a mystery, but Brodhead conceived it his duty to give the artillerymen whatever support he could, "and make a stand." He crossed the Bedford Road with his truncated battalion and formed his men into line by the guns.[16]

Brodhead's men were quickly overwhelmed, but from a wholly unexpected quarter. Wyllys's and Chester's regiments, hearing commotion to their left rear, had left Bedford Pass and were now streaming up the road. They had not been routed, nor had they even been engaged; they were spurred only by the soldier's dread of being attacked from one direction while facing another. The Yankees passed through Brodhead's line, sweeping some of his riflemen along with them. "I did all in my power to rally the musquetry & Riflemen, but to no purpose," Brodhead reported later. The retreating column, which could now see the light infantry bearing down on them, veered left off the Bedford Road and, hugging the foot of the morain's northern slope, raced across country for the Flatbush Road and gained it before the grenadiers got there. Brodhead kept his position with fifty men till everyone had run by, fired three rounds at the British—who were now within rifle range—and then followed after. The guns were captured, and it may have been here that Captain-Lieutenant John Johnston and/or cadet-volunteer John Callender of the Artillery Regiment were taken prisoners. Wyllys's and Chester's New Englanders got back to the lines with very few losses, one of them being Major Levi Wells of Wyllys's. Brodhead later tallied a captain, six lieutenants and 47 men lost, but it is impossible to tell how many were captured here and how many with the other,

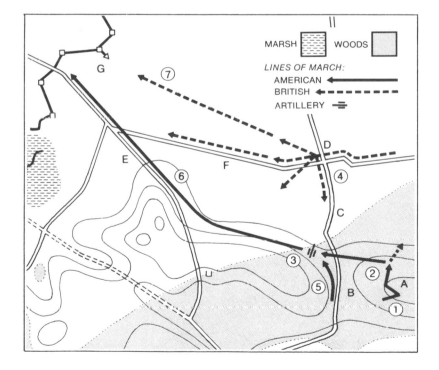

WITHDRAWAL FROM BEDFORD PASS, 8:00 — 10:00 AM. (A) Eastern wood, (B) Bedford Pass, (C) Bedford Road, (D) Bedford, (E) Flatbush Road, (F) Jamaica Road, (G) Fort Putnam. (1) Lt. Col. Brodhead, with 2nd Battalion Pennsylvania riflemen, searches for Col. Miles in the wood. (2) Battalion splits into two sections. (3) Brodhead forms his section of the battalion at artillery. (4) British light infantry approaches from Bedford. (5) Column from Bedford Pass sweeps through Brodhead's line. (6) Column gains Flatbush Road; retreats to the lines. (7) British grenadiers pursue column; demonstrate against Fort Putnam.

separated section.[17]

The officer Miles had sent to warn General Putnam tried to rejoin his battalion, but once outside the works he met Wyllys's and Chester's regiments bounding up the Brooklyn Ferry Road. Some distance behind them he made out another party, "dressed in hunting shirts." He assumed them to be from his own unit, and started in their direction. But the New Englanders insisted "they were the enemy in our dress; on this I prevailed on a Sergeant and two men to halt and fire on them, which produced a shower of bullets, and we were obliged to retire." His first assumption was correct; the shirtmen could only have been Brodhead's detachment bringing up the rear. That they returned his fire is extraordinary, but not improbable. Taking accidental fire from one's own side is an especially exasperating combat experience, in this case heightened by the regional animosity between Yankees and Pennsylvanians. Aside from this, however, the story has a more significant point. Neither the New Englanders nor the Pennsylvanians were so panic-ridden as to throw away their weapons in flight, which is the usual practice of terrorized fugitives.[18]

The grenadiers—and the 33rd Foot—were mortified to see the Bedford Pass column escape with virtually a whole skin. They closed the pursuit as vigorously as they could, following Brodhead's rear guard "within long shot" of the prepared works, and started to engage the American lines with small arms fire. The grenadiers, their adrenalin pumping, were so emotionally and physiologically primed to storm the Brooklyn lines that their commander, Major General John Vaughan, asked leave to do just that. Clinton was willing to let them go, but Howe was not about to let the battle get so far out of control. Vaughan "stormed with rage," but the grenadiers, who were now taking fire from Fort Putnam and its lunette battery, were ordered to break off and retire out of range. There was time enough to take the American lines and it would be done cheaply, with systematic approaches.[19]

As soon as General von Heister heard the two-gun signal from over the Heights he set his Hessian division in motion. The jaegers fired a volley "into the woods directly in front of them," and then led the way into Flatbush Pass. They were followed by Donop's grenadier battalions and then by the infantry brigades, each unit pulling along its support artillery. "Our Hessians marched like Hessians," one officer proudly recalled; "they marched incorrigibly." Their drums were beating the march step, and the ranks were so tightly formed that the men carried their muskets—with bayonets fixed—at shoulder arms. But when the jaegers fronting Stirn's brigade approached the American breastworks they were greeted by no blast of grapeshot, no hail of musket balls from embattled defenders. The works were completely deserted; the guns had been spiked and the ammunition wagons overturned. Mirbach's jaegers entered the encampment on the left, across the road from the empty battery, just in time to surprise a knot of "fifty or sixty men" who "were forming in column." It was Sullivan's rear guard.[20]

General Sullivan not only had heard Howe's signal guns, but the popping of Miles's and/or Brodhead's firefights as well. He understood their message, and may also have convinced himself than von Heister's artillery barrage was only a feint to hold his attention till his rear became enveloped. At any rate, the spiked guns at the breastworks bear mute testimony that (1) the withdrawal from Flatbush Pass was a deliberate move, (2) Sullivan did not intend to return, and (3) he did not plan to make a stand against the enemy forces on the plateau; the spiked guns were light enough to have been dragged along. If he planned any action at all, it was to give the Americans already embroiled, whatever relief he could in passing. One subaltern wrote home the next day that "after hearing a very hot fire for some time we whare ordered to march for the fire." The troops at Flatbush Pass did not resort to panic; their general was physically present and he had worked out an orderly if risky withdrawal to the safety of the lines.[21]

WITHDRAWAL FROM FLATBUSH PASS, 9:00—11:00 AM. (A) Flatbush Pass, (B) Breastworks, (C) Flatbush Road, (D) Byroad, (E) Gowanus Road, (F) Milldam, (G) Fort Putnam. (1) Gen. von Heister advances on Flatbush Pass, but finds the breastworks abandoned and the artillery spiked. (2) American column from Flatbush Pass retreats up the byroad and crosses Gowanus Creek at milldam. (3) British light infantry fires on column. (4) Light infantry and Highlanders join Hessians in Flatbush Pass. (5) Grenadiers break off demonstration against Fort Putnam, but fail to cut off American column.

Sullivan could not have known that the Flatbush Road was crawling with British grenadiers between himself and the lines. But by the time he was ready to start, the light infantry was approaching across country from the Bedford Road on the right, where they had just gobbled up Brodhead's artillery. They were now closely supported by the 71st Highlanders and by four companies of Guards, and their looming presence cancelled out the Flatbush Road as a safe line of retreat. There was, however, an alternate route; a byway that came down from the tidemills on Gowanus Creek. It intersected the Gowanus Road and then cut diagonally across the plateau to join the Flatbush Road just below the American campsite. Even the terrain seemed willing to cooperate. A rising ground to the right of the lane would screen the retreating column from the grenadiers on the plateau, and so give it an odds-on chance to reach the Gowanus Road intersection without being cut off. Sullivan fed his column onto the lane.[22]

The run home did not go off without incident. Presently the light infantry gained the rising ground, firing into the column's right flank so that it sustained "a Verry heavy fire for two miles." But there was no attempt to close with the bayonet, nor did the musket fire do any great damage except to sharpen natural feelings of anxiety. At the far end of the lane the column crossed the Gowanus Road, ran up a spit of dry land to the right of Denton's millpond and then plunged into the chest-high creek, wading across to the safety of the other side. Here a number of them drowned, weighed down by their equipment, possibly not far from where some had once playfully displayed their naked manhood to the local farm women. Others—perhaps most—were able to cross dry shod over the milldam, where protective fleches had been thrown up last spring. The grenadiers sighted the column too late, and could only fire at it ineffectually from a distance. The 17th Light Dragoons were also slow in coming up; they arrived only in time to inspire a final sprint for safety by Knowlton's rangers. The cavalrymen could not take their mounts into the hoof-sucking wetlands for a closer pursuit and the Death-or-Glory sabers stayed clean.[23]

Not everyone got away. The Americans who had been surprised by Mirbach's jaegers were now caught in a hammer-and-anvil squeeze, pushed from all sides as Hessians, Highlanders and light infantry closed in. Most of them surrendered, or at least tried to, and those who hesitated were put to the bayonet without compunction. Their total number remains uncertain, and so does their identity. The Hessians, noting their hunting shirts, assumed them to be the riflemen who had been harassing Donop's brigade since last week (Hand's people were no longer there, of course). There may have been some skulkers among them from the different regiments, but the majority were probably either New Jersey levies or sentries come down too late from the communication line along the ridge—or both. Four officers were present. Two lieutenants, both captured, were of the 11th Continentals and the Jersey levies. Another, Colonel Philip Johnston of New Jersey, was mortally wounded by a Hessian grenadier's bayonet. The fourth was General Sullivan himself, who had stayed too long to see the last of his command out of the pass. He was taken in a cornfield, trying to make his way to the lines.[24]

After mopping up, the Hessians formed in line and pushed their left flank down Gowanus Heights toward General Grant's division. At the same time the light infantry and Highlanders returned to their primary mission of securing the plateau. It was now about 11 o'clock.[25]

We left General Stirling and General Grant on the Gowanus Road four hours ago, in the nearest arrangement each could manage to a classical line of battle. Stirling had his troops posted along a lateral ridge: Smallwood's and Haslet's regiments on the right, under himself; Atlee's Pennsylvanians and Huntington's 17th Continentals in a wood on the left, under General Parsons. Kachlein's riflemen were deployed as skirmishers in front of the entire line. On the other side, Grant's 4th Brigade held the British left, "formed in two lines" on a rising ground opposite Stirling; Agnew's 6th Brigade the British right, opposite Parsons. Grant could draw on the 42nd Highlanders for a reserve, while Stirling had his Flying Camp men.[26]

The intervening ground was part of the northern slope of Gowanus Heights, giving Parsons's and Agnew's brigades a higher vantage point than their respective fellow countrymen. The space between the two elevated brigades was relatively open, with a scattering of brush or "hedges," except the top of the slope near the ridgeline was more heavily wooded. The space between Stirling and the British 4th Brigade, however, was partially covered by a morass; a section of the Gowanus Road crossed this marshy area as a causeway. A little way up the slope, but still in Stirling's front, was a stand of apple trees.

By and large, the two opposing lines were out of each other's effective musket range. Kachlein's Associators, however, were far enough ahead to bring Grant well within range of their Pennsylvania rifles. As a countermove, Grant had to establish a skirmish line of his own, posting them as close as 150 yards of the main American line. This at least served to bring Kachlein's people within range of their smoothbore muskets. These advanced troops were identified by the Americans as light infantry, which suggests they were dressed somewhat differently from their fellows. Inasmuch as Grant had no regular light troops with his division, they may therefore have been the two New York provincial companies.[27]

For the next two hours the opposing skirmishers kept up a small arms fight, concentrating their fire on each other rather than on the troops in the rear. It was rifles against muskets, with the range and accuracy of the rifles gaining the upper hand. Both sides took advantage of the terrain. Some of the British found cover in the apple orchard on their left front; those on the lower flank even crossed the morass to the American side. But many of the riflemen were in the wood at the top of the slope, giving them a better view of prospective targets and the chance to inflict more casualties. The firefight broke off rather abruptly about 9 o'clock, when Grant called the skirmishers back to his line.

The artillery of either side had been in action all along, but was now felt all the more keenly by the lack of any other visible activity on the main front. Captain Carpenter's two Continental pieces were posted on the face of the slope; Grant had a gun on his own left, close to his line, and another up the slope on his right, but somewhat further back. The troops of both sides stood—literally stood—in position, the Americans spaced in more extended order than the British simply because there was less of them to cover their front. None of the Americans and few of the British, as individual soldiers, had ever been in a formal combat situation before. In keeping with the traditional ritual, neither commander sought cover for his men. One Marylander recalled incoming rounds to consist of round shot and mortar shells, both of which "flew very fast, now and then taking off a head." The danger to each army, however, lay not in the number of actual casualties—which were not heavy at all—but in the ghastly effect cannonballs have on living flesh, and the natural horror of those who so witness the bloody pulping of a messmate. Green troops could normally be expected to snap, break ranks and flee. Yet they all stood the ordeal like veteran campaigners for the better part of two hours more; "not even one of them shewed a Disposition to shrink." The Delawares even looked the part, fitted out in blue regimental coats and with their colors snapping.[28]

It does not appear that Stirling ever heard General Howe's two-gun signal behind the masking effect of the artillery immediately at hand. Grant, for his part, seems to have been working on a fixed schedule. Even before his skirmishers had been called in—before, that is, the signal had been fired at Bedford—elements of both his brigades were sent over the ridge to probe the feasibility of a link-up with the Hessians, who were supposed to work their way down from Flatbush Pass. Once this connection was made, Stirling could be enveloped and bagged at will. But Stirling caught sight of the activity and assumed it to be an attempt to turn his left flank. He sent two companies of Delawares up the slope to General Parsons, with orders for him to "file off farther to the left" and head off the flanking movement.[29]

When Parsons got his two regiments through the woods to the summit he could see that this section of the Gowanus Heights morain was broken into a network of interlocking hills, each with its own crest and—where the drainage was poor—with swampy glens between. One bald hilltop, about 300 yards off, promised to command the entire chain. Parsons determined to occupy it before the British got there.

He was too late. The hill was already occupied by elements of the 17th, 23rd and 44th British Regiments; their highest ranking officer known to be present was Lieutenant Colonel James Grant (not the general) of the 40th Foot. The crest formed a natural semi-circular breastwork, and from its cover the redcoats poured "a very heavy fire" on the Americans. In firing downhill there is a natural tendency to overshoot, so Parsons got off with little or no damage. Even so, there was a general scurrying back from the shock. The two Delaware companies—all but two lieutenants and 16 men—remembered they had to rejoin their regiment, and some of Atlee's Pennsylvanians went off with them. Parsons nonetheless had Atlee form the troops for another go at the hill, with

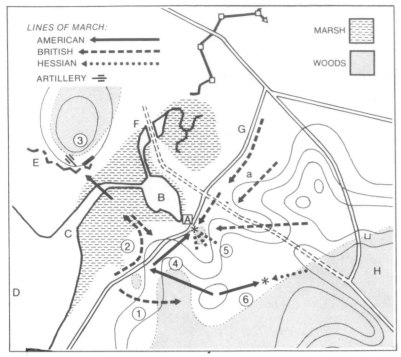

GOWANUS ROAD SECTOR, 7:00 — 11:30 AM. (A) Upper Mills, (B) Denton's Millpond, (C) Gowanus Creek, (D) Gowanus Cove, (E) Entrenchments, (F) Milldam, (G) Gowanus Road, (H) Flatbush Pass. (a) Grant's line, (b) Stirling's line, (c) Gist's detachment from Stirling's column, (d) Cornwallis's detachment from British main force. (1) Gen. Grant and Lord Stirling face each other in line of battle. (2) Grant detaches Lt. Col. Grant to make a juncture with the Hessians. (3) Stirling detaches Gen. Parsons. (4) Lt. Col. Grant and Parsons clash on bald hilltop; Grant is killed and British are thrown back. (5) Stirling withdraws from his position. (6) Stirling, with Maj. Gist's detachment, clashes with Lord Cornwallis at the Upper Mills. (7) Remainder of Stirling's column retreats across marshes. (8) Hessians advance through the hills of Gowanus Heights.

orders for them to hold their fire till the last possible moment. The determined charge and close fire surprised and unnerved the British defenders, who retired in panic to a stone fence sixty yards in their rear, leaving their dead and wounded on the field. The Americans had to be restrained from pursuit (they too had adrenal glands), and for some minutes a firefight kept up between the hilltop and the wall before Colonel Grant pulled further back to regroup.[30]

The short fight—it had lasted half an hour—left the Americans in better shape than their enemy. Their only casualty was Lieutenant Colonel Caleb Parry of Atlee's regiment, shot through the head. But ammunition was running dangerously low, and the pinch was only slightly relieved by stripping the British dead and wounded of their equipment. While plundered cartridges were being distributed, Parsons deployed his troops around the hilltop and posted lookouts. The inevitable counterattack came after a twenty-minute wait: "the enemy was observed marching down to make a second attempt for the hill. The Sentinels gave the alarm. Officers and men immediately flew to arms." Musket fire was exchanged for a quarter of an hour; again the British retired "in precipitous flight" and again left their casualties to be stripped of muskets and cartridge boxes. Somebody picked up a dead officer's hat and found Colonel Grant's name marked inside the crown. The Americans, to their satisfaction, concluded they had not only avenged Parry but had killed the Yankee-hating redcoat general into the bargain. Parsons's only casualty was a private in the Pennsylvania regiment.[31]

Atlee's adjutant, Francis Mentges, was sent back to the brigade to report on the morning's engagements and to request help. Stirling had already heard the banging during a lull on his own front, and Mentges was sent back with hefty detachments of riflemen and Flying Camp men under Lieutenant Colonels Kachlein and Lutz. Just as important, they toted along the 17th Continentals' ammunition cart and its load of fresh cartridges. Everybody was quickly supplied "with a sufficient stock to sustain another attack, if the enemy should think proper to make it." The enemy thought proper, and in half an hour the lookouts were once more sounding the alarm. The new wave of British was "received as usual, and as usual fled" after another fifteen-minute action.

Parsons had grown confident enough to let his troops pursue, only to have them run into the 42nd Highlanders covering the latest retreat of their fellows. There was a hasty falling in to make a line, but no new action developed. The Scots had been instructed to press the attacks no further, and when the Americans returned to their hilltop position they found out why. The noise of "an exceeding heavy fire" was rolling in from the direction of Flatbush Pass. This confirmed reports already made by "some scattering soldiers"—probably some of last night's sentries on the communication line—that Hessians were advancing through the hills to cut them off. Adjutant Mentges was sent out once more for Stirling's orders, but this time he never came back.

Stirling must have concluded, from Mentges's report and other evidence, that Parsons was already cut off and beyond his help. The other evidence was the Flatbush Pass column, now running across the plateau in Stirling's rear. The commotion warned that he himself was about to fall into the same trap. In order to save his own command he would have to break off action with Grant's superior force, turn about and quick-march up the Gowanus Road without breaking into wild-eyed flight. Once he fell back from his position on the ridge, of course, the rising ground would temporarily conceal him from Grant's view. The trick was to get everybody onto the road in good order. In the light of subsequent events it is reasonable to surmise that the Delawares filed off first and took the lead, followed by the Marylanders. Such remnants of the Flying Camp previously sent up the slope to fill in for Parsons's regiments had to be brought down again, along with any of Kachlein's riflemen that may have been left. It would have been appropriate, too, for Captain Carpenter's two guns to cover the retreat as long as possible. But the rear-guard Pennsylvanians could hardly have gained the road before the Delawares, only a quarter of a mile up front, were once again formed for battle.[32]

Earlier this morning we saw Lord Cornwallis's grenadiers fail completely to cut off and capture the Americans retreating out of Bedford Pass. Then, instead of pressing on with their assigned mission, they wasted so much time railing against the prepared American works that they failed again—this time with Sullivan's column out of Flatbush Pass. Now they were lumbering up to the Gowanus marshes, where their last quarry had just flown by, anxious not to let Stirling's brigade escape as well. Cornwallis sent Lieutenant Colonel Henry Monckton down the Gowanus Road with the 2nd Grenadier Battalion to hit Stirling in the rear while Grant held him fixed in position. Monckton had barely started out when he saw the Delawares coming up the road towards him. He halted in some confusion. The troops in the road were all wearing blue uniforms, which made them so unlike any ragtag rebels seen heretofore that they surely must be Hessians. But if they were Hessians, then what happened to the rebels they were supposed to be driving ahead of them like flushed game? Two grenadier companies—one of them a detachment of Marines were sent ahead to meet them and find out.[33]

They found out. The Delawares' quarter-mile march had put them farther up Gowanus Creek. Salt marshes bordered the creek its entire length, except where the ovoid expanse of Denton's millpond jutted out almost to the Gowanus Road. The original American intention had been to go around the pond and cross dry-shod at the dam, where part of Sullivan's column had got over. But now the way was blocked by Monckton's grenadiers, supported by the 71st Highlanders. A good portion of them had taken cover in an orchard at the head of the millpond—the Upper Mills—and had brought up artillery and Lord Cornwallis. Major Thomas McDonough had no way of knowing his regiment's blue coats were the source of confusion, so he got the Delawares into line and waited for Stirling to come up with the rest of the column. Still, there were those two advanced grenadier companies bearing down on him with surprisingly little show of hostility. When they were at eyeball distance the Delawares delivered a volley that killed both company commanders "on the spot." The grenadiers fell back immediately, but the Marine company had approached so close that they lost a lieutenant, a sergeant and 21 men prisoners. The British line, feeling itself somehow betrayed, let fly a barrage of small arms and artillery fire that shredded the Delaware colors and forced McDonough to fall back on Stirling for support.[34]

When Stirling arrived, he drew up his brigade out of musket range and assessed his position. A platoon of Delawares was already crossing the salt marshes with their prisoners, intending to swim the creek and gain the safety of the American entrenchments on the other side. But should the brigade follow suit—and there was no real alternative—then the entire column would be vulnerable to an attack on its exposed right flank and rear. Stirling therefore deemed it "absolutely necessary" to keep Cornwallis occupied at the Upper Mills. He detached Major Mordecai Gist with five Maryland companies, "ordering all the other troops to make the best of their way through the creek." They kept formation down to the edge of the marsh, and then dispersed in the wet ground. Gist's detached companies, with Stirling at their head, marched on in equally good order to take on Cornwallis in his orchard. Their immediate goal was to break through, if possible, and make their way around Denton's millpond to the dam. In any event, the Marylanders would provide a screen, and behind them the rest of the brigade could get over the creek in relative safety.[35]

It was a truly heroic act of self sacrifice. Cornwallis's people clumsily tried to avenge their fancied "betrayal" by drawing the Marylanders into a trap of their own. A party of them went forward as bait, with arms reversed and hats removed in a gesture of capitulation. But the bait apparently lost its nerve at sixty yards distance when "they presented their pieces and fired," and then retired under American fire to the British line "that was laying in ambuscade." At this point Cornwallis counterattacked, and "after a warm and close engagement for near ten minutes," the Marylanders broke and fell back toward Gowanus Heights to regroup. Gist formed his detachment in a wood and started a fresh assault, but by this time Howe's juggernaut was on the scene. The Marylanders broke again in the face of overwhelming numbers and "were drove with much precipitation and confusion." In short, they disintegrated. Major Gist, Captain Ford and nine men made it to the marsh and escaped over the creek, but the rest were captured: Captain Bowie, ten lieutenants and about 250 men. Lord Stirling was chased running into the hills; he managed to shake off his pursuers, but had to surrender in the end to the Hessian von Heister. Within hours he was aboard the *Eagle* flagship where, as plain Billy Alexander, he could compare battle notes with an old friend named Henry Clinton.[36]

General Grant, far more circumspect in the field than he had once been in the House of Commons, was anything but vigorous in his pursuit of Stirling's brigade. The Americans had got off to a good head start, of course, and Grant had to rearrange his left flank so as to get it over the morass in his front via the Gowanus Road causeway. To keep this column from being enfiladed he would have had to send a party to neutralize the Continental artillery, and it may have been here that Captain Carpenter was killed and, perhaps, his company captured or dispersed.

Moreover, it appears at least one more regiment—the 57th—was sent into the hills where Parsons was still at large, joining the five already there. At any rate, Grant did not overtake Stirling's brigade till it was well into the salt marshes. He followed along part way, when Americans posted on the other side of the creek opened up on him with a combination of musketry, rifle fire and artillery. The pursuers, unable to form a line in the churned-up muck, fell back to dry land "where they continued parading within six hundred yards," till all of Stirling's people got over except for an inevitable few who drowned. Thanks to the lost battalion of Maryland heroes, the grenadiers had been foiled again.[37]

When Adjutant Mentges failed to return, General Parsons concluded his detachment was surrounded and he determined to fight his way back to Stirling's line. The wounded British prisoners had already received first aid; now they were left as comfortable as possible for their own comrades to find (the wounded Pennsylvania soldier, shot twice through the body, must have been left with them). Exactly what happened after that is lost in a maze of conflicting testimony, from which it can only be deduced that, by accident or design, Parsons's command broke up into its separate parts.[38]

The general took Atlee's Pennsylvania musketeers back to the morning's first battleground, only to discover the field entirely deserted. He then quick-marched up the Gowanus Road, somehow missing Grant (who may have been at that moment in the salt marshes), and reached Gist's forlorn hope just as it was disintegrating. Atlee's unit suffered much the same fate as the Marylanders, although all but the colonel, four captains, five subal-

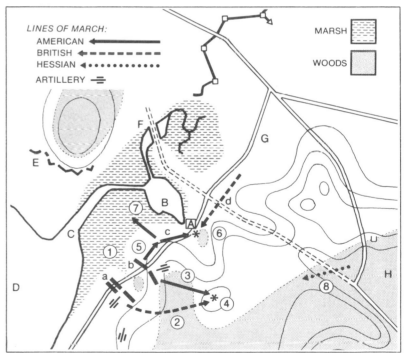

MAP FOR CAPTION ON OPPOSITE PAGE.

GOWANUS ROAD SECTOR, 11:00 AM—12:30 PM. (A) Upper Mills, (B) Denton's Millpond, (C) Gowanus Creek, (D) Gowanus Cove, (E) Entrenchments, (F) Milldam, (G) Gowanus Road, (H) Flatbush Pass. (a) Elements of British main force. (1) Gen. Grant sends additional British units into the hills of Gowanus Heights. (2) Grant pursues American column into the marshes. (3) Col. Smallwood covers American retreat; drives Grant from the marshes. (4) Col. Atlee returns to original American position and finds it deserted; joins Lord Stirling in clash with Lord Cornwallis. (5) Maj. Gist's detachment is ultimately dispersed and captured. (6) Lt. Col. Clark pushes through hills; clashes with the Hessians and surrenders.

terns and 77 men eventually got back to the lines. Colonel Atlee tried to cut over to the southern plain and make his way to Newtown ferry with 23 followers. After spending the afternoon alternately dodging Highlanders and Hessians, his party gave up hope of escape and surrendered to the Scots at 5 o'clock.[39]

Lieutenant Colonel Joel Clark apparently never took the 17th Continentals out of the hills, but instead got caught in a series of running fights with the Hessian Mirbach brigade. In the confusion his regiment began to fall apart. Those officers still with Clark, satisfied they were cut off from Stirling, gathered long enough to decide their best course was to force their way eastward and somehow break through the Hessians. Having thus underestimated the depth of their opposition, they eventually came under the crossfire of two different Hessian units and had to fall back. After another hurried council they agreed to split into small groups, "& Each one Take care for Himself." Colonel Clark surrendered his colors to the Rall regiment with sixty men, all of them fully expecting to be slaughtered where they stood. Other parties got gobbled up in detail. Some concluded they would stand a better chance of survival if they avoided the Hessians altogether. Instead they gave themselves up to one or another of Grant's regiments, who were still picking their way through Gowanus Heights. In all the 17th lost the lieutenant colonel, six captains, twelve subalterns, the adjutant, the surgeon and 186 men.[40]

How the rest of the American units were taken is not recorded. Haller's Flying Camp regiment lost Lieutenant Colonel Nicholas Lutz, three captains and 38 men (some of whom had been captured with Major Burd at the Red Lion last night). Cunningham's lost only a lieutenant and an unknown number of men, if any. The riflemen's casualties were Lieutenant Colonel Peter Kachlein, three captains, three lieutenants and 21 known men. Finally, the Delawares reported two lieutenants and 25 men missing; both officers and most of the men were those who had stayed with Parsons after this morning's first repulse from the bald hilltop.[41]

General Parsons started with Atlee's regiment, but then got separated. He was adroit enough to evade enemy patrols all day and then hide all night, making his way to the lines with seven men on Wednesday morning. All the others who escaped capture did much the same thing. There were enough of them so that no regiment of the Continental Army was so decimated as to lose its identity.[42]

CHAPTER X

Deliverance

General Howe was in a position not only to shape his battle as the events unfolded, but he was also able to keep his adversary occupied in New York City for much of the morning. His brother, the admiral, had assigned Sir Peter Parker to demonstrate against the city with *Preston, Eagle, Renown, Asia, Roebuck, Rainbow, Repulse* and *Mercury* (lately arrived from Halifax), plus the bomb vessels *Carcass* and *Thunder*. But the wind was cranky, "veering to the Northward soon after the Break of Day." The squadron had hardly come abreast of Gowanus Cove when the tide turned as well, and the signal was made to drop anchor. From their station the seamen could watch, in scenic panorama, the morning's action between Grant and Stirling. But only *Roebuck*, with an "especially shallow draft," could fetch high enough to exchange some random fire with the American battery at Red Hook, before hauling off to join her sister ships in line of battle.[1]

Nonetheless, it was a close-run thing. The main channel of the East River had been stopped with hulks only as a hasty, last-minute precaution. Recent experience with the Hudson River obstructions was not very reassuring, even given the powerful batteries at the Grand Battery and Governor's Island. Moreover,

the *Washington* and *Spitfire* galleys had returned to Rhode Island, slipping past Ferguson's squadron in Long Island Sound. This left the two Continental and three Connecticut galleys to cover the flatboats as they transported the morning's reinforcement to Brooklyn.[2]

These units seem to have been the 19th Continentals from McDougall's brigade, plus the remaining three regiments of Connecticut levies and the remaining regiment and a half of New York levies. With all their units now on Long Island, Brigadiers Wadsworth and Scott crossed as well, and so did Major General Spencer. For a back-up, General Mercer was ordered to bring the entire Flying Camp to Paulus Hook, along with whatever New Jersey militia he could scrape together. In addition, General Mifflin's combat team was brought down to New York from Bloomingdale.[3]

Washington crossed over with his staff late in the morning, now convinced that Long Island was the main show and not just a diversion. Whatever the aim of the stalled British squadron, it was not to land troops; no transports accompanied the men-of-war. But once in Brooklyn, the commander-in-chief found he could do no more than Putnam to influence the course of the battle, which is to say not very much at all. Sullivan's column had just come in, and the plateau in front of the lines teemed with British soldiers.

Stirling's brigade was still out, however, and Colonel William Smallwood, faced with the prospect of losing his entire regiment, asked for troops "to march out to support and cover their retreat." Instead he was sent down to Gowanus Creek with Douglas's Connecticut levies and Thomas's independent Maryland company—both units fresh over from New York—and with two field pieces. He found the trenches by the creek already occupied by Brodhead's 2nd Battalion of riflemen, who had been posted there immediately after their run for the lines earlier on. Thus it was Smallwood and his pick-up detachment of Yankees and Pennsylvanians who fired over the heads of the retreating Americans and drove Grant's pursuing column out of the marsh, keeping the redcoats at bay while Thomas's Marylanders helped Stirling's people through the mire.[4]

From the pimple of Cobble Hill Washington could watch not only this last retreat but the sacrifice of Gist's detachment as well. Even discounting the histrionics of popular tradition ("Good God! what brave fellows I must this day lose!"), it must have been a depressing, soul-searing experience. One old soldier later recalled the general walking along the lines, alternately instructing the regimental commanders, encouraging the troops, and threatening to shoot skulkers: "I will not ask any man to go further than I do; I will fight as long as I have a leg or an arm." A general assault on the works was expected at any moment. The troops manning the lines were ordered not to fire till the enemy entered the established killing ground. The grenadiers of Lasher's regiment—the original New York City Independents—stood at regular intervals, each with his slow match burning and with six grenades in his pouch.[5]

But the moment for an assault had already past. General Howe contented himself with sorting out his forces and unloading the baggage train, while search parties ferreted out whatever rebels were still uncaught. Prisoners, as quickly as they were taken, were herded through a gauntlet of verbal and physical abuse, stripped of everything but the basic essentials of clothing, and confined in one of the reception depots at Bedford, Flatbush or Gowanus villages. Hospital facilities were set up at New Utrecht for the wounded prisoners—nine officers and 58 men—and they lay there for ten days "wallowing in their own filth." Finally an American loyalist physician, Richard Bayley, was sent from Staten Island to care for them, with the captured surgeon's mate of the 17th Continentals as his assistant. Doctor Bayley, it turned out, was the antithesis of the malevolent Tory stereotype; he attended his patients with such skill and humanity that his postbellum career in New York was unaffected by his wartime politics.[6]

On Tuesday afternoon Commodore Parker tried once more to beat up to New York, but the elements remained against him. By nightfall white tents dotted the plateau at a distance of a mile and a half from the American lines. Washington posted a picket guard in front of the works, and everybody spent the night under the open sky. In the morning General Mifflin's ad hoc brigade of Pennsylvania Continentals and New York levies was brought over from New York. With them was a body of Miles's riflemen, who yesterday had made it to the Newtown ferry and were now reporting in. With them, too, was the 14th Continentals of Essex County, Massachusetts, filled with blue water fishermen and experts in the handling of small craft. The reinforcement "inspired no inconsiderable degree of confidence."[7]

The continuing north wind brought in a new meteorological system on Wednesday. Yesterday's cloudy but moderate weather deteriorated into "a searching drizzle," punctuated by cloudbursts. Even so, the day was marked by a sporadic exchange of artillery and by scattered firefights between the opposing pickets from one end of the lines to the other: "Hot skirmishes between different Parties in which the success is sometimes One Way & sometimes another." By late evening, however, a more determined push on the American left drove in the pickets from a piece of high ground some 600 yards in front of Fort Putnam. This time the British held the field and started digging in. The maneuver told its own story. This was the first opening of regular, systematic approaches to take the American lines scientifically. From now on it would be an engineer's game; there was to be no second battle of Bunker's Hill after all.[8]

The game was one the Americans could not hope to win, even with the bulk of the Continental Army now on Long Island. They had lost confidence in the fruits of their own labors. The Brooklyn lines—that impregnable barrier against which the British enemy was meant to dash himself—seemed in the end to be a frail defense indeed. The breastworks connecting the redoubts to each other and to the wetlands on either flank came in for the heaviest criticism. Scott's New York brigade held the section between Fort Greene and the Oblong Redoubt, where the Brooklyn Ferry Road passed through and provided the main—perhaps only—sally port. Here the ground was so low, said Scott, "that the rising ground immediately without it, would have put it in the power of a man at 40 yards distance to fire under my horse's belly." Mifflin's brigade was posted on the left flank, between the northern redoubt and Wallabout Bay. "There was a fraised ditch in front," complained Captain Graydon of the 3rd Pennsylvania, "but it gave little promise of security, as it was evidently commanded by the ground occupied by the enemy." The corresponding section on the right flank, between Fort Box and the Gowanus marshes, was completed by Gay's regiment as the battle raged on the plateau. Colonel Hitchcock urged the quick erection of a second line, "for their bombs will drive us out of Fort Putnam." But Major Tallmadge of Connecticut best summed up the American change of heart. "Our intrenchment was so weak," said he, "that it is most wonderful the British general did not attempt to storm it soon after the battle."[9]

At least three factors had combined to undermine American morale. First, a sense of defeat. The Army had just been outsmarted and whipped, and now nothing was going according to plan. Second, the incessant rain soaked everyone and everything for two days, and there was no escaping it for even a moment. Few if any tents were set up; the situation was critical enough to demand everyone's unrelenting vigilance. But the constant discomfort was almost too much to bear. Some of Scott's New Yorkers stood waist deep in the flooded trenches, and even in the redoubts water sloshed over a man's ankles and into his shoes. Keeping cartridges dry and muskets in working order called for infinite care. Not only had the locks to be perfectly dry, but water

could not be allowed to trickle down the bore. Even so, the level of exhaustion was so great that men fell asleep sitting in the mud, with the rain pelting down on them. Third, food was scarce and what there was had to be eaten cold and raw. The last reinforcements had been given ships biscuit to carry in their knapsacks, and this was the first to be consumed. After that there was salt pork, just as it came from the brine—and green corn. One of Wednesday's skirmishes—over by the Gowanus marshes—was fought for possession of a cornfield which Douglas's levies hoped to glean.[10]

By Thursday morning British sappers, having labored all night in the rain, had opened a parallel trench "60 rods long." They were already at work on a second approach, which shot off at a shallow angle from the southern end of the first, edging toward Fort Putnam's lunette. On top of this immediate threat, Captain Ferguson's squadron had run the length of Long Island Sound and was now off Westchester County, snapping up cattle from some of the islands east of Hell Gate. General George Clinton deployed his New York levies to discourage any foraging on the mainland, at least until they could be relieved by the Westchester militia. A Connecticut seaman, whose sloop was destroyed by the squadron, had been aboard the *Halifax* brig. He learned that Ferguson's objective was to drop anchor at Flushing Bay in Queens County, and there cover General Howe as his forces crossed the East River and seized Kingsbridge. The seaman took his story to the New York Committee of Safety, and it got to Washington the same day.[11]

Taking everything together, Long Island seemed no longer worth the awesome risk that holding it would involve. Sometime on Thursday, while the skirmishers' muskets were still banging in the rain, General Washington chaired a council of war which included Major Generals Putnam and Spencer, and Brigadiers Mifflin, McDougall, Parsons, Scott, Wadsworth and Fellows. The proposition was submitted and unanimously agreed upon; the Army would retire to New York City. Eight reasons were cited for the move; if nothing else they reflect the collective mood and its most compelling obsessions. They were (1) loss of Gowanus Heights, "where we expected to make a principal Stand;" (2) heavy losses in personnel, which tended to deplete morale; (3) weather conditions which rendered muskets unworkable, spoiled ammunition, wore the men down and eroded their discipline; (4) the continuing menace of Commodore Parker's squadron in Gowanus Cove; (5) prospects that Parker's ships might run the East River obstructions, or even pass—as least the smaller frigates—through Buttermilk Channel; (6) even less of a guarantee that the lines could not be taken by assault; (7) the "precarious" division of the Grand Army into two sections, making constant vigilance at all the works all the time a fatiguing business; (8) Ferguson's squadron at or approaching Flushing Bay, and the consequent threat to Kingsbridge. The formal siege operations opened last night were not even mentioned.[12]

Washington had grown astute enough in the intelligence game to know the retreat, if it was to be successful, had to be both swift and secret—more secret, even, than Clinton's march to Jamaica Pass last Monday night. An augmentation of the normal flatboat complement would be needed, and gathering the extra craft would attract a good deal of attention. So a cover story was circulated that the more frazzled units now on Long Island would be relieved by fresh troops from Mercer's Flying Camp at Paulus Hook. The sick and wounded, as "an encumbrance to the Army," were to be evacuated immediately to the General Hospital with their arms and equipment. Deputy Quartermaster Hugh Hughes was called on to collect everything afloat between Hell Gate and Spuyten Duyvil and have it all at New York by dark. General Heath was advised to send down all the craft at his post in northern Manhattan "without the least delay." Moreover, they were to be manned by the 27th Continentals, another regiment of Massachusetts fishermen from Essex County. Its sister unit, the

14th, was earmarked to be brought off the lines and also take part in handling the assembled flotilla. Every regiment in camp was ordered to parade at 7 o'clock and "wait for Orders," each happy in the anticipation that it was one of those selected to be relieved.[13]

The withdrawal was a masterpiece of organization, apparently pulled off without arousing the slightest curiosity on General Howe's part. Even the early evacuation of the invalids played its role; it was a perfectly natural thing to do and it served to make potential tale-bearers unwary about additional cross-river traffic. Smith's and Remsen's Long Island levies also went over early, finally released to state jurisdiction and under orders for trans-shipment to Queens County. Everybody else, though, had to wait till dusk. General Mifflin had command of the rear guard during the retreat, keeping with him his provisional brigade, the 1st Continentals, Haslet's Delawares, Smallwood's Marylanders and Chester's Connecticut levies. In case the lines were overrun during the night, they were to fall back and rally at Brooklyn Church, just behind the lines and on the ferry road. There a kneeling front rank, carrying pikes from each redoubt's arsenal, would try to prevent the Army's being run down by the 17th Light Dragoons.[14]

It would have been logical for the reserve units—those without any assigned works to defend—to draw off first, and then the relatively less sensitive garrisons at Red Hook, Cobble Hill and Brooklyn Heights. But that does not appear to have been the case. Gay's Connecticut regiment left the right of the lines by 9 o'clock Thursday evening. Some of Scott's brigade started to get edgy and spread their restiveness to the 1st Continentals; the Yorkers were taken off early at Colonel Hand's request. Douglas's levies were pulled from the Gowanus Creek entrenchments sometime before 3 in the morning, but the Fort Stirling garrison remained on station all night to help supply cover against a naval attack. As each unit was removed from the lines, the remainder spread out to fill the consequent breach in the perimeter and in the picket line outside. Speaking—even coughing—was prohibited, and orders were relayed in whispers.[15]

The tormenting rain had stopped, but a residual cloud cover made for a black, moonless night. Fires were begun on the lines so as to give the impression of a natural appearance. From that point, however, the men had to grope their way down to the ferry slip, toting not only their personal gear but all the regimental baggage and camp equipment as well. Whatever materiel could be taken was taken. The artillerymen worked the brass field pieces, with their powder and shot, down to the slip and stowed them aboard the flatboats. All they left were iron garrison guns, some of which were mounted on naval carriages and could not be hauled through the mud.[16]

The Yankee seamen-soldiers plied their craft back and forth over the mile-wide stretch of water all night, without running lights and hampered by a swift-flowing tide. Their flanks were covered by the five row galleys and by the East River batteries, which screened them from the sight of Parker's squadron. In spite of every effort, however, dawn found much of the rear guard still on Long Island sweating it out. In the early morning hours they had been taken from the lines en masse, only to learn their removal had been caused by an aide's foul-up and they would have to go back again. With the cover of darkness gone, their only security lay in a drop in air temperature which created enough condensation to blanket the entire area in heavy fog. The atmosphere grew so thick, recalled Chester's major, that one "could scarcely discern a man at six yards' distance." Nerves tautened almost to the snapping point, and when the second retirement order came down, the men "very joyfully bid those trenches a long adieu." The last troops at the ferry clogged the street "with waggons and Carts to Prevent the Light Horse from Rushing Down upon us," and then had to wait anxiously on the stairs till boats came to pick them up. Even so, as they clambered aboard they could make out the tall figure of their commander-in-chief:

"General Washington saw the last over himself."[17]

At 4 o'clock Friday morning a curious British patrol noted the absence of American pickets and was game enough to climb through the abatis and inspect the breastworks. They were empty; the hour suggests that the rear guard was away on its aborted first withdrawal. Incredibly, however, there was no follow-up on their report for another three or four hours, at which time a detachment of Hessians crossed the lines—by now occupied by last night's pickets—and probed their way across the Brooklyn peninsula. They reached the north shore just in time to see the last boats pull away, and rushed down to the ferry slip to fire their volleys into the foggy river. Four Americans were wounded in this hair-raising getaway, the only casualties of the retreat other than the Continental Army's pride.[18]

Before noon two 6-pounders were taken out of *Roebuck* with a quantity of powder and shot, snaked up to Red Hook and put into action against the American position on Governor's Island. In the early evening that post was evacuated as well, the 4th and 7th Continentals retiring under the cover of a row galley with all their baggage and equipment. By this time the fog had dissipated, and the amphibious column drew fire from Brooklyn Heights on one side and Parker's squadron on the other. But the guns in the abandoned works were left mounted. On Saturday a party of artillerymen returned to the island and kept the British vessels occupied while all the row galleys picked their way through the East River obstructions, rounded the tip of Manhattan and worked up the Hudson. Once the American ships were clear the doughty gunners crossed over to New York, running much the same gauntlet as the day before. The British did not occupy Governor's Island till Monday. After that the Royal Navy had free access to the East River anchorage through Buttermilk Channel, entirely screened from the Grand Battery's guns.[19]

With Kings County under British control, the rest of Long Island became all but untenable. But its takeover did not happen without incident. On Tuesday, the day of battle, General Woodhull ran cattle out of Newtown in northwestern Queens and sent his light horse cowboys to drive them off to the Hempstead Plains. By this time refugees were arriving from Kings to escape the proximity of combat. In some way they gave Woodhull the impression that General Howe had merely extended his right flank from Flatlands to Jamaica Pass and dug in. The militia general, apparently still unaware that a major battle was raging, established a base at Jamaica and waited there for help from the New York Convention. His small contingents from the Queens and Suffolk regiments were rapidly melting away in the rain, and he hoped the Convention could somehow get Smith's and Remsen's levies around the British lines. Either that, or find some other augmentation for him.[20]

On Wednesday Howe detached Sir William Erskine with the 71st Highlanders and the 17th Light Dragoons, and sent him forth to secure the Island's submission. Erskine made a beeline for Jamaica, hoping to catch General Woodhull and Joseph Robinson, an active committeeman and lieutenant colonel of the 1st Queens County Regiment. Robinson was already on his way to Connecticut, but Woodhull stayed behind in a barn belonging to Lieutenant Increase Carpenter of the Jamaica militia company. With the general was the remnant of his command—the lieutenant and four men—and all were taken prisoners. It was not done gently. Somewhere in the process Woodhull raised his hands protectively, and got sliced on both arms and on his head. The wounds were superficial in themselves, but through early neglect one of his arms grew gangrenous and had to be removed by Doctor Bayley. He never recovered. In a little more than three weeks after his capture the President of the New York Convention was dead, and the Death-or-Glory boys had blooded their sabers at last.[21]

The Convention, unaware of its President's capture, was desperately making efforts to reinforce him. Remsen's levies could no longer be used; they were now on the eve of their legal expiration. Colonel Remsen was told to attach himself to George Clinton's brigade and reorganize his regiment under new enlistments. Once that was done he could furlough whatever men he deemed trustworthy "to visit or remove their families from Long Island," provided they did not take their muskets. Colonel Smith, unable to find adequate shipping this side of Mamaroneck, crossed Long Island Sound on Sunday night and landed at Smithtown. There he grasped the deteriorating situation on the island and released his men to remove their families and household effects. Neither regiment was ever heard from again as an operative unit, except for 68 of Smith's people who regrouped in Connecticut under Lieutenant Colonel Benjamin Birdsall.[22]

From his Jamaica headquarters General Erskine sent the 17th Light Dragoons fanning out through Newtown, Flushing and Hempstead, ferreting out prominent Whigs like a mirror image of Isaac Sears. Committeemen, militia officers and light horse troopers—at least those who were still at home—were enthusiastically fingered by their neighbors and placed under arrest. The Oyster Bay committee met only to dissolve itself, when some of its members escaped across Long Island Sound with other Queens patriots who had not been bagged. The remnants of Woodhull's light horse troops, still dutifully driving stock out of the northern reaches of the township, finally gave up the chase and joined in the flight to Connecticut, leaving their mounts behind. By Thursday Queens was a British county once more; its elated citizenry—some of them just now emerging from the swamps—displayed their loyalty by sporting pieces of red material on their hats.[23]

Erskine did not choose to break his communication with Howe by invading Suffolk County. Instead he sent out a proclamation of his own, ordering the revolutionary committees to disband, the militia to disarm, and the county at large to bring in their livestock, horses and wagons. If this were not done he would "be under the necessity of marching the force under my command without delay into the county, and lay waste the property of the disobedient." It was a bluff, but for the most part it worked. The New York Convention had sent a two-man committee to rally the militia for Woodhull; they were now trying to organize a defense at Huntington. The men seemed willing enough but the early summer drafts had reduced their strength by over fifty per cent, and their own officers were beginning to renounce their commissions. In the 1st Regiment—the one nearest Queens—Colonel William Floyd (a Signer) was away at Congress, "Lieut. Col. Potter is gone off with himself, and first Major Smith has resigned." Only 2nd Major Jesse Brush seemed inclined to buck up. Colonel David Mulford of the 2nd Regiment was sent for to fill Woodhull's position as brigade commander, but he never arrived. The committee decided to continue their efforts further east, where help might be expected from Connecticut.[24]

But there was to be no more active resistance. The only viable force left on Long Island was Colonel Livingston's three companies of the 2nd New York, posted on the south fork from Southampton to Montauk Point. Livingston resolved, without waiting for orders, to quit his assigned station and march his detachment to Huntington, join with Connecticut forces he had asked Governor Trumbull to send, and then give Washington some relief by creating a diversion in Howe's rear. He got as far as Riverhead, where he learned about the evacuation of Kings County. There was an attempt to rally the Southold militia, but the officers "dismissed their men and prepared to submit to the enemy." Livingston disarmed about seventy of the slackers, seized the township's four pieces of artillery, retired up the north fork and crossed the Sound to Saybrook with the guns and his regimental baggage.[25]

The colonel kept faith with his men—they were all east Islanders—by letting them go back for their families, and they repaid his trust by reporting in with only a handful of desertions. After that Livingston's Yorkers, finally aided by detachments of Connecticut regulars, returned to Long Island again and again to bring off livestock and cover the massive exodus of Suffolk County patriots.[26]

By the last day of August General Washington had his Grand Army dried out and reorganized for a last-ditch defense of New York City. "Now is the time for every man to exert himself," the troops were warned, "and make our Country glorious, or it will become contemptable." At the same time General Howe quit Kings County altogether. Von Heister's Hessians were left to occupy the old American position at Brooklyn, supported by Grant's division at Bedford village. But Howe took the juggernaut itself through Bushwick township and on to Newtown, where he established his headquarters overlooking Hell Gate. General Lee's collapsed defense plan was not even to be tested in reverse; there would be no cannonade of the city from Brooklyn Heights. Instead, Fort Thompson and northern Manhattan lay waiting across the East River. The battle for Long Island was over, but the struggle for the North American continent had scarcely begun.[27]

BIBLIOGRAPHY

Short title

AmM—Peter J. Guthorn, *American Maps and Map Makers of the Revolution*, Monmouth Beach, 1966

Baker—William S. Baker, *Itinerary of General Washington from June 15, 1775 to December 23, 1783*, Philadelphia, 1892

Balderston—Marion Balderston and David Syrett, editors, *The Lost War: Letters from British Officers during the American Revolution*, New York, 1975

Bangs—Edward Bangs, editor, *Journal of Lieutenant Isaac Bangs, April 1 to July 29, 1776*, Cambridge, 1890

Baurmeister—Bernhard A. Uhlendorf, editor, *Revolution in America: Confidential Letters and Journals 1776-1784 of Adjutant General Major Baurmeister of the Hessian Forces*, New Brunswick, 1957

BrM—Peter J. Guthorn, *British Maps of the American Revolution*, Monmouth Beach, 1972

Cal. Mss.—State of New York, *Calendar of Historical Manuscripts Relating to the War of the Revolution in the Office of the Secretary of State*, Albany, 1868

Clinton—William B. Willcox, editor, *The American Rebellion: Sir Henry Clinton's Narrative of His Campaigns, 1775-1782*, New Haven, 1954

Clinton Papers—Papers of Sir Henry Clinton, Clements Library, Ann Arbor

Collier—Louis L. Tucker, Editor, "To My Inexpressible Astonish- ment: Admiral Sir George Collier's Observations on the Battle of Long Island," *The New York Historical Society Quarterly*, XLVIII, 1964

Elting—John R. Elting, *The Battle of Bunker's Hill*, Monmouth Beach, 1975

Fernow—Berthold Fernow, editor, *Documents Relating to the Colonial History of the State of New York*, XV, (State Archives, I), Albany, 1887

Field—Thomas W. Field, *The Battle of Long Island* (Memoirs of the Long Island Historical Society, II), Brooklyn, 1869

Fitch—W.H.W. Sabine, editor, *The New York Diary of Lieutenant Jabez Fitch*, New York, 1954

Force—Peter Force, editor, *American Archives,* Fourth and Fifth Series, Washington, 1837-1853

George 3rd—Sir John Fortescue, editor, *The Correspondence of King George the Third from 1760 to December 1783,* London, 1927-1928

Graydon—John S. Littell, editor, *Alexander Graydon's Memoirs of His Own Time,* New York, 1969

Greene Papers—Richard K. Showman, editor, *The Papers of General Nathanael Greene,* Chapel Hill, 1976

GW—John C. Fitzpatrick, editor, *The Writings of George Washington,* Washington, 1931-1944

Heath—William Abbott, editor, *Memoirs of Major General William Heath,* New York, 1901

Hodgkins—Herbert T. Wade and Robert A. Lively, editors, *This Glorious Cause: Letters of Lieutenant Joseph Hodgkins,* Princeton, 1958

Huntington—*Letters Written by Ebenezer Huntington during the American Revolution,* New York, 1914

JCC—Worthington C. Ford, editor, *Journals of the Continental Congress,* Washington, 1904-1937

Johnston—Henry P. Johnston, *The Campaign of 1776 around New York and Brooklyn* (Memoirs of the Long Island Historical Society, III), Brooklyn, 1878

Kemble Papers—New York Historical Society, *The Stephen Kemble Papers,* New York, 1884-1885

Kipping—Ernst Kipping, *The Hessian View of America 1776-1783* Monmouth Beach, 1971

Lee Papers—New York Historical Society, *The Charles Lee Papers,* New York, 1872-1875

Leggett—Charles I. Bushnell, editor, *The Narrative of Major Abraham Leggett,* New York, 1865

LIHS—Manuscript collections of the Long Island Historical Society, Brooklyn, New York: *Calendar of Manuscripts of the Revolutionary Period 1763-1783,* New York, 1977

Linn & Egle—John B. Linn and William H. Egle, editors, *Pennsylvania in the War of the Revolution, Battalion and Line 1775-1783* (Pennsylvania Archives, Second Series, X and XI), Harrisburg, 1880

Lowell—Edward J. Lowell, *The Hessians and Other German Auxiliaries of Great Britain in the Revolutionary War,* New York, 1884

Mackenzie—*Diary of Frederick Mackenzie,* Cambridge, 1930

Martin—George F. Scheer, editor, *Private Yankee Doodle: a Narrative of . . . a Revolutionary Soldier, Joseph Plumb Martin,* New York, 1962

Muenchhausen—Ernst Kipping and Samuel Stelle Smith, editors, *At General Howe's Side 1776-1778: The Diary of General William Howe's Aide de Camp, Captain Friedrich von Muenchhausen,* Monmouth Beach, 1974

Murray—Eric Robson, editor, *Letters from America 1773 to 1780: Being the Letters of a Scots Officer, Sir James Murray,* New York, c. 1950

NA—National Archives, Record Group 93, Revolutionary War Rolls, Pennsylvania (Microcopy 246, Roll 84)

Nav. Doc.—William B. Clark et al, editors, *Naval Documents of the American Revolution,* Washington, 1964-1976

NYPC—State of New York, *Journals of the Provincial Congress, Provincial Convention, Committee of Safety and Council of Safety* of the State of New York, 1775-1776-1777, Albany, 1842

O'Callaghan—Edmund B. O'Callaghan, *Documents Relative to the Colonial History of the State of New York,* Albany, 1856-1887

Onderdonk Q—Henry Onderdonk, *Documents and Letters Intended to Illustrate the Revolutionary Incidents of Queens County,* New York, 1846

Onderdonk S/K—Henry Onderdonk, *Revolutionary Incidents of Suffolk and Kings Counties,* New York, 1849

PA—Commonwealth of Pennsylvania, *Pennsylvania Archives,* Second Series, Harrisburg, 1874-1890

Robertson—Harry M. Lydenberg, editor, *Archibald Robertson: His Diaries and Sketches in America 1762-1780,* New York, 1930

Serle—Edward H. Tatum, editor, *The American Journal of Ambrose Serle 1776-1778,* San Marino, 1940

Smith—W.H.W. Sabine, editor, *Historical Memoirs of William Smith 1763-1776,* New York, 1956

Sparks—Jared Sparks, editor, *Correspondence of the American Revolution,* Boston, 1853

Stokes—I.N. Phelps Stokes, *The Iconography of Manhattan Island,* New York, 1915-1928

Tallmadge—*Memoir of Col. Benjamin Tallmadge,* New York, 1858

Webb—Worthington C. Ford, editor, *Correspondence and Journals of Samuel Blatchley Webb,* New York, 1893

Willard—Margaret W. Willard, editor, *Letters on the American Revolution 1774-1776,* Boston, 1925

WO—War Office Papers, London

NOTES

Notes: Preface

1. The classification system appears in *The British Navy 1775-1783,* Division of Publications, National Park Service, U.S. Dept. of the Interior, Washington, 1976.

Notes: Chapter I

1. The Bay's channel was constricted by extensive sand banks between Constable Point and Paulus Hook off New Jersey, and between Yellow Hook and Red Hook off Long Island. "A Sketch of the Operations of His Majesty's Fleet and Army under the Command of Vice Admiral the Rt. Hble. Lord Viscount Howe and Genl. Sr. Wm. Howe, K.B. in 1776. Publish'd according to Act of Parliament Jany. 17. 1777, by J.F.W. Des Barres Esq." The source is "The Atlantic Neptune, Published for the Use of the Royal Navy of Great Britain, By Joseph F.W. Des Barres Esqr. Under the Directions of the Right Honble. the Lords Commissioners of the Admiralty. London, MDCCLXXX."
2. Adams-Washington 1/6/76: Sparks I, 113. For a corresponding British appraisal see Tryon-Dartmouth 11/11/75: O'Callaghan VIII, 644.
3. 4 Force II, 468, 604-605. O'Callaghan VIII, 601-603. The companies were similar to those which had been chartered by Gov. Tryon for the city militia in 1772; some may have been the same companies, but not all.
4. Tryon-Dartmouth 11/11/75: op. cit. Tryon's recruits seem to have been originally intended for the regiment of Royal Highland Emigrants; see NYPC II, 5, 160.
5. Graves-Vandeput 5/1/75: Nav. Doc. I, 255.
6. Nav. Doc. I, 1206, 1217, 1221-1227, 1239, 1249.
7. Vandeput-Graves 8/24/75: Nav. Doc. I, 1224. Graves-Vandeput 9/10/75: ibid II, 71. *Phoenix* journal 12/17/75: ibid, 1008.
8. Parker-Tryon 12/18/75: Nav. Doc. III, 159. Tryon-Hicks 12/18/75: ibid, 159, 160.
9. JCC III, 335, 416.
10. For local reaction to Sears's raid see the minutes of the Committee for the City and County of New York, 4 Force IV, 186-187.
11. Washington-Reed 1/4/76: GW IV, 212. The rumor about New York's perfidy appears in Smith, 260-261.
12. Lee-Washington 1/5/76: Lee Papers I, 234-236.
13. Washington-Hancock 1/4/76: GW IV, 209.
14. Washington-Lee 1/8/76: GW IV, 221-223.

15. GW IV, 217-221, 226-227, 229.
16. NYPC I, 249-250.
17. Tryon-Dartmouth 2/8/76: O'Callaghan VIII 667. NYPC I, 258-259. 4 Force IV, 958. Smith, 263-264.
18. NYPC I, 259.
19. Lee Papers I, 235-269 passim. The terms of the Connecticut enlistments are in 4 Force IV, 931. Waterbury's regiment had first been raised to take part in the Queens County expedition described in Chapter III, but its services were subsequently deemed unnecessary and it was discharged just before Lee showed up. See JCC IV, 27, 47-48.
20. Lee-N.Y. Committee of Safety 1/23/76: Lee Papers I 256-258. Also see ibid, 259, 268, 272-274. Lee's cavalry was extemporaneously organized, rather than a formal detachment of light horse from the Connecticut militia establishment.
21. NYPC I, 277, 279.
22. Lee-Washington 2/5/76: Lee Papers I, 271. NYPC I, 270. Pa. Evening Post, 2/6/76: Stokes IV, 913. Clinton, 24. *Phoenix* journal 2/4/76: Nav. Doc. III, 1125.
23. Lee-Washington 2/5/76: op. cit. For a calendar of early Clinton/Lee correspondence see Willcox, 23n.
24. Clinton Papers, Memoranda, fols. 40-42.
25. Lee-Washington 2/11/76: Lee Papers I, 283. *Phoenix* and *Asia* journals, 2/11/76: Nav. Doc. III, 1217, 1218.

Notes: Chapter II

1. Lee-Washington 2/19/76: Lee Papers I, 309.
2. Blackwell's and Montresor Islands are now Roosevelt and Ward's Islands, respectively.
3. Lee-Washington 2/5/76 and 2/14/76: Lee Papers I, 272, 296. NYPC I, 283, 284.
4. Lee-Washington 2/19/76: op. cit. "Report on the Defence of New York, March, 1776," ibid, 354, 356.
5. GW IV, 222. Stirling-Lee 2/4/76: Lee Papers I, 271.
6. Lee Papers I, 276-279, 321. NYPC I, 288. 4 Force V, 203. JCC IV, 127, 128, 151, 163, 166-167. Linn & Egle I, 115. Pennsylvania did not have a militia law until March 1777; the organization which served in the interim was a voluntary "association" rather than a true militia. Service in the ranks was not legally obligatory. However, the Pennsylvania Associators were fully sanctioned by the provincial government, and responsive to its bidding. Those of Philadelphia were even uniformed, and enjoyed an especially good reputation at this point.
7. Lee-N.Y. Congress 2/20/76: Lee Papers I, 315.
8. NYPC I, 194, 228-231, 269-270, 277, 284, 332.
9. N.Y. Congress-Lee 2/20/76: Lee Papers I, 315.
10. Lee-Hancock 2/11/76: Lee Papers I, 283. O'Callaghan VIII, 641-642. Smith, 264-265. NYPC I, 291
11. Lee Papers I, 257, 295, 341. Nav. Doc. III, 1135. Smith, 264-265. Lee's estimate was correct: Parker did not feel as free to open hostilities as he pretended. Vandeput's firing on the city in August had not been received enthusiastically by his superior, Vice Admiral Samuel Graves, although he was not censured for it. See Nav. Doc. II, 70-72, 840-841.
12. Parker-Shuldham 2/25/76: Nav. Doc. IV, 76. Lee Papers I, 301, 308-309, 315, 350-352. NYPC I, 327, 332.
13. NYPC I, 294, 312; also 255-332 passim.
14. Lee-Washington 2/29/76: Lee Papers I, 337. BrM 80:29 Montressor. BrM 100:8 Sauthier.
15. Lee-Morris and Lee-Washington, both 2/14/76: Lee Papers I, 295, 296. Descriptions of the proposed works in this and the following paragraphs are from Lee's "Report," ibid, 354-357. BrM 100:6 Sauthier. BrM 92:3 Ratzer.
16. NYPC I, 301, 303. Lee-Washington 2/29/76: op. cit. BrM 75:9 Mackenzie.
17. Lee-Washington 2/29/76: op. cit. N.Y. Packet 2/29/76: Stokes

IV, 916. NYPC I, 309, 327, 332.
18. GW IV, 222. Lee-Washington 2/29/76: op. cit. NYPC I, 253, 255. AmM 44 Smith.
19. JCC IV, 174, 180. NYPC I, 343. Stirling-Washington 3/11/76: 4 Force V, 183.

Notes: Chapter III

1. JCC IV, 181. The standard modern biography is Alan Valentine, *Lord Stirling*, New York, 1969.
2. Washington-Lee 2/26/76: GW IV, 352.
3. Lee-N.Y. Congress 3/4/76: Lee Papers I 344-345. NYPC I. 336-337.
4. Nav. Doc. III, 486; IV, 237-238. NYPC I, 348, 349, 353. *Schuyler's* skipper was Capt. James Smith.
5. NYPC I, 336, 342, 355.
6. Lee-Hancock 3/5/76: Lee Papers I, 346-347. "Return of all the Troops at New York" 3/13/76: 4 Force V, 203.
7. Moylan-Stirling 3/9/76: Nav. Doc. IV, 253.
8. JCC IV, 163, 204. Hancock-Stirling 3/15/76: 4 Force V, 232.
9. 4 Force V, 78-80, 202, 215-216, 246-247, 397-398, 401-402, 447-448. The Connecticut replacements were commanded by Col. Gold Selleck Silliman and Col. Matthew Talcott.
10. NYPC I, 360-361. 4 Force V, 217-221.
11. JCC III, 187-190. Militia Bill 8/22/75: Fernow 30-34.
12. 4 Force III, 708, 738.
13. Cal. Mss. I, 225. 4 Force III, 1205; IV, 690. See Appendix B for militia commanders.
14. 4 Force V, 218. O'Callaghan VIII, 457. Fernow, 286. Appendix B.
15. 4 Force III, 68. Fernow, 287-289. Appendix B.
16. NYPC I, 438. Onderdonk Q, 35-36. The Jamaica minutemen were commanded by Capt. John Skidmore, and the Newtown light horse by Capt. Daniel Lawrence.
17. A form of the General Association for Queens County appears in Onderdonk Q, 30-31; the apparent prototype in NYPC I, 5.
18. NYPC I, 149-150, 156-157.
19. Onderdonk Q, 39-42. 4 Force IV, 203. NYPC I, 215-216. Nav. Doc. III, 157.
20. NYPC I, 230. JCC IV, 27-28. Onderdonk Q, 44-45. Thomas Jones, *History of New York during the Revolutionary War,* New York, 1884-1885, I, 69, 70. Nav. Doc. III, 1015.
21. Lee Papers I, 345-346, 352, 359. NYPC I, 355. 4 Force V, 220.
22. 4 Force V, 218. Appendix B.
23. NYPC I, 227, 230, 263, 310; II, 121, 176. 4 Force IV, 1589.
24. Cal. Mss. I, 274. Appendix B.
25. NYPC I, 269, 272, 307. Cal. Mss. I, 233.
26. Stirling-Hancock 3/16/76: Nav. Doc. IV, 363. Carroll-Carroll 3/29/76: ibid, 565. General Orders 3/16/76: 4 Force V, 220.
27. General Orders 3/14/76: 4 Force V, 220. Silliman-his wife 3/29/76: Nav. Doc. IV, 564. The honorary title of "Colonel" appears to have been conferred on Engineer Smith, thereby giving him sufficient status to carry out his duties without having militia field officers pull rank on him.
28. General Orders 3/13/76: 4 Force V, 221. Silliman-his wife: op. cit. Fish-Varick 4/9/76: Johnston II, 128. "State of the Fortifications at New York" (an intelligence report to Capt. Parker): Nav. Doc. IV, 738-739. Official names of the works are in General Orders 5/22/76: GW IV 73-74. The Battery became the Grand Battery to distinguish it from the other batteries.
29. Stirling-Hancock 3/19/76: 4 Force V, 247. "A Return of the Batteries in and near the City of New York" 3/24/76: ibid, 480.
30. Stirling-Washington 3/20/76 and 4/1/76: 4 Force V, 437, 750. NYPC I, 401. Nav. Doc. IV, 725-726.
31. 4 Force V, 402, 475, 508. Nav. Doc. IV, 770.
32. Brigade Orders 3/25/76: Nav. Doc. IV, 506.

Notes: Chapter IV

1. Washington-Greene 3/25/76: GW IV, 430-431
2. Washington-Putnam 3/29/76: GW IV, 442-443. General Orders 3/13-31/76: ibid, 389-444 passim. 4 Force V, 1193-1194.
3. Heath-Hancock 4/3/76: Nav. Doc. IV, 646. Tryon-Germain 4/6/76: O'Callaghan VIII, 675.
4. Putnam-Hancock 4/7/76: Nav. Doc. IV, 698. Tryon-Germain 4/15/76: O'Callaghan VIII, 675-676. Nav. Doc. IV, 698-699, 725-726, 770-771, 1310-1311.
5. General Orders, 4/8/76: Nav. Doc. IV, 722-723. *Asia* journal 4/14/76: ibid, 819. Tryon-Germain 4/15/76: op. cit.
6. Willard, 301. General Orders 4/8/76: 4 Force V, 796. JCC IV, 272. Washington-Hancock 4/15/76: GW IV, 480.
7. For details of organizational data see the author's series, "Notes on Troop Units of the Continental Army" in *Military Collector and Historian,* XXIII/3, 71-74; XXV/1, 18-21; XXXVI/2, 86-97.
8. JCC II, 89-90
9. General Orders 6/14/76: GW V, 134-135.
10. General Orders 4/15 & 27/76, 6/26/76: GW IV, 479, 535; V, 180. Brigade Orders 6/20/76: Johnston II, 18.
11. General Return 5/5/76: 4 Force V, 1197. Artillery Regt. return 5/19/76: ibid, VI 527. JCC IV, 204. GW IV, 509, 522-524. General Orders 4/29/76: ibid, 535-536. This was actually the second brigade arrangement within the month. The first had to be altered after the departure of Sullivan and his six regiments to Canada.
12. "A Return of the state of Arms and Accoutrements" 6/24/76: 4 Force VI, 1121-1122. Ritzema-N.Y. Congress 5/17/76: ibid, 493. NYPC I, 355, 455-456.
13. "A Return of the disposition of the Cannon" 6/10/76: 4 Force VI, 920-921. Washington-Hancock 4/15/76: Nav. Doc. IV, 836. NYPC I, 256. Stokes IV, 918. Nav. Doc. IV, 711-712; V, 199.
14. Nav. Doc. IV, 721. Onderdonk S/K, 117.
15. GW V, 67, 100. Glover Correspondence: Stokes IV, 923.
16. The names of the posts are in Brigade Orders 6/1 & 20/76, 7/2 & 16/76: Johnston II, 15, 18, 20, 22. Col. Putnam apparently assumed the principal assault would be against the perimeter's low point, by way of the Brooklyn Ferry Road. Four of the five redoubts were situated so as to concentrate their fire on this area. BrM 107:5 Sproule.
17. Washington-Putnam 5/21/76: GW V, 68. Johnston II, 18, 22.
18. Brigade Orders 6/17/76: Johnston II, 17. Clinton, 41.
19. "Plan for General Putnam's Consideration:" Nav. Doc. V, 232. NYPC I, 411. Appendix C.
20. Tryon-Germain 4/18/76: O'Callaghan VIII, 677. Nav. Doc. IV, 1393; V, 22-23, 156, 228, 397.
21. Washington-Putnam 5/21/76: GW V, 67. JCC IV, 385ff.
22. JCC IV, 412-414. General Orders 7/2/76: GW V, 211.
23. Washington-Schuyler 5/22/76: GW V, 74. JCC IV, 412-414, 424.
24. JCC IV, 359, 419; V, 448.
25. Washington-Hancock 6/20/76: GW V, 161. 5 Force I, 27-28. Baker, 39. Heath, 39.
26. Graydon, 152.
27. Stirling-Washington 6/1/76: 4 Force VI 672-674ff. Livingston-Stirling 6/11/76: ibid, 818. Washington-Clinton 6/14/76: GW V, 138-139.
28. Washington-Essex Committee 6/17/76: GW V, 154-155. Essex Committee-Washington 6/25/76: Nav. Doc. V, 735-736. Bangs, 48.
29. N.Y. Committee for Disaffected Persons 6/15-29/76: 4 Force V, 1152-1183. "Proceedings of a Court Martial of the Line . . . for the Trial of Thomas Hickey and others" 6/26/76: Carlos E. Godfrey, *The Commander-in-Chief's Guard,* Washington, 1904, 27-30. Forbes's contact and financial backer was Mayor David Mathews of New York City.
30. Washington-Hancock 6/28/76: GW V, 193.

31. Washington-Hancock 6/10/76: GW V, 121. Ibid, 97, 129, 155. Tupper-Washington 6/21/76: Nav. Doc. V, 663. Bangs, 45.
32. Davidson-Washington 6/27/75: Nav. Doc. V, 770. Ibid, 381-383, 661, 789-790.

Notes: Chapter V

1. Howe-Dartmouth 3/21/76: 4 Force V, 459. Howe-Germain 5/7/76: Nav. Doc. IV, 1436. Ibid, 488, 1293.
2. Kemble Papers I, 328-378 passim.
3. "Board of General Officers" 3/4/71: *Journal of the Society for Army Historical Research,* XV, 250. Royal Warrant 12/19/68: Charles M. Lefferts, *Uniforms of the American, British, French and German Armies in the War of the American Revolution,* New York, 1926, 183, 184, 185.
4. War Office 12/17/75: Edward E. Curtis, *The Organization of the British Army in the American Revolution,* New Haven, 1926, 163. Return of 29th Foot 12/17/73: H. Everard, *History of Thos. Farrington's Regiment,* Worcester, 1891, 73-74. "Stoppages" comprised a system of payroll deductions imposed on the hapless soldier by his grateful king. A staggering list of charges against the enlisted man's pittance appears in Curtis, 22.
5. General Orders 5/16/76: Kemble Papers I, 355. George III-North 8/26/75: George 3rd III, 251. Casualty return 3/17/75: 4 Force II, 1098-1099. Elting 51,52.
6. Kemble Papers I, 353, 382. M.E.S. Laws, *Battery Records of the Royal Artillery 1716-1859,* Woolwich, 1952, 42, 47. H.G. Parkyn, *Shoulder-Belt Plates and Buttons,* Aldershot, 1956, 51.
7. Kemble Papers I, 366, 374, 377. NYPC II, 5-7, 160. Recruiting warrant for Royal Highland Emigrants 4/3/75: O'Callaghan VIII, 562-563.
8. Howe-Germain 5/7/76: Nav. Doc. IV, 1435-1436. Ibid V, 149. The British ordnance vessel *Hope* was captured by the American schooner *Franklin,* Capt. James Mugford, on 17 May. *Franklin* was part of a naval squadron Washington had organized at Cambridge in 1775. Nav. Doc. V, 134-135.
9. Howe-Germain 5/7/76: op. Cit. *Chatham* journal 6/10/76: ibid, 446. "Troops Embarked at Halifax, Fit for Duty" 6/4/76: WO 36-3-X/LO 7646.
10. Germain-Howe 1/5/76, 2/1/76, 3/28/76: 4 Force IV, 574, 903; V, 526. All these letters were received by 12 May: ibid V, 1080; VI, 431.
11. Washington-Hancock 6/17/76: GW V, 152.
12. *Chatham* journal 6/10/76: op. cit. Feilding-Denbigh 6/7/76: Balderston, 83. Bowater-Denbigh 6/8/76, 7/7/76: ibid, 85, 87-88. Nav. Doc. V, 469, 975, 816.
13. Howe-Germain 6/7/76, 7/7/76: 4 Force VI 729; 5 Force I, 105. Nav. Doc. V, 919.
14. Howe-Germain 7/7/76: op. cit. "Owing to representations made by General [James] Robertson the plans were changed." Stuart-Bute 7/9/76: Nav. Doc. V, 989.
15. Ships' journals 7/2/76: Nav. Doc. V 895-896. Chadd-Stephens 7/8/76: ibid, 976. Robertson, 86.
16. Trumbull-Wadsworth 7/4/76: Nav. Doc. V, 918. Ibid, 894, 1011, 1285. Robertson, 87. Balderston, 88. GW V, 215-216. On 17 June Congress expanded the Maryland/Virginia rifle companies into a regiment with the three captains as field officers: Col. Hugh Stephenson, Lt. Col. Moses Rawlings, Maj. O.H. Williams. The reinlistees were formed into a provisional company but, inasmuch as this unit disappears from the record, it is probable the men were furloughed home. By September Stephenson was dead, apparently of natural causes. The new regiment, now under Rawlings, did not join the Army till early October.
17. *Chatham* journal 7/3/76: Nav. Doc. V, 897. *Asia* journal 7/4/76: ibid, 921. Greene-Washington 7/5/76: ibid, 935. Ibid, 920-973. For an evaluation of the effective ranges of rifles and artillery of the period, see John R. Elting's *The Battles of Saratoga,* Monmouth Beach, 1977, 85, 87.

18. Birdsall-N.Y. Convention 11/25/76: NYPC II, 334-335. Nav. Doc. V, 895-897, 919-921, 936-937. References to *Mifflin* are all but nonexistent; it is not known when she quit her station at Rockaway Inlet. By September she had joined company with *Schuyler* and *Montgomerie,* apparently operating out of Providence, Rhode Island. Nav. Doc. VI, 854.
19. Kemble Papers I, 79, 355. Robertson, 87. Webb I, 152.
20. Tryon-Germain 7/8/76: O'Callaghan VIII, 681. Nav. Doc. V, 921, 936, 975. Robertson, 87-88. Kemble Papers I, 79. Balderston, 88. The sometime delegate was Richard Lawrence. Col. Christopher Billop, who had commanded the Richmond County militia before the war, now resumed that position.
21. Washington-Hancock 6/28/76: GW V, 194.
22. Mifflin-Washington 7/5/76: 5 Force I, 27. GW V, 198-199, 209-211. Heath, 40-41. The New Jersey regiments posted to Long Island were the 2nd Essex County and an unidentified unit under Lt. Col. Thomas Cadmus. Johnston II, 20.
23. General Orders, 6/29 & 30/76: GW V, 198, 205-207.
24. Washington-Hancock 7/10/76; GW V, 250. General Orders 6/30/76-7/7/76: ibid, 206-230 passim. Bangs, 58.
25. Shuldham-Stephens 7/8/76: Nav. Doc. V, 975.
26. *Phoenix* and *Rose* journals 7/12/76: Nav. Doc. V, 1037-1038. Ibid, 1089. Robertson, 89-90.
27. *Phoenix* and *Rose* journals: 7/12/76: op. Cit. Robertson, 89. Serle, 28. Bangs, 58. Nav. Doc. V, 1038, 1089, 1131, 1189.
28. Nav. Doc. V, 1042, 1089-1090. Kemble Papers I, 80. Bangs, 58-59. Graydon, 152. Drowne-his sister 7/13/76: Stokes V, 994. *Phoenix* carried 44 guns and *Rose* 20; *Tryal* probably carried 6 carriage guns and 10 swivels, the normal complement for a schooner. Nav. Doc. IV, 1090-1091.
29. Bangs, 59-60. General Orders 7/13/76: GW V, 268-269.
30. Serle, 28. Declaration 6/20/76: Nav. Doc. V, 634-635.
31. Washington-Hancock 7/14 & 17/76: GW V, 273-274, 297. Minutes of the interview with Col. Paterson are in ibid, 321-323n.
32. Proclamation 7/14/76: Nav. Doc. V, 1075-1076. General Orders 7/9/76: GW V, 245. Bangs, 57. Webb I, 153.

Notes: Chapter VI

1. GW V, 214. Nav. Doc. V, 991.
2. NYPC I, 478-479, 483-484, 487.
3. NYPC I, 508; II, 302. Onderdonk Q, 55, 71.
4. LIHS, documents 352-360. NYPC I, 504. Greene Papers I, 241-242, 244-245. The Jamaica minutemen were now a standard company in the 1st Queens County Regiment.
5. Scott-Sands 6/11/76: LIHS, documents 345, 346.
6. Trumbull-Washington 7/3/76: 4 Force VI, 1254. Ibid V, 1612; VI, 869, 871.
7. "Conference of General Officers" 7/8/76: 5 Force I, 224. Seymour-Trumbull 7/11/76: ibid, 205. Washington-Seymour 7/16/76: GW V, 286. 5 Force I, 236-237, 317, 417. GW V 228-229. It is interesting that Washington, who has been accused of insufficient appreciation of the uses of light cavalry for not holding Seymour, sought and received permission to take Capt. Leary's city troop into Continental pay. At the same time, Gen. Greene did not hesitate to make use of the Kings County troops. One factor often overlooked is Seymour's orders to return home as soon as a sufficient number of Wadsworth's levies had arrived.
8. Washington-Livingston 6/19/76, 7/5/76: GW V, 198-199, 224-226. Washington-Mercer 7/4/76: ibid, 217-218. 4 Force VI, 1619-1620.
9. 5 Force I, 287-289. GW V, 363, 364.
10. 4 Force VI, 1507.
11. JCC V, 520. Linn & Egle I, 193-253 passim.
12. JCC V, 519-520, 523. 4 Force VI 964-965. 5 Force I, 885, 894. There were 53 regiments in the Pennsylvania Association, eight of them in the exempt counties of Westmoreland, Bedford and Northumberland. A number of counties sent out special compos-

ite units, rather than their standing regiments. 2 PA XIII, 257-258.
13. "Conference of General Officers" 7/12/76: 5 Force I, 224.
14. Mercer-Hancock 7/26/76: Nav. Doc. V, 1233-1234. Ibid, 1158-1159, 1245-1246. 5 Force I, 369-370, 413, 443-444, 600-601.
15. Nav. Doc. V, 1102-1285 passim. GW V, 276-277, 292-293. NYPC I, 512. 5 Force I, 355-356. William Smith of Havestraw—that singular anomaly, a loyalist Whig—reported in his Memoirs that the tender had been hulled by a 32-pound shot from Fort Montgomery, but he was subsequently contradicted by a Marine officer belonging to *Phoenix*. Nav. Doc. V, 1240.
16. NYPC I, 527, 528. Nav. Doc. V, 1187-1189.
17. Heath, 40. Nav. Doc. V. 1157-1158, 1169, 1170, 1214. Sparks I, 270-271.
18. Nav. Doc. V, 1098, 1113, 1169-1170, 1178, 1260, 1273. Bangs, 63. GW V, 337. 5 Force I, 186.
19. Tupper-Washington 8/3/76: Nav. Doc. VI, 37-38. *Phoenix* and *Rose* journals 8/3/76: ibid, 38-39. Ibid, 49, 121. GW V, 370. Flagship *Hester* drops from the record after July; she may have been trapped in Raritan Bay. *Putnam* held her station off Monmouth County, plagued with disrepair and mutiny, till she was ordered sold in October. NYPC I, 665.
20. Heath-Washington 8/18/76: Nav. Doc. VI, 226. Washington-Trumbull 8/18/76: ibid, 227. *Phoenix* and *Rose* journals 8/16 & 18/76: ibid, 206, 225-226. Heath 41, 45-46. N.Y. Mercury 8/19/76: Stokes V, 1000.
21. GW V, 307-308. Heath, 44-45. 5 Force I, 224.
22. NYPC I, 524, 525-526. GW V, 298, 309.
23. GW V, 255, 363, 404. JCC V, 631. 5 Force I, 885.
24. Trumbull-Washington 7/6/76, 8/13/76: 5 Force I, 45, 936-937.
25. General Orders 8/12/76: GW V, 422-424.
26. Sundry returns: 5 Force I, 763-764, 963-964; II, 327-330, 449-452.
27. Sundry returns: 5 Force I, 787-788, 963-964; II, 296; III, 679-680. 4 Force VI, 1649-1650. New Jersey had thirty regiments on its militia establishment, but the alternating divisions were to be made up of composite rather than standing units. 4 Force VI, 1662.

Notes: Chapter VII

1. "Return of Troops Embarked at Halifax . . . & Joined at Sea" 6/11/76: WO 36-3-X/LO 7646. Nav. Doc. IV, 925. George 3rd III, 311. 4 Force IV, 574.
2. T.C. Smout, *A History of the Scottish People,* New York, 1969, 342. 5 Force I, 1111-1112.
3. Examination of Isaac Favier 8/14/76: 5 Force I, 996. Willard, 334-335. Balderston, 89. Four of the transports, with Lt. Col. Archibald Campbell and part of the 71st, were taken by Washington's Massachusetts squadron. The other two, with parts of both regiments, were taken by the Continental Navy brig *Andrea Doria*. These troops were crowded into one of the transports, but subsequently overpowered the American prize crew. Then they headed south to join Lord Dunmore, only to be captured again by the Virginia Navy. Nav. Doc. V, 564-566, 619-620, 686-688.
4. Farley's Bristol Journal 10/12/76: Willard, 351. Kemble Papers I, 83. 5 Force I, 789. The 50th Foot arrived from Jamaica (West Indies), but was drafted and sent home.
5. "Disposition of his Majesty's Ships and Vessels" 8/13/76: Nav. Doc. VI, 167, 169.
6. C.T. Atkinson, "British Forces in North America, 1774-1781" *Journal of the Society for Army Historical Research,* XVI, 7. Muenchhausen, Appendix 73-79.
7. "Troops of Hesse Cassel, 1783" WO 36-3-X/LO 7646. Kipping 5-7. "Translation of a Treaty between his Majesty and the Landgrave of Hesse Cassel" 1/15/76: 4 Force VI, 273-276. A.W. Haarmann, "The Hessian Army & the Corps in North America,

1776-1783" *Military Collector and Historian,* XIV/3, 69-75.
8. "A List of the Hessian Troops arrived at Spithead" 4/26/76: Nav. Doc. IV, 1063-1064.
9. Muenchhausen, 75-76. Kipping, 39-45. A. W. Haarmann, "Contemporary Observations on the Hesse-Cassel Troops Sent to North America, 1776-1781" *Journal of the Society for Army Historical Research,* LIV, 130-134.
10. Nav. Doc. IV, 1062-1063, 1103, 1131-1132.
11. 5 Force I, 788, 813, 1110-1111. Serle, 44.
12. Robertson, 88, 89. Nav. Doc. VI, 124.
13. Serle, 56-57, 65. Rawdon-Huntington 8/5/76: Great Britian Historical Manuscripts Commission, *Report on the Manuscripts of the Late Reginald Rawdon Hastings,* London, 1930-1947, III, 179-180. 5 Force I, 813, 1110-1111.
14. Morning Chronicle and London Advertiser 6/7/76: Willard, 301-302. Brigade Orders 5/18/76, 7/28/76: Greene Papers I, 215, 268. Martin, 20-22. Bangs, 43-44.
15. Baldwin-his wife 6/12/76: Loammi Baldwin Papers, Houghton Library, Cambridge. Bangs, 29-30. The Holy Ground is supposed to have been so named because it occupied real estate owned by Trinity Church.
16. General Orders 8/1/76: GW V, 361-362. Graydon, 147-149.
17. NYPC I, 401. Heath, 38. GW IV, 477; V, 25, 63, 82-84, 346.
18. Brigade Orders, 7/28/76: op. cit. Drowne-his sister 8/9/76: Stokes V, 999. GW V, 353, 369.
19. Heath, 44. GW V, 345. N.Y. Mercury 7/29/76. Stokes V, 997. NYPC I, 568. See Appendix A.
20. Washington-Hancock 8/16/76: GW V, 439-440. The disability rate is derived from the monthly returns. By contrast, the British Army on Staten Island remained extraordinarily healthy, a phenomenon cited by a number of its chroniclers. The Highlanders may have brought in some cases of smallpox; if so, they were quickly contained. Some of Clinton's Virginia refugees may have had yellow fever, but this did not spread either; any infected mosquitoes must not have survived the trip north. A few cases of scurvy appeared among the Hessians, brought on by an extended shipboard diet. One Royal Navy officer sniffed incongruously that this was because they, "being foreigners, were naturally dirty." Collier, 300.
21. GW V, 299, 407, 409-410. Greene Papers I, 286-287. Bangs, 55, 58. Graydon, 152.
22. GW IV, 484; V, 208-209, 422-424. Johnston II, 17, 21, 25, 27, 75-76. Greene Papers I, 287.
23. NYPC I, 567-568. Greene Papers I, 288.
24. NYPC I, 533-534, 563, 566, 568. LIHS, documents 370, 377, 378, 385.
25. Greene-Washington 8/15/76: Greene Papers I, 287-288. Ibid, 289.
26. Greene-Washington 8/15/76: op. cit. Ibid, 291. Johnston II, 25.

Notes: Chapter VIII

1. Serle, 62. Nav. Doc. VI, 183. Baurmeister, 32. Robertson, 93. Field, 426.
2. "Extract of a Letter from an Officer in General Frazier's Battalion" 9/3/76: 5 Force I, 1259-1260. Nav. Doc. VI, 130. JCC V, 654. 5 Force I, 1160. The leaflets, however disguised, did not get into Staten Island until after all the Hessians had left except for one brigade. They do not appear to have made any great impression. Baurmeister, 41.
3. Nav. Doc. VI, 167, 306-307, 316. That Capt. Ferguson had the command appears from *Halifax's* journal 9/1/76: ibid, 640.
4. Hodgkins-his wife 8/25/76: Hodgkins, 214. GW V, 467. 5 Force I, 1068-1070.
5. Reed-Livingston 8/30/76: 5 Force I, 1231. GW V, 649.
6. Division Orders 8/21/76: Johnston II, 27.
7. The road system of western Long Island appears in Taylor's and Skinner's "Map of New York and Staten Island, and Part of Long Island." BrM 112:3.
8. GW V, 494.
9. Kemble Papers I, 84. Baurmeister, 35.
10. Hand-Nixon 8/21/76: 5 Force I, 1111. Livingston-Washington 8/21/76: ibid, 1110-1111.
11. "Letter from New York" 8/22/76: 5 Force I, 1111-1112. GW V, 474-475. Johnston II, 113.
12. Nav. Doc. VI, 267-269. Collier, 302.
13. Howe-Stephens 8/31/76: Nav. Doc. VI, 374. Serle, 72. Embarkation Return 8/-/76: WO 36-3-X/LO 7646. Nav. Doc. VI, 267.
14. Serle, 71. Howe-Germain 9/3/76: 5 Force I, 1256. Clinton, 40. Kemble Papers I, 85. Baurmeister, 35.
15. Howe-Germain 9/3/76: op. cit.
16. Chambers-his wife 9/3/76: Linn & Egle I, 306-307. GW V, 475. 5 Force I, 1111-1112.
17. Washington-Heath 8/23/76: GW V 475-476. Ibid, 299.
18. Washington-Hancock 8/23/76: GW V, 476-477. Ibid, 473-479. Johnston II, 52-53, 60-61. Fitch, 25.
19. Ewing-Yeates, 8/30/76: Johnston II, 50. Fitch, 25.
20. Chambers-his wife 9/3/76: op. cit. Fitch, 26. 5 Force I, 1136-1137. Hessian officer's account from "Die Neuesten Staatsbegebenheiten," 1777: Lowell, 61.
21. Proclamation 8/23/76: LIHS, Document 410. Serle, 82.
22. Washington-Hancock 8/24/76: GW V, 481. Washington-Heath 8/22 & 23/76: ibid, V, 473, 474, 476. 5 Force I, 1121-1122, 1144-1146. Leggett, 11-12.
23. Division Orders 8/23 & 24/76: Johnston II, 27-28. Hodgkins, 214.
24. Hessian officer's account: Lowell, 61. GW V, 486-488, 491.
25. Washington-Hancock 8/26/76: GW V, 491. Johnston II, 28-29.
26. Washington-Hancock 1/30/76: GW IV, 290.
27. Washington-Putnam 8/25/76: GW V, 486-489.
28. Washington-Trumbull 8/24/76: GW V, 485-486.
29. NYPC I, 587-588.
30. Howe-Stephens 8/31/76: op. cit. Baurmeister, 37. Hessian officer's account: Lowell, 62.
31. Diary of Ens. Caleb Clap: Nav. Doc. VI, 254, 308. GW V, 382-383, 491. NYPC I, 598. 5 Force I, 1144.
32. NYPC I, 589-591. Woodhull-N.Y. Convention 8/27/76: ibid II, 273.
33. Potter-Woodhull 8/26/76: NYPC II, 295. Nav. Doc. VI, 306-307.
34. GW V, 494. Field, 387. New England officer's account: Stokes V, 1003.
35. Court Martial on Colonel Zedwitz 8/25/76: 5 Force I, 1159-1162. Zedwitz had been assigned to translate Congress's propaganda leaflet into High German. He wrote to Gov. Tryon of his activities, dropped some intelligence tidbits, and offered his services as a spy for 2,000 pounds sterling. However, his messenger betrayed him and he was arrested. Zedwitz pleaded that he was working a confidence scheme to retrieve 2,000 pounds the British government had owed him since the last war. After his dismissal he was placed under confinement.
36. Harrison-Hancock 8/27/76: GW V, 494. Stokes V, 1003. Johnston II, 35, 58.
37. Parsons-Adams 10/8/76: Johnston II, 35. Ibid I, 137n; II, 29-30. 5 Force I, 1251. Hodgkins, 215.
38. NYPC I, 598. Kemble Papers I, 85. Johnston II, 59-61.
39. Johnston II, 50-51. It is not clear if Col. Haller or Col. Cunningham had been assigned their regiments as yet. At any rate, the units were actually commanded by Lt. Col. Nicholas Lutz and Lt. Col. William Hay, respectively.
40. New England officer's account: Stokes V, 1003.

Notes: Chapter IX

1. Clinton, 40-41.
2. Clinton, 41n.
3. Clinton, 41-42. Nav. Doc. VI, 309. The colonel of the 71st Highlanders was Maj. Gen. Simon Fraser of Lovat. In his absence Erskine, lieutenant colonel of the 1st Battalion, had command of the entire regiment with the rank of Brigadier General.
4. Howe-Germain 9/3/76: 5 Force I, 1256-1257.
5. Murray-his sister 8/31/76: Murray, 33-34. Kemble Papers I, 85. NYPC II, 273.
6. Clinton, 42. Field, 405-406, 419. Johnston I, 178-179n. Onderdonk S/K, 139. Mackenzie I, 37-38.
7. Clinton, 42. "Memo. of the affair of Brooklyn" 8/29/76: Clinton Papers.
8. Part of the day's tradition is that Stirling actually witnessed Grant's gasconade in Parliament. Stirling, however, was back in America by the end of 1761, and it does not appear that he ever returned to England.
9. Letter of a Pennsylvania officer 8/27/76: Field, 485-486. Johnston II, 48-49.
10. Parsons-Adams 8/29/76, 10/8/76: Johnston II, 33-35. Atlee was the only full colonel present. Smallwood's regiment was commanded by Maj. Mordecai Gist, Haslet's by Maj. Thomas McDonough, Huntington's 17th Continentals by Lt. Col. Joel Clark.
11. Atlee journal: 5 Force I, 1251. Stirling-Washington 8/29/76: ibid, 1245. Fitch, 30.
12. Baurmeister, 37. Field, 432. Lowell, 62-63. Onderdonk S/K, 140.
13. Miles journal: Johnston II, 60-63. 5 Force I, 1195-1196. Miles claims that he had all along anticipated Howe's descent along the Jamaica Road. If so, his initial actions on Tuesday morning do not reflect his concern. The officer sent to warn Putnam says that Howe's approach was discovered by "our scouting parties."
14. Miles journal: op. cit. Murray, 33. Clinton, 42-43. Robertson, 93. 5 Force I, 1250.
15. Harris journal: Field, 406. 5 Force I, 1256-1257. Robertson, 93.
16. Brodhead letter 9/5/76: Johnston II, 63-66.
17. Brodhead letter 9/5/76: op. cit. 5 Force I, 1250, 1256-1257. Chester's regiment was commanded by Lt. Col. Solomon Wills. There does not, however, appear to have been any field officers with the Bedford Pass column, or Brodhead would have been obliged to work through them in forming his "rally." That the New Englanders failed to respond does not necessarily mean their company officers had lost control of them (although that possibility certainly obtains). They may have been under Col. Wyllys's prior orders to proceed directly to the lines, or they may have judged that taking a stand would have been a purposeless self-sacrificing gesture.

When and where Johnston and Callender were captured is uncertain. Callender had been an artillery captain himself last year, but was cashiered for misconduct at Bunker's Hill. This year he attached himself to one of Col. Knox's companies as a volunteer. His actions on Long Island were heroic enough to win him the return of his commission upon his exchange. Johnston, however, had been so severely wounded that he never rejoined the service.

18. Letter of a Pennsylvania officer 8/28/76: 5 Force I, 1195-1196. Why the New Englanders should have taken the riflemen to be disguised British soldiers cannot be readily explained. If they were, then they would have had to be between Brodhead's detachment and the lines. In that case, Brodhead could not have retreated directly to the lines without interference—which he says he did: "as the Enemy's main body was then *nearly* between us and the lines, I retreated to the lines." (Johnston II, 65; italics added.)

But there is a possibility the British ranks did indeed hold some shirtmen. On 30 August Lt. Ewing of the 1st Continentals wrote: "Several Companies of their Light Infantry are cloathed exactly as we are, in hunting shirts and Trowsers." (Linn & Egle, I, 310) And even before the battle, one newspaper reported that in Cornwallis's detachment at Flatbush, "Many of the Regulars are in rifle dresses." (*Military Collector and Historian, XXIX, 119*) There is, however, no corroboration in British sources. Redcoats were not above modifying their dress to suit field conditions, but such a radical departure from proper military attire is highly unusual. American riflemen had been deserting to Staten Island by two's and three's all summer, but there is no record they were formed into a distinct loyalist corps. In any case, there would not have been enough of them to form even a company.

19. Smallwood-Md. Convention 10/12/76: 5 Force II, 1012-1013. London Chronicle: Onderdonk S/K, 138. Clinton, 43-44. Conventional wisdom charges Howe with a Bunker's Hill complex for not giving the grenadiers their head. But his decision, if not bold, was militarily sound. However, from this point forward Howe steadily lost the confidence of his admirers.
20. Baurmeister, 37. Hessian officer's account: Lowell, 63-64. Field, 432-433. The parade ground charge was not done for martial display. The Germans theorized that the surest way to hold down losses in the long run was to maintain tight unit integrity.
21. Hodgkins-his wife 8/28/76: Hodgkins, 215. Hitchcock's 11th Continentals were commanded by Lt. Col. Ezekiel Cornell, Little's 12th by Lt. Col. William Henshaw.
22. 5 Force I, 1257.
23. Hodgkins-his wife 8/28/76: op. cit. Robertson, 93. Johnston I, 186; II, 45, 47.
24. Heeringen-Lossberg: Lowell, 65-67. Johnston II, 178. Kipping, 21. 5 Force I, 1259-1260. Field, 436. The hunting shirt, derived from the English farmer's smock, was worn by a large part of the American forces other than the riflemen.

Luridly overdrawn tales of massacre in Flatbush Pass quickly circulated among all three armies. Much of the seemingly gratuitous bayoneting, however, may have involved what some behaviorists term *critical reaction,* when the individual British, Hessian or Scots soldier came on the American quite suddenly in extremely close quarters. The American was not able to flee, and therefore made gestures of self defense. According to the critical reaction theory, both parties acted instinctively, and the aggressor was compelled to strike to kill. See John Keegan, *The Face of Battle,* New York, 1976, 165-167.

The capture of two Jersey officers is significant in identifying the trapped men. There are no figures to show New Jersey losses, and they may have been quite heavy (see Appendix E). An early biography of Stephen Olney contains a garbled account, which suggests the previous night's out-guards were also present. The words are ostensibly Olney's, but they seem to have been reworked considerably. At any rate, it appears that part of Capt. William Tew's company, 11th Continentals, was detached from the regiment just before the retreat "to protect our sentries." One of the subalterns captured in the pass, John Blunt, can be identified as Tew's first lieutenant. Field, 516-517; 4 Force IV, 637-638.

25. Baurmeister, 37. Johnston II, 43.
26. Activities on the Gowanus Road are from six principal sources. Stirling-Washington 8/29/76: op. cit. Atlee journal; op. cit. Parsons-Adams 8/29/76, 10/8/76: op. cit. Letter of a Maryland officer 9/1/76: Field, 487-490. Gist letter 8/30/76: 5 Force I, 1232-1233. Fitch, 30. There appears to have been a gap between the two American brigades from the outset. Moreover, Parson's wing, following the tree line, would have curved slightly toward the British right, giving the entire American line an arc-like appearance, especially on its extreme left.
27. The New York companies, as we know, had been equipped at Halifax. Unless they continually wore the same civilian apparel they enlisted in, they must also have drawn clothing out of the

British stores. If so, they would now have been dressed in red coats—possibly short light infantry coats. They suffered a disproportionate number of casualties compared to the rest of Grant's division; these high losses cannot otherwise be readily accounted for than their presence on the skirmish line. 5 Force I, 1259.

28. Letter of a Maryland officer 9/1/76: op. cit. Haslet-Rodney 10/4/76: 5 Force II, 882. The Marylanders had red uniform coats for parade, but today were clad in functional hunting shirts. Atlee's regiment wore blue coats, and the Cambridge Army regiments—the 17th Continentals was one—wore brown. It is not likely, though, that either Atlee's or the 17th was completely uniformed, or even close to it.

29. Atlee journal: op. cit. Atlee leaves the impression that he was in charge of the left wing and initiated all its activities. That responsibility, of course, belonged to General Parsons.

30. Activities in the Gowanus hills are from the Atlee journal, supplemented by the Parsons letters and by Fitch.

31. Col. Grant's hat was taken to Washington's headquarters, and the misinformation that General Grant had been killed spread through the Continental Army.

32. Stirling-Washington 8/29/76: op. cit. Gist letter 8/30/76: op. cit.

33. Howe-Germain 9/3/76: op. cit. Robertson, 94. Two companies of Marines had been attached to the 2nd Grenadier Battalion at Halifax, and did not rejoin their parent units left in garrison there. Kemble Papers I, 353.

34. Murray-his sister 8/31/76: op. cit. Haslet-Rodney 10/4/76: op. cit. Letter of a Maryland officer 9/1/76: op. cit. 5 Force I, 1258, 1259.

35. Stirling-Washington 8/29/76: op. cit. Gist letter 8/30/76: op. cit. 5 Force II, 1012-1013. Onderdonk S/K, 151-152. The five Maryland companies were those of Captain Peter Adams, Barton Lucas, Benjamin Ford and Daniel Bowie from the battalion, and Capt. Edward Veazey's independent company. Adams and Lucas were sick absent (the camp fever again), while Veazey had been killed earlier in the day. Col. Smallwood later complained that the mill dam had been destroyed by New England troops, giving us another sample of regional backbiting. The dam was no longer of any use to Stirling's column; the ground before it was already occupied by British forces.

36. Gist letter 8/30/76: op. cit. Stirling-Washington 8/29/76: op. cit. Clinton, 43. Johnston II, 177, 179.

37. Smallwood-Md. Convention 10/12/76: op. cit. 5 Force I, 1257. Grant's artillery did continue "playing upon" the American column during its quarter-mile withdrawal, and even during its flight across the salt marsh. Field, 488-489.

38. Parsons-Adams 8/29/76: op. cit.

39. Atlee journal: op. cit. 5 Force I, 1250. Johnston II, 38-39.

40. Fitch, 30-31. Field, 434-435. Heeringen-Lossberg: Lowell, 67. Johnston II, 176-179 passim, 180-182. Hessian accounts neither identify Lt. Col. Clark nor the 17th Regiment, but no other unit could have surrendered so many men with a commanding officer at one time. The captured flag was of red damask with the LIBERTY motto.

41. Johnston II, 176-178 passim, 186. 5 Force II, 882. "A Return of Col. Hallers Battalion" 9/20/76: NA, Jacket 78, No. 4.

42. Parsons-Adams 8/29/76: op. cit.

Notes: Chapter X

1. Howe-Stephens 8/31/76: Nav. Doc. VI, 374-375. Ibid, 324-325, 353-354. Collier, 304. Muenchhausen, 24. A number of Americans conceived the notion that Grant received a strong reinforcement from the squadron. But neither Lord Howe's report nor the several ships' journals make any mention of it, and a sizeable debarkation could hardly have been made without bringing up transports. In any event, the only reserve available was Lossberg's Hessian brigade, which remained on Staten Island.

2. Nav. Doc. VI, 370.

3. Johnston I, 189n. 5 Force I, 1193-1194. Spencer's division was made up of Parsons's and Wadsworth's brigades.

4. Smallwood-Md. Convention 10/12/76: 5 Force II, 1012-1013. Johnston II, 65. Martin, 26.

5. Munsell account: Field, 502. Ibid, 489. Onderdonk S/K, 150. Another of the day's traditions is that Putnam encouraged the men on the lines by reliving last year's glories. "Gentlemen, by your dress I conclude you are country-men," he is supposed to have said, "and if so, are good marksmen. Now don't fire till you see the white of their eyes." Onderdonk Q, 92.

6. Holmes statement, Onderdonk S/K, 40. Independent Gazette, or the New York Journal Revived, 12/20/83: William H. W. Sabine, *Suppressed History of General Nathaniel Woodhull*, New York, 1954, 135ff. 5 Force I, 1254, 1258. Johnston II, 167, 168. Fitch, 31. Some American prisoners were used by the Hessians to haul their battalion guns, thereby relieving German soldiers of that duty—demeaning, perhaps, but not intentionally brutal. Other captives—officers and men—were subjected to taunts, physical abuse, stripping of personal effects and mock hanging. More shocking still was the occasional bayoneting of already wounded men. Among the most vituperative captors were the camp women, some of whom had lost husbands in the engagement; it is interesting that they were permitted to follow the Army right into an active combat zone. The Marines captured by the Americans were sent to Fairfield County in Connecticut.

7. Graydon, 163-164. Nav. Doc. VI, 325. Leggett, 11. Johnston II, 43, 54. 5 Force I, 1196, 1257.

8. Graydon, 165. Silliman-his wife 8/29/76: Johnston II, 54. Ibid, 43. 5 Force I, 1257.

9. Scott-Jay 9/6/76: Johnston II, 37. Graydon, 164-165. Munsell account: op. cit. Hitchcock-Little 8/29/76: Johnston II, 76. Tallmadge, 10. Ironically, at least one British professional held a higher opinion of the Brooklyn lines than the American defenders. When examined by Parliament about them three years later, Capt. John Montresor of the Engineers stated the lines "were about a mile and a half in extent, including the angles, cannon proof, with a chain of five redoubts, or rather fortresses, with ditches, as had also the lines that formed the intervals, raised on the parapet and the counterscarp, and the whole surrounded by a most formidable abbatties." When asked if the left flank might have been turned, he answered that "Sir William Howe, on the enemy's evacuating, followed the road to the point, to examine and see if he could get out at that part, which he could not do, and we were obliged to return and go out of a sally port of the lines." He said further that the redoubts "could not be taken by assault, but by approaches, as they were rather fortresses than redoubts." Johnston I, 73-74n. But General Clinton remained unconvinced that the lines could not have been stormed at the "close of the action," especially on one or both of the extended flanks where there were no redoubts. His remarks, penned on Sproule's "A Plan of the Environs of Brooklyn," appear in full on this map reproduced elsewhere in this volume. The lines were demolished by the British shortly after their acquisition.

10. Graydon, 165. Johnston II, 37. Field, 518-519. Martin, 23, 27. Leggett, 11.

11. Little-his son 9/1/76: Johnston II, 43. BrM 107:5 Sproule. Heath, 47. NYPC I, 593, 597. 5 Force I, 1185, 1215.

12. Council of General Officers 8/29/76: GW V, 508-509; 5 Force I, 1246. Generals Nixon and Heard, who commanded the two brigades of the "permanent" Long Island garrison, were not at the council; presumably their duties kept them on the lines. McDougall's presence suggests that the 1st and/or 3rd New York Regiments may have been at Brooklyn; these two units plus the 19th Continentals and a provision regiment of artificers made up his brigade. By the same token, Fellows's brigade of Mas-

sachusetts levies may have been present as well.

13. General Orders 8/29/76: Johnston II, 30-31. Mifflin-Heath 8/29/76: Johnston I, 218. Washington-Hughes 8/22/84: Isaac Q. Leake, *Life and Times of General John Lamb*, Albany, 1857, 362-363.

14. 5 Force I, 1211, II, 882. NYPC I, 601. Smith diary 8/29/76: Frederic G. Mather, *The Refugees of 1776 from Long Island to Connecticut*, Albany, 1913, 1012. Graydon, 167. Leggett, 11-12. Tallmadge, 10-11. Linn & Egle I, 307-308. Chester's regiment had been at Bedford Pass on Tuesday. Its inclusion in the rear guard is another indication there had been no panic-stricken withdrawal from that post.

15. Field, 503. Linn & Egle I, 308. Martin, 28-29. Tallmadge, 10. Onderdonk S/K, 165.

16. Linn & Egle I, 307. Field, 519. GW V, 506.

17. Chambers-his wife 9/3/76: Linn & Egle I, 308. Tallmadge, 10-11. Leggett, 12. Onderdonk S/K, 165.Yet another tradition describes a melodramatic shift in wind about midnight, immobilizing all the sailing craft and causing some anxious moments. Contemporary accounts of the event, however, do not appear to be extant. At any rate the greater part of the evacuation fleet, in terms of capacity, must have been the flat-bottomed boats which had been built during the summer and which were operated by sweeps.

18. Montresor Journals: New York Historical Society, *Collections*, XIV, 122. Field, 442-443, 462-465. Baurmeister, 40-41. Linn & Egle I, 309. Tallmadge, 11. Leggett, 12.

19. Nav. Doc. VI, 377-378, 655. Nash journal: Stokes V, 1006. Between Long Island and Governor's Island, Howe captured 26 pieces of iron ordnance that had not been removed: six 32-pounders, one 24, four 18's, two 12's, two 9's, eight 6's and three 3's. Six brass field pieces had already been taken during the battle: a 5½-inch howitzer, four 6-pounders and a 3-pounder. Thus each of the three artillery detachments known to have been engaged had two guns. Despite the effort to take all portable materiel to New York, Howe also captured an uninventoried quantity of shot, shells, ammunition, tools, small arms, pikes, ammunition carts, "and many other articles." Return 9/3/76: 5 Force I, 1258.

20. NYPC II, 273, 274.

21. Robertson, 94. Onderdonk Q, 103-104. NYPC I, 617, 619. Scott-Jay 9/6/76: Henry P. Johnston, editor, *The Correspondence and Public Papers of John Jay*, New York, 1896, I, 78-83. There is some indication that Gen. Woodhull was persuaded to formally surrender Suffolk County to his captors. On 27 September the *Connecticut Gazette* published some intercepted correspondence of Brig. Gen. Oliver DeLancey, recently appointed to command the loyal New York militia. DeLancey identifies Woodhull as one of two prominent Suffolk men "who have signified . . . that the Inhabitants of said County are desirous of laying down their Arms and again becoming loyal and obedient Subjects," The entire correspondence appears in 5 Force II, 504-506.

22. NYPC I, 603-604; II, 227, 228, 334. Smith diary: Mather, *Refugees of 1776*, 1012. Birdsall was the lieutenant colonel of the 2nd Queens County Regiment and had served as a company commander in Smith's levies. His detachment in Connecticut was attached to Livingston's New York Continentals.

23. NYPC I, 620. Onderdonk Q, 102ff, 114-115. Gen. Heath could see the British dragoons in Flushing and organized a party to disperse them, but it was prevented from crossing by the heavy weather. 5 Force I, 1216, 1238.

24. Erskine-Suffolk County 8/29/76: 5 Force I, 1211-1212. Hobart & Townsend-N.Y. Convention 8/30 & 31/76: NYPC II, 291, 292. 5 Force I, 1261. NYPC I, 596, 597-598.

25. Livingston-Conn. Council 9/4/76: 5 Force II, 170. Ibid I, 1235-1236, 1260-1262.

26. 5 Force II, 252, 265, 296, 336. Estimates have been made that some 35% of the population of Suffolk County took refuge in Connecticut in 1776. Mather, *Refugees of 1776*, 187.

27. General Orders 8/30-31/76: GW V, 499-504. Robertson, 95.

APPENDIX A

"Putrid Fever" and the Continental Army

In the loose medical terminology of the day, putrid fever also went by the names of camp fever, jail fever, ship fever and hospital fever, depending on the circumstance of its incidence. In terms of modern identification the likeliest candidates—typhoid fever and epidemic typhus—are so similar in their outward manifestations that they were not distinguished as two different ailments until 1837. But distinct they are. A key factor in the spread of typhoid fever is fecal contamination; the causative microbe is passed out of the victim's body in his excreta. The disease may then be carried indirectly by water, food, flies, by contact with sick patients or even with "carriers" who are themselves infected but who display no apparent symptoms. Epidemic typhus, on the other hand, is passed from one person to another by the transfer of lice. The insect becomes infected from a sick host, then carries the microbe to a new host whose blood stream is introduced to the disease at the next feeding.[1]

The very existence of microbes, of course, was unsuspected by contemporary medicine, but it was recognized that sanitation had something to do with inhibiting the spread of infection. General Washington ordered his officers not only to keep themselves and their quarters clean, but to inspect the men's quarters and "impress on them the necessity of frequently changing their linen." A frequent change of shirts and breeches (and "drawers", for those who had them) would indeed have been an excellent prophylactic measure for either typhoid fever or typhus. In the case of typhoid, contamination might have been removed to a great extent in the process of laundering and sun-drying. In the case of typhus, lice might have been washed out of clothing seams where they commonly breed. But even assuming an inclination to do so, the private soldier had precious little extra clothing to change into. Months of grueling labor on the fortifications had left him tattered and grimy. Unlike his British counterpart, the Continental was denied the services of so many camp women per company to handle the laundry, cooking and general cleaning up. For parades and inspections he was very apt to take the easy course and simply put on his cleanest dirty shirt.[2]

There is some circumstantial evidence that the infection may have been introduced from the Continental Navy. In April, when the Cambridge Army was passing through Connecticut en route to New York City, two hundred soldiers were detached at New London to serve aboard the fleet. Commodore Hopkins had just returned from a cruise to the Bahamas, and so many of his seamen were down with a "malignant fever" that naval operations were brought to a standstill. It was hoped the augmentation would help keep the fleet active, but new cases of fever developed at a rapid rate and Hopkins could do little more than shift his base to Providence. Meanwhile, when Washington ultimately discovered the weak state of his own forces he called for the return of the borrowed men, and Lieutenant John Paul Jones delivered the bulk of them to New York on 18 May. Two months later General Greene could observe: "Those that were on board the fleet brought a putrid fever into the Camp at their return from the Ships, that has raged to a prodigious degree." It is possible, of course, that the Navy connection is entirely coincidental, and that the seamen were infected with a mosquito-borne tropical disease such as malaria or yellow fever.[3]

1. Geoffrey Marks and William K. Beatty, *Epidemics,* New York, 1976, 164-167; Frederick E. Cartwright, *Disease and History,* New York, 1972, 84. Cartwright maintains the United States was not infected with typhus until early in the nineteenth century.
2. General Orders 7/11/76: GW V, 263.
3. Greene-Cooke 7/22/76: Greene Papers I, 260. Nav. Doc. IV, 1252, 1358; V, 151-153, 199.

APPENDIX B:

Ground Forces in the New York Theater

TABLE OF ORGANIZATION: THE GRAND ARMY

Gen. George Washington, Commander-in-Chief
Col. Joseph Reed, Adjutant General

DIVISION: MAJ. GEN. ISRAEL PUTNAM

Brigade: Brig. Gen. James Clinton[1]
3rd Continentals: Col. Ebenezer Learned (Mass.)
13th Continentals: Col. Joseph Read (Mass.)
23rd Continentals: Col. John Bailey (Mass.)
26th Continentals: Col. Loammi Baldwin (Mass.)
2nd New York Continentals: Lt. Col. Henry B. Livingston[2]

Brigade: Brig. Gen. John Morin Scott
New York Levies: Col. John Lasher
New York Levies: Col. William Malcolm
New York Levies: Col. Samuel Drake
New York Levies: Col. Cornelius Humphrey[3]
New York State Artillery: Capt. Alexander Hamilton

Brigade: Brig. Gen. John Fellows
Massachusetts Levies: Col. Jonathan Smith
Massachusetts Levies: Col. Simeon Cary
Massachusetts Levies: Col. Jonathan Holman
14th Continentals: Col. John Glover (Mass.)

DIVISION: MAJ. GEN. WILLIAM HEATH

Brigade: Brig. Gen. Thomas Mifflin
3rd Pennsylvania Continentals: Col. John Shee
5th Pennsylvania Continentals: Col. Robert Magaw
11th Continentals: Col. Daniel Hitchcock (R.I.)[4]
16th Continentals: Col. Paul Dudley Sargent (Mass.)
27th Continentals: Col. Israel Hutchinson (Mass.).
Connecticut Continentals: Col. Andrew Ward[5]

Brigade: Brig. Gen. George Clinton
New York Levies: Col. Levi Pawling
New York Levies: Col. Jacobus Swartwout
New York Levies: Col. Morris Graham
New York Levies: Col. Thomas Thomas
New York Levies: Col. Isaac Nicoll

DIVISION: MAJ. GEN. JOSEPH SPENCER

Brigade: Brig. Gen. Samuel Holden Parsons
10th Continentals: Col. John Tyler (Conn.)
17th Continentals: Col. Jedediah Huntington (Conn.)
20th Continentals: Col. John Durkee (Conn.)[6]
21st Continentals: Col. Jonathan Ward (Mass.)
22nd Continentals: Col. Samuel Wyllys (Conn.)

Brigade: Brig. Gen. James Wadsworth
1st Connecticut Levies: Col. Gold Selleck Silliman

2nd Connecticut Levies: Col. Fisher Gay[7]
3rd Connecticut Levies: Col. Comfort Sage
4th Connecticut Levies: Col. Samuel Selden
5th Connecticut Levies: Col. William Douglas
6th Connecticut Levies: Col. John Chester
Connecticut State Regulars: Col. Philip Burr Bradley[8]

DIVISION: MAJ. GEN. JOHN SULLIVAN

Brigade: Brig. Gen. William Alexander (Lord Stirling)
Delaware Continentals: Col. John Haslet
Maryland State Regulars: Col. William Smallwood
Pennsylvania State Riflemen: Col. Samuel Miles
Pennsylvania State Musketry: Col. Samuel Atlee
1st Pennsylvania Flying Camp: Col. James Cunningham
2nd Pennsylvania Flying Camp: Col. Henry Haller
Pennsylvania Associators: Lt. Col. Peter Kachlein

Brigade: Brig. Gen. Alexander McDougall
1st New York Continentals: Lt. Col. Herman Zedwitz[9]
3rd New York Continentals: Col. Rudolphus Ritzema
19th Continentals: Col. Charles Webb (Conn.)
Continental Artificers: Col. Jonathan Brewer[10]

DIVISION: MAJ. GEN. NATHANAEL GREENE

Brigade: Brig. Gen. John Nixon
1st Continentals: Col. Edward Hand (Pa.)
4th Continentals: Lt. Col. Thomas Nixon (Mass.)
7th Continentals: Col. William Prescott (Mass.)
9th Continentals: Col. James Mitchell Varnum (R.I.)
12th Continentals: Col. Moses Little (Mass.)
New York Levies: Col. Josiah Smith
New York Levies: Col. Jeromus Remsen

Brigade: Brig. Gen. Nathaniel Heard
New Jersey Levies: Col. Philip van Cortland
New Jersey Levies: Col. David Forman
New Jersey Levies: Col. Ephraim Martin
New Jersey Levies: Col. Philip Johnston
New Jersey Levies: Col. Silas Newcomb

WESTERN DIVISION, CONNECTICUT MILITIA

Brigade: Brig. Gen. Oliver Wolcott
1st Connecticut Militia: Maj. Roger Newberry
2nd Connecticut Militia: Lt. Col. Jabez Thompson
4th Connecticut Militia: Lt. Col. Ichabod Lewis
6th Connecticut Militia: Col. Elizur Talcott
9th Connecticut Militia: Lt. Col. John Mead
10th Connecticut Militia: Lt. Col. Jonathan Baldwin
13th Connecticut Militia: Col. Benjamin Hinman
15th Connecticut Militia: Lt. Col. Selah Heart
16th Connecticut Militia: Col. Joseph Platt Cook
17th Connecticut Militia: Col. Epaphrus Sheldon
18th Connecticut Militia: Col. Jonathan Pettibone
19th Connecticut Militia: Lt. Col. George Pitkin
22nd Connecticut Militia: Col. Samuel Chapman
23rd Connecticut Militia: Col. Matthew Talcott

ARTILLERY

Continental Artillery: Col. Henry Knox
New York Continental Artillery: Capt. Sebastian Bauman

For an analysis of the strength of the Grand Army and its components see Chapter VI. It would be reasonable to assume a 30%

disability rate by the end of August, from camp fever and other causes. Thus the probable effective strength would be reduced from 34,800 to approximately 24,400.

1. Gen. Clinton concurrently served as commandant in the Highlands; in his absence Col. Read acted as brigade commander.
2. Five companies of the 2nd New York were posted to the Highlands; Lt. Col. Livingston and the remaining three companies to Suffolk County.
3. Col. Humphrey and five of his ten companies were posted to the Highlands.
4. The 11th Continentals did not join the brigade, but remained at its former post in Brooklyn.
5. Ward's Connecticut was posted to Burdett's Ferry (Fort Lee).
6. The 20th Continentals was posted first to Bergen Neck and then to Paulus Hook.
7. Col. Gay died of natural causes, 22 August.
8. Bradley's Connecticut was posted to Bergen Neck.
9. Lt. Col. Zedwitz was cashiered, 26 August.
10. Except for three permanent companies, the artificer regiment was a provisional unit made up of skilled men on temporary assignment from their parent regiments.

TABLE OF ORGANIZATION: NEW YORK MILITIA

1st New York Brigade
1st New York County: Col. Henry Remsen
2nd New York County: Col. John Jay
3rd New York County: Col. Abraham P. Lott
1st Independents: Col. John Lasher
2nd Independents: Col. William Malcolm
New York County Light Horse: Capt. John Leary
Kings County: Col. Rutgert van Brunt
Kings County Light Horse: Capt. Adolph Waldron
Kings County Light Horse: Capt. Lambert Suydam
Richmond County: Col. Abraham Jones

3rd New York Brigade: Brig. Gen. Nathaniel Woodhull
1st Queens County: Col. Jeromus Remsen
2nd Queens County: Col. John Sands
Queens County Light Horse: Capt. Daniel Lawrence
1st Suffolk County: Col. William Floyd
2nd Suffolk County: Col. David Mulford
3rd Suffolk County: Col. Thomas Terry
Suffolk County Minutemen: Col. Josiah Smith
Suffolk County Artillery: Capt. William Rogers

The following fundamental changes took place in June and early July, as described in the text: (1) The Suffolk County minutemen were ''abolished'' and the men returned to their parent units. (2) The 1st and 2nd New York City Independents were drafted into Continental service as New Levies. (3) The Richmond County regiment ended its existence with the British occupation of Staten Island.

Quotas Levied on the 1st and 3rd Brigades
18 February: Continental service (voluntary enlistment only). 8 companies of 4 officers and 86 men from New York County, 3 from Suffolk, 1 from Queens, 1 between Kings and Richmond.
7 June: Scott's Brigade. 1,200 men from New York County, 200 from Suffolk, 175 from Queens, 58 from Kings, 57 from Richmond.
20 July: Smith's Regiment. 25% of remaining militia from Suffolk, Queens, Kings.
10 August: Remsen's Regiment. 50% of remaining militia from Queens, Kings.

TABLE OF ORGANIZATION: THE BRITISH ARMY

Gen. William Howe, Commander-in-Chief
Lt. Col. James Paterson, Adjutant General

Lt. Gen. Henry Clinton
Lt. Gen. Hugh Earl Percy

1st Brigade: Maj. Gen. James Robertson
4th King's Own: Lt. Col. Henry Blunt
15th Regiment of Foot: Lt. Col. John Bird
27th Inniskillings: Lt. Col. John Maxwell
45th Regiment of Foot

2nd Brigade: Maj. Gen. Robert Pigot
5th Regiment of Foot: Lt. Col. William Walcott
28th Regiment of Foot
35th Regiment of Foot: Lt. Col. Robert Carr
49th Regiment of Foot: Lt. Col. Sir Henry Calder

3rd Brigade: Maj. Gen. Valentine Jones
10th Regiment of Foot: Maj. John Vatass
37th Regiment of Foot: Lt. Col. Robert Abercromby
38th Regiment of Foot: Lt. Col. William Butler
52nd Regiment of Foot: Lt. Col. Mungo Campbell

4th Brigade: Maj. Gen. James Grant
17th Regiment of Foot: Lt. Col. Charles Mawhood
40th Regiment of Foot: Lt. Col. James Grant
46th Regiment of Foot: Lt. Col. Enoch Markham
55th Regiment of Foot: Maj. Cornelius Cuyler

5th Brigade: Brig. Gen. Francis Smith
22nd Regiment of Foot: Lt. Col. John Campbell
43rd Regiment of Foot: Lt. Col. George Clerk
54th Regiment of Foot: Lt. Col. Alured Clark
63rd Regiment of Foot: Maj. Francis Sill

6th Brigade: Brig. Gen. James Agnew
23rd Royal Welsh Fusiliers: Lt. Col. Benjamin Bernard
44th Regiment of Foot: Maj. Henry Hope
57th Regiment of Foot: Lt. Col. John Campbell
64th Regiment of Foot: Maj. Robert McLeroth

Reserve Corps: Lt. Gen. Charles Cornwallis
33rd Regiment of Foot: Lt. Col. James Webster
42nd Royal Highlanders: Lt. Col. Thomas Sterling

Brigade of Grenadiers: Maj. Gen. John Vaughan
1st Grenadier Battalion: Lt. Col. William Medows
2nd Grenadier Battalion: Lt. Col. Henry Monckton
3rd Grenadier Battalion: Maj. James Marsh
4th Grenadier Battalion:

Brigade of Light Infantry: Brig. Gen. Alexander Leslie
1st Light Infantry Battalion: Maj. Thomas Musgrave
2nd Light Infantry Battalion: Maj. John Maitland
3rd Light Infantry Battalion: Maj. Henry Johnson

Unbrigaded Units
Detachment, Brigade of Foot Guards: Brig. Gen. Edward Mathew
71st Fraser's Highlanders: Brig. Gen. Sir William Erskine
17th Light Dragoons: Lt. Col. Samuel Birch
1st New York Provincial Company: Capt. Archibald Campbell
2nd New York Provincial Company: Capt. Alexander Grant

Detachment, Royal Artillery: Brig. Gen. Samuel Cleaveland

In 1776 senior officers were temporarily upgraded, presumably to prevent their being outranked by Hessians of the same grade. Thus Major General Howe was elevated to full General; Major Generals Clinton, Percy and Cornwallis to Lieutenant General; Brigadiers Vaughan, Pigot, Jones, Grant and Robertson to Major General; full Colonels to Brigadier General. The inflated rank was effective from 1 January, and operated only in America. 4 Force IV, 902-903; Kemble Papers I, 351.

TABLE OF ORGANIZATION: THE HESSE-CASSEL ARMY

Lt. Gen. Leopold Philipp von Heister, Commander-in-Chief
Maj. Carl Leopold Baurmeister, Adjutant General

Brigade: Maj. Gen. Werner von Mirbach
Fusilier Regt. v. Knyphausen: Col. Henrich v. Borck
Fusilier Regt. v. Lossberg: Col. Henrich A. v. Heeringen
Grenadier Regt. Rall: Col. Johann G. Rall

Brigade: Maj. Gen. Johann Daniel Stirn
Musketeer Regt. v. Donop: Col. David U. v. Gosen
Musketeer Regt. v. Mirbach: Col. Johann A. v. Loos
Musketeer Regt. Erbprinz: Col. Carl W. v. Hachenberg

Brigade: Col. Friedrich Wilhelm von Lossberg
Fusilier Regt. v. Ditfurth: Col. Carl v. Bose
Musketeer Regt. v. Trumbach: Col. Carl E. v. Bischhausen
Prinz Carl Musketeer Regt.: Lt. Col. George E. v. Lengercke
Leib Infantry Regt.: Col. Friedrich W. v. Wurmb

Brigade: Col. Carl Emil von Donop
Grenadier Bn. v. Linsing: Lt. Col. Otto C. v. Linsing
Grenadier Bn. v. Block: Lt. Col.—v. Block
Grenadier Bn. v. Minnegerode: Lt. Col. Friedrich L. v. Minnegerode
Jaeger Company: Capt. Carl A. v. Wreden

Artillery Corps: Maj. George H. Pauli

APPENDIX C:

Naval Vessels in the New York Theater

AMERICAN NAVAL FORCES AT NEW YORK

Lt. Col. Benjamin Tupper, Commodore

OUTER SQUADRON

Continental Vessels
Sloop	*Hester*	Capt.------Burr
Schooner	*Mifflin*	
Sloop	*Schuyler*	Capt. Charles Pond

New York State Vessels
Sloop	*Montgomerie*	Capt. William Rogers
Schooner	*Putnam*	Capt. Thomas Cregier

INNER SQUADRON

Continental Vessels
Row Galley	*Lady Washington*	Capt. Robert Cook
Row Galley	*Independence*	Capt. Jøhn Baker

Connecticut State Vessels
Row Galley	*Shark*	Capt. Theophilus Stanton
Row Galley	*Crane*	Capt. Jehiel Tinker
Row Galley	*Whiting*	Capt. John McCleave

Rhode Island State Vessels
Row Galley	*Washington*	Capt.------Hill
Row Galley	*Spitfire*	Capt. John Grimes

Schuyler began service as a New York state vessel under Capt. James Smith, but by June had been transferred to Continental ownership. *Putnam* remained a state vessel, but was ordered by the Provincial Congress to place herself under Commodore Tupper's immediate command. *Montgomerie* remained under state jurisdiction throughout, but she carried a commission from the Continental Congress and eventually wound up in company with *Schuyler,* off southern Long Island.

According to one of her payrolls, *Putnam* had a crew of 30, including officers. *Montgomerie's* complement was 60, and she mounted six carriage guns. Nav. Doc. V, 32; Fernow, 529-533.

BRITISH NAVAL FORCES AT NEW YORK

Vice Admiral Richard Lord Viscount Howe
Vice Admiral Molyneaux Shuldham
Commodore Sir Peter Parker
Commodore William Hotham

Rate	Name	Guns	Men	Commander
3rd	*Eagle*	64	520	Capt. Henry Duncan
	Asia	64	500	Capt. George Vandeput
4th	*Chatham*	50	370	Capt. John Raynor
	Preston	50	367	Capt. Samuel Uppleby
	Bristol	50	367	Capt. Toby Caulfield
	Centurion	50	350	Capt. Richard Brathwaite
	Renown	50	350	Capt. Francis Banks
	Experiment	50	300	Capt. William Williams
5th	*Rainbow*	44	280	Capt. Sir George Collier
	Phoenix	44	280	Capt. Hyde Parker, Jr.
	Roebuck	44	280	Capt. Andrew Snape Hamond
	Emerald	32	220	Capt. Benjamin Caldwell
	Repulse	32	220	Capt. Henry Davis
	Flora	32	220	Capt. John Brisbane
	Brune	32	220	Capt. James Ferguson
	Niger	32	220	Capt. George Talbot
6th	*Greyhound*	28	200	Capt. Archibald Dickson
	Solebay	28	200	Capt. Thomas Symonds
	Syren	28	200	Capt. Tobias Furneaux
	Rose	20	160	Capt. James Wallace
	Mercury	20	160	Capt. James Montagu
	Lively	20	160	Capt. Thomas Bishop.
Sloop	*Tamar*	16	125	Lieut. Christopher Mason
	Kingsfisher	14	125	Capt. Alexander Graeme
	Senegal	14	125	Capt. Roger Curtis
	Swan	14	125	Capt. James Ayscough
Bomb	*Thunder*	8	80	Capt. Anthony Molloy
	Carcass	8	70	Lieut. Robert Dring
Brig	*Halifax*	6	40	Lieut. William Quarme
Schooner	*St. Lawrence*	6	30	Lieut. John Graves
	Tryal	6	30	Lieut. John Brown
Fireship	*Strombolo*	—	45	Capt. Charles Phipps
Storeship	*Adventure*	4	40	Lieut. John Hallum

Besides the carriage guns listed above, *Halifax, St. Lawrence* and *Tryal* carried 10 swivel guns and *Adventure* 8 swivel guns.

Estimated Effective Combat Strengths, 27 August

AMERICAN FORCES ON THE OUTER PERIMETER

Gowanus Road

17th Continentals: Lt. Col. Joel Clark	300	
Del. Continentals: Maj. Thomas McDonough	450	
Md. Regulars: Maj. Mordecai Gist	525	
Pa. Regulars: Col. Samuel Atlee	250	
1st Pa. Flying Camp: Lt. Col. William Hay	175	
2nd Pa. Flying Camp: Lt. Col. Nicholas Lutz	175	
Pa. Associators: Lt. Col. Peter Kachlein	225	
	2,100	

Flatbush Pass

11th Continentals: Lt. Col. Ezekiel Cornell	250	
12th Continentals: Lt. Col. William Henshaw	275	
N.J. Levies: Col. Philip Johnston	275	
Conn Partisans: Lt. Col. Thomas Knowlton	100	
	900	

Bedford Pass and Eastern Wood

22nd Continentals: Col. Samuel Wyllys	300	
6th Conn. Levies: Lt. Col. Solomon Wills	250	
Pa. Riflemen: Col. Samuel Miles		
1st Battalion: Lt. Col. James Piper	325	
2nd Battalion: Lt. Col. Daniel Brodhead	275	
	1,150	
	4,150	
Artillery	120	
	4,270	

There are no hard figures for the Americans actually engaged; any analysis has to fall back, in the end, on arbitrary speculation. What effects did the camp fever infection have on any given unit by 27 August? How many men were likely to have been on assignment outside the regiment—in the artillery, for example, or the artificers, or the sea service? What was the probable rate of recruitment versus attrition? By September the 1st Pennsylvania Flying Camp had three companies of Bucks County Associators attached to it; had they been there in August? And so forth.

The dated general returns closest in time to the battle—before and after—are those of 8 August and 21 September. Neither the Delaware Continentals nor any of the Maryland or Pennsylvania state units appear on the former, while the New Levies are seen coming in piecemeal from New Jersey and Connecticut. By the latter part of September the picture is no clearer; the Army had evacuated New York City and was still in a relatively unstable condition.[1]

The three artillery companies engaged outside the lines present yet another problem. Each was commanded, as far as we know, by a captain-lieutenant (usually an artillery officer, who ranked just below captain). But most if not all of the full captains were still present, probably at the stationary batteries, so it is likely that these mobile units were in fact detachments of less than company strength. Such mobile detachments—at least four—had been formed in early August to serve with different brigades. As it happens, Captain-Lieutenants Carpenter and Johnston were two of the detachment commanders appointed to this service. Each such unit engaged on Long Island had two field pieces and would have required about 30 matrosses to work them; officers, sergeants, corporals, drums and fifes may have brought the figure close to 40—or 120 in all.[2]

BRITISH FORCES ON LONG ISLAND

Gen. Clinton's Vanguard

1st Brigade	1,185	
Grenadiers	1,440	
Light Infantry	1,115	
33rd Foot	315	
71st Highlanders	1,250	
17th Light Dragoons	120	5,525
Gen. Percy's Division		
2nd Brigade	1,235	
3rd Brigade	1,175	
5th Brigade	1,240	
Guards	1,100	4,750
Gen. Grant's Division		
4th Brigade	1,255	
6th Brigade	1,225	
42nd Highlanders	605	
New York Companies	80	3,165
		13,340
Artillery		*500*
		13,840

Figures for the Grenadiers, 3rd Light Infantry, 33rd Foot, 42nd Highlanders and the 3rd, 4th, 5th and 6th Brigades are from an embarkation return dated August. Those for the 1st and 2nd Light Infantry and the 1st and 2nd Brigades are from an embarkation return dated 11 June, with estimates of the missing Charleston regiments (15th and 28th) factored in. That for the 71st Highlanders is estimated, based on the regiment's known strength in 1777; there had been no extraordinary losses in the interim. Both Highland units were far below their established strengths, even allowing for the prisoners lost at sea and in Boston harbor. The Guards, on the other hand, did not have to rely on recruiting at large and so must have been at their establishment or close to it.[3]

Captain Grant had almost 40 New Yorkers (or Scottish emigrants to New York) enlisted by late February. There is no evidence he got any more; even so, this represents a fair-sized company as British companies went. If Captain Campbell had very many less it is unlikely his would have been commissioned the senior company of the two.[4]

HESSE-CASSEL FORCES ON LONG ISLAND

Gen. von Heister's Division[5]

Mirbach's Brigade	2,055	
Stirn's Brigade	2,080	
Donop's Brigade	1,795	5,930
Artillery		*240*
		6,170

1. These two returns are in 5 Force I, 763-764; II, 449-452. Also helpful are: Flying Camp return 7/25/76, ibid I, 475; Smallwood letter 10/12/76, ibid II, 1011-1014; undated return of Kachlein's battalion in *Pennsylvania Archives, Second Series* XIV, 571-572; sundry regimental returns in National Archives Record Group 93
2. General Orders 8/9/76: GW V, 407. The four captain-lieutenants were Benajah Carpenter, John Johnston, Winthrop Sargent and Joseph Crane. It is possible that Crane, of the New York Continental company, commanded the artillery at Flatbush Pass.
3. WO 36-3-X/LO 7646. Figures for the 17th Light Dragoons and the Artillery are from Kemble Papers I, 84.
4. NYPC II, 160. Kemble Papers I, 377.
5. "A List of the Hessian Troops arrived at Spithead" 4/26/76: Nav. Doc. IV, 1063-1064. Estimates of the missing regiments (Rall and Mirbach) are factored in.

American, British and Hessian Casualties

AMERICAN CASUALTIES

Specific information about American casualties is as difficult to come by as any other American statistical data concerning the battle. We are ultimately obliged to turn to a British source: a return compiled by Joshua Loring, the British Commissary of Prisoners, purporting to show the precise numbers captured in each grade. Loring's return contains its share of flaws, but it presents a reasonably accurate picture for all that, and has since formed a basis for subsequent revisions and identifications. The breakdown of captured officers is especially comprehensive. With corrections, it appears the British captured 3 general officers, 3 colonels, 4 lieutenant colonels, 2 majors, 19 captains, 1 captain-lieutenant, 50 subalterns, 5 staff officers and 4 volunteers. The generals, of course, are Sullivan, Stirling and Woodhull. The field officers are Colonels Miles, Atlee and Johnston; Lieutenant Colonels Clark, Piper, Lutz and Kachlein; Majors Wells and Burd.[1]

At least six officers and an uncommissioned volunteer are known to have been killed in action. These are Lieutenant Colonel Caleb Parry and Volunteer Joseph Moore of Atlee's regiment, Captain Edward Veazey of the 7th Maryland Independent Company, and Captain-Lieutenant Benajah Carpenter of the Continental Artillery. All four were in Stirling's division. Lieutenant Joseph Jacquet of Miles's 1st Battalion fell in the woods east of Bedford Pass. Lieutenants David Sloan and Charles Taylor of the 2nd Battalion were lost either at the same place or by the Bedford Road. In addition, Brigadier General Nathaniel Woodhull of the New York militia, Colonel Philip Johnston of the New Jersey levies, Captain Joseph Jewett of the 17th Continentals, and Lieutenant Joseph Butler of the Maryland Regiment died of their wounds in captivity.[2]

Details of wounded but uncaptured officers can only be gleaned from scattered letters, journals and regimental returns. The list is probably incomplete, but at least we know of Major McDonough and two Delaware lieutenants hit while facing the 2nd Grenadiers, one of Atlee's lieutenants at Gist's last rally, a captain of Miles's 1st Battalion, and a lieutenant of the 11th Continentals.[3]

The Continental Army had no systematic way to determine how many enlisted men had been killed and how many captured; all had to be lumped together as "missing." Only the superficially wounded could have made it to the lines without help; the more seriously injured necessarily had to be left behind (Loring returned 58 wounded prisoners). General Washington's initial estimate of his losses was between 700 and 1,000, which he later narrowed down to "about 800 Men; more than three fourths of which were taken Prisoners." Which is to say, 200 killed and 600 captured. Finally, on 8 October, he called for exact returns to be made by the units engaged.[4]

Figures for most of the Pennsylvanians were already in. On 8 September the regulars returned 120 missing in Miles's 1st Battalion, 47 in the 2nd, and 77 in Atlee's. The 2nd Flying Camp returned 38. There are no losses known in the 1st Flying Camp, but Kachlein's Associators reported 21. By November the 11th Continentals returned 10 men missing; the 12th, 3; the 17th, 186; the 22nd, 9; the 6th Connecticut Levies, 12. Also, 3 men were missing from the 21st Contimentals and 4 from the 2nd Connecticut Levies; both these units had been posted on the lines. Another 4 were lost on 28-30 August. Major Gist reported 247 Maryland casualties (excluding officers), and Colonel Haslet 25 Delawares. Thus the total number of known American missing—killed or prisoners—is 806.[5]

There are no figures, however, for the New Jersey levies. That Colonel Johnston was captured suggests his unit was among the last out of Flatbush Pass. For the rest of the campaign it remained the weakest regiment in Heard's brigade, running about 125 men below average. And the extent of Continental Artillery losses is reflected only in Colonel Knox's pensive remark to his wife: "I have met with some losses in my regiment. They fought like heroes and are gone to glory." Taking a liberal estimate, the casualties of the Jersey levies and the artillerymen *might* bring the total to 900, more or less.[6]

This contrasts with Commissary Loring's return of 1,006 living prisoners. But his list includes General Woodhull and two Long Island militia lieutenants, who were not properly part of the Continental Army. This suggests his total for enlisted men includes whatever militiamen might have been arrested in Kings and Queens Counties as notorious rebels. The light horse companies were on the proscribed list, and probably the Jamaica minutemen as well. Then there is the possibility that Loring's figure is purposely inflated. Unlike their officers, enlisted men remained largely anonymous, and there would have been great potential for graft by drawing extra rations. Loring, after all, was unabashedly in it for the money; his wife was currently on loan to his commander-in-chief.[7]

With only scattered reports about individual soldiers to go by, the true extent of Americans killed in action will perhaps never be determined. On 3 September General Howe reported with a straight face that "their loss is computed to be about 3,300 killed, wounded, prisoners and drowned"—which would have put the mortalities at better than 2,000! But he really didn't have a true body count either. As late as 2 September American corpses had been seen "scattered up and down the Fields," decomposing where they had fallen. There is no reason to believe they were ever gathered and properly buried.[8]

BRITISH AND HESSIAN CASUALTIES

By 3 September General Howe had in hand a comprehensive return of the casualties he had suffered, complete with a unit-by-unit breakdown and the names of the officers. Only five officers were dead. Captains Andrew Neilson and George Logan had been killed when their grenadier companies went to investigate the blue Delaware uniforms. Lieutenant Colonel James Grant and Captain Sir Alexander Murray lost their lives fighting Parsons for the bald hilltop off the Gowanus Road. Lieutenant Lovell of the Royal Artillery probably belonged to General Grant's division as well; Grant's batteries are the only ones known for certain to have been under fire.[9]

Aside from the mortalities, eleven British officers were wounded and one captured, all of them either in Clinton's vanguard or in Grant's division. Those wounded in the vanguard were of the 2nd Light Infantry (1 captain, 2 lieutenants), or the 2nd Grenadiers (Lt. Col. Monckton, 1 captain, 3 lieutenants). The captured officer was Lieutenant John Ragg of the 2nd Grenadiers, who was hurried across the Gowanus Creek morass. Those wounded in Grant's division all belonged to the four regiments— 17th, 23rd, 42nd and 44th—that had been engaged with Parsons in the hills: 1 captain, 4 lieutenants. The Hessians suffered only three officers wounded: Maj. Pauli of the Artillery, 1 captain, 1 lieutenant.

The enlisted men suffered 58 killed, 268 wounded and 30 missing (including the 22 Marines captured with Lieutenant Ragg). Again, the heaviest concentrations are in Clinton's vanguard and in Grant's division:

	K	W	M
1st Brigade	—	2	—
Grenadiers	12	50	22
Light Infantry	11	58	1
33rd Foot	—	4	—
71st Highlanders	3	11	6
17th Light Dragoons	—	—	—

2nd Brigade	—	—	—
3rd Brigade	1	11	1
5th Brigade	2	1	—
Guards	—	—	—
4th Brigade	4	32	—
6th Brigade	18	45	—
42nd Highlanders	—	9	—
New York Companies	4	17	—
Royal Artillery	1	5	—
Hessians	2	23	—

The relatively high casualties sustained by the light infantry and by the 71st Highlanders suggest that the Americans caught in Flatbush Pass gave a better account of themselves than they are usually given credit for. The grenadier losses fall mainly on the 2nd and 4th Battalions, and were probably taken while fighting Gist's Marylanders at the Upper Mills. Those in the 4th and 6th Brigades are principally in the regiments that were engaged with Parsons. The exceptionally high rate in the two New York companies—perhaps 25%—supports the supposition that they formed Grant's skirmish line; at least they must have been under concentrated fire for a considerable period. The Hessian losses were mostly jaegers and grenadiers.

1. "Return of Prisoners taken on Long Island, August 27, 1776" 5 Force I, 1258. Also, a list of captured American officers 9/5/76: ibid I, 1250-1251. With only one detected omission, the names of all the officers are worked out in Johnston II, 176-179.
2. 5 Force I, 1233, 1258. Linn & Egle I, 201, 218, 226. Fitch, 34.
3. 5 Force I, 1254; II, 882; III, 505. Linn & Egle I, 200.
4. Washington-Hancock 8/31/76: GW V, 507. Washington-Mass. General Court 9/19/76: ibid VI, 75. General Orders 10/8/76: ibid VI, 179.
5. 5 Force I, 1233, 1250; II, 882; III, 716-728 passim. Johnston II, 180-186. NA Jacket 78, No. 4.
6. Johnston I, 198.
7. 5 Force I, 1258. The captured Long Island lieutenants were Jonathan Coe and Increase Carpenter, both of Queens.
8. Howe-Germain 9/3/76: 5 Force I, 1257. Serle, 88.
9. "Return of the Killed, Wounded, and Missing, . . August 27. 1776" 5 Force I, 1258-1259.

INDEX OF NAMES

A
Agnew, Brig. Gen. James 40, 43
Alexander, Brig. Gen. William (see Lord Stirling)
Asia 5, 6, 9, 12, 14, 19, 22, 46
Atlee, Col. Samuel 26, 28, 36, 37, 40, 43, 45

B
Bayley, Dr. Richard 46, 48
Birdsall, Lt. Col. Benjamin 49
Blanchard, Capt. John 22
Bowie, Capt. 45
Bradley, Col. Phillip Burr 26
Bristol 29
Brodhead, Lt. Col. Daniel 46
Brodhead, Lt. Luke 41, 42
Brune 30, 32
Brush, Maj. Jesse 49
Burd, Maj. James 38, 40, 46

C
Callender, Cadet John 41
Campbell, Capt. Archibald 19
Carcass 30, 34, 46
Carpenter, Capt.-Lt. Benajah 40, 43, 44, 45
Carpenter, Lt. Increase 48
Centurion 22
Chatham 22
Chester, Col. John 36, 37, 40, 41, 42, 48
Clark, Lt. Col. Joel 45, 46
Clinton, Brig. Gen. George 28, 35, 47, 49
Clinton, Lt. Gen. Henry 7, 9, 10, 12, 19, 21, 22, 24, 29, 34, 38, 39, 40, 42, 45
Clinton, Brig. Gen. James 15, 18, 28
Connecticut General Assembly 26
Continental Congress 5-8, 10, 11, 12, 14-17, 28, 32
Cornwallis, Lt. Gen. Charles 29, 34-37, 39, 41, 44, 45
Covenhoven, Lt. Col. Nicholas 37, 38
Crane 27
Cunningham, Col. James 36, 38, 46

D
Donop, Col. Carl Emil von 34, 35, 37, 42, 43
Douglas, Col. William 46, 48
Drake, Col. Samuel 26, 36
Duchess of Gordon 5, 14, 16
Dunmore, Lord 29

E
Eagle 24, 45, 46

Emerald 30
Erskine, Brig Gen. William 39, 48, 49
Evelyn, Capt. W.G. 39
Experiment 29

F
Faucitt, Col. William 30
Fellows, Brig. Gen. John 26, 28, 47
Ferguson, Capt. James 36, 37, 46, 47
Flora 29
Floyd, Col. William 49
Forbes, Gilbert 18
Ford, Capt. 45

G
Gates, Adj. Gen. Horatio 15, 17, 33
Gay, Col. Fisher 31, 36, 37, 47, 48
George III 24, 29
Germain, Lord George 19
Gist, Maj. Mordecai 44, 45, 46
Grant, Capt. Alexander 19
Grant, Lt. Col. James 43, 44
Grant, Maj. Gen. James 38-41, 43-46
Graydon, Capt. Alexander 47
Greene, Maj. Gen. Nathanael 14, 15, 16, 22, 24, 28, 30-33, 36
Greyhound 18, 19, 22, 34

H
Halifax 32
Haller, Col. Henry 36, 38, 46
Hamilton, Capt. Alexander 15
Hamilton, Capt. James 35
Hand, Col. Edward 13, 22, 26, 31, 34, 35, 37, 43, 48
Haslet, Col. John 37, 40, 43, 48
Heard Brig. Gen. Nathaniel 12, 26, 28, 36
Heath, Maj. Gen. William 13, 14, 15, 28, 35, 47
Heister, Lt. Gen. Leopold von 29, 36-42
Hester 16, 18, 27
Hewlett, Capt. Richard 12, 24
Hickey, Thomas 18, 23, 37
Hitchcock, Col. Daniel 47
Hopkins, Commo. Esek 15
Hotham, Commd. William 25, 30, 32, 34
Howe, Vice Adm. (Lord) Richard 19, 24, 25, 27, 32, 34, 35, 46
Howe, Gen. William 18, 19, 21-24, 29, 30, 31, 32, 34-37, 40, 41, 42, 46-49
Hughes, Dep. 2M. Huch 47
Humphrey, Col. Cornelius 26
Huntington, Col. Jedediah 40, 43

I

Independence 27

J

Jersey 30
Johnston, Capt.-Lt. John 41
Johnston, Col. Philip 36, 37, 38, 43
Jones, Maj. Gen. Valentine 40

K

Kachlein, Lt. Col. 3, 37, 40, 43, 44, 46
Kingfisher 32
Knowlton, Maj. Thomas 26, 27, 37, 39, 43
Knop, Col. Henry 15, 16, 19

L

Lady Washington 27
Lasher, Col. John 5, 9, 11, 12, 13, 24, 26, 36, 37, 38, 40, 46
Leary, Capt. John 26
Lee, Maj. Gen. Chas. 6-13, 16, 21, 24, 26, 34, 49
Lively 16
Livingston, Col. Henry B. 36, 49
Livingston, Brig. Gen. William 34
Lossberg, Col. Friedrich von 37
Lutz, Lt. Col. Nicholas 44, 46

M

McDonough, Maj. Thomas 45
McDougall, Brig. Gen. Alexander 15, 28, 46, 47
Malcolm, Maj. William 10, 11, 16, 24, 26
Martin, Col. Ephriam 36
Mathew, Brig. Gen. Edward 40
Mentges, Adj. Francis 44, 45
Mercer, Brig. Gen. Hugh 17, 26, 27, 28, 46, 47
Mercury 7, 9, 12, 16, 46
Mifflin 16, 18, 22
Mifflin, Brig. Gen. Thomas 17, 23, 28, 31, 35, 46, 47, 48
Miles, Col. Samuel 3, 26, 27, 28, 35-38, 40, 41, 42, 47
Mirbach, Maj. Gen. Werner 36, 37, 40, 42, 43
Monckton, Lt. Col. Henry 44, 45
Montgomerie 16, 18
Montresor, Capt. John 21
Moylan, Col. Stephen 17
Mulford, Col. David 49

N

N.J. Committee of Safety 13, 30
N.J. Provincial Congress 11, 12, 26
N.Y. Committee of Safety 7, 8, 9, 12
N.Y. Provincial Congress 3, 5, 6, 7, 9, 10, 11, 15, 18, 22, 24, 28
Nicoll, Col. Isaac 18
Niger 29, 32
Nixon, Brig. Gen. John 28, 31, 36

O

Orpheus 16

P

Parker Jr., Capt. Hyde 5, 9, 10, 14, 18, 22, 23, 24, 27, 32, 34
Parker, Commd. Peter 29, 46, 47, 48
Parry, Lt. Col. Caleb 44
Parsons, Brig. Gen. Samuel. H. 28, 36, 38, 40, 43-47
Peterson Lt. Col James 24
Percy, Lt. Gen. Hugh 38, 40, 41
Phoenix 5, 6, 9, 10, 14, 16, 22, 23, 25, 27, 34
Pigot, Maj. Gen. Robert 40
Piper, Col. James 41
Potter, Lt. Col. 49
Preston 30, 34, 46
Putnam 16, 18
Putnam, Maj. Gen. Israel 14, 15, 28, 36, 37, 38, 42, 46, 47
Putnam, Lt. Col. Rufus 16

R

Rainbow 30, 34, 46
Read, Col. Joseph 17, 28

Reed, Adj. Gen. Joseph 33
Remsen, Col. Jeromus 32, 36, 37, 48, 49
Renown 29, 46
Repulse 30, 32, 46
Ritzema, Col. Rudolphus 15
Rivington, James 6
Robertson, Capt.-Lt. Archibald 25
Robertson, Maj. Gen. James 39
Robinson, Joseph 48
Roebuck 29, 46, 48
Rogers, Maj. Robert 29, 34, 36, 37
Rose 6, 22, 23, 25, 27, 34

S

St. Lawrence 29
Savage 14, 16, 19, 25
Schuyler 10, 16, 18, 22
Schuyler, Maj. Gen. Philip 5
Scott, Brig. Gen. John M. 26, 28, 29, 47, 48
Sears, Capt. Isaac 6, 7, 12, 26, 49
Senegal 22
Serle, Ambrose 25
Seymour, Lt. Col. Thomas 26
Shark 27
Shuldham, Vice Adm. Molyneux 22, 29
Sillman, Col. Gold 35, 36
Smallwood, Col. William 26, 28, 37, 40, 43, 45, 46, 48
Smith, Maj. 49
Smith, Brig. Gen. Francis 40
Smith, Col. Josiah 32, 36, 37, 48, 49
Smith, Capt. William 8-11, 13, 16, 18
Solebay 29
Spencer, Maj. Gen. Joseph 14, 15, 28, 46, 47
Spitfire 27, 46
Sproule, Lt. George 21
Stephenson, Capt. Hugh 13, 14, 22, 25
Stirling, Brig. Gen. (Lord) 10-13, 15, 18, 28, 40, 43-46
Stirn, Maj. Gen. Johann 36, 37, 40, 42
Strombolo 30
Sullivan, Maj. Gen. John 14, 15, 33, 34, 36, 40, 42-46
Swan 22
Syren 29

T

Tallmadge, Maj. Benjamin 47
Thomas, Capt. John A. 46
Thompson, Brig. Gen. William 13, 14, 15
Thunder 29, 34, 46
Trumbull, Gov. Jonathan 26, 28, 36, 49
Tryal 22, 23, 27
Tryon, Gov. William 5, 6, 7, 9, 14, 18, 19, 22, 37
Tupper, Lt. Col. Benjamin (Commo.) 16, 18, 27

V

Van Brunt, Col. Rutgert 31
Vandeput, Capt. George 5, 22
Vaughan, Maj. Gen. John 42

W

Wadsworth Jr., Brig. Gen. James 26, 28, 47
Ward, Col. Andrew 7, 8, 10-13, 28
Ward, Col. Jonathan 21
Washington 27, 46
Washington, Gen. George 5-8, 13, 14-19, 22, 24, 27, 28, 31, 32, 34-39, 46-49
Waterbury, Col. David 7-11
Wells, Maj. Levi 41
Whiting 27
Williams, Maj. Ennion 40
Wolcott, Brig. Gen. Oliver 28
Woodhull, Brig. Gen. Nathaniel 36-40, 48, 49
Wreden, Capt. Carl von 40
Wyllys, Col. Samuel 38, 40, 41, 42

Z

Zedwitz, Lt. Col. Herman 37

ERRATA

Page 13L: ". . . some of these <u>Continental</u> companies . . ."

44/45: transpose situation maps (captions remain)

61R: "Gen. Clinton's Vanguard . . . <u>5,425</u>"

62R: ". . . <u>twelve</u> British officers <u>were</u> wounded . . ."

62R: ". . . in the hills: 1 captain, <u>3</u> lieutenants."